The
Psych
101
series

James C. Kaufman, PhD, Series Editor

Director, Learning Research Institute
California State University at San Bernardino

HI ELGA-
HOPE YOU GET A KICK
OUT OF THIS! THANKS FOR
YOUR INTEREST.

Mitch

Mitch Earleywine, PhD, is a professor of psychology at the State University at Albany (SUNY), where he teaches courses on clinical research methods, and drugs and human behavior. Prior to his current appointment, Dr. Earleywine was an assistant professor of psychology (1991–1997) and an associate professor of psychology (1997–2005) at the University of Southern California, where he won numerous teaching and mentoring awards. He was also the director of clinical training at USC from 1998–2000. He received his BA in psychology from Columbia University (1986), his PhD from Indiana University (1990), and his clinical internship training at the University of Mississippi Medical Center (1991). He is on the editorial board of *Cognitive and Behavioral Practice*, *Journal of Research in Personality*, *Journal of Studies on Alcohol*, and *Psychology and Addictive Behaviors*. He has published over 90 peer-reviewed journal articles, and three books with Oxford University Press: *Understanding Marijuana* (over 13,000 copies sold in hardcover and paperback), *Mind-Altering Drugs*, and *Pot Politics*. Dr. Earleywine has given over 70 conference presentations and has been widely quoted in mainstream media outlets such as *The Economist*, the *San Francisco Chronicle*, the *Chicago Tribune*, *The New York Times*, *Los Angeles Times*, *USA Today*, *Time* magazine, *Rolling Stone*, and *The Nation*.

Professor Earleywine performed stand-up comedy in Los Angeles while he was a professor at USC. He appeared at The Comedy Store on Sunset Boulevard, The Ice House Comedy Club in Pasadena, the Long Beach Chuckle Hut, and the Ha Ha Comedy Club's talent competition in North Hollywood. His comedic skills in the classroom are well documented on www.Ratemyprofessor.com. He developed this book for a course, titled "Human Talents: Learning, Humor, and Creativity."

HUMOR
101

Mitch Earleywine, PhD

SPRINGER PUBLISHING COMPANY
NEW YORK

Springer Publishing Company, LLC
11 West 42nd Street
New York, NY 10036
www.springerpub.com

Acquisitions Editor: Nancy S. Hale
Senior Editor: Rose Mary Piscitelli
Cover design: Mimi Flow
Project Manager: Ashita Shah
Composition: Newgen Imaging

ISBN: 978-0-8261-0608-7
E-book ISBN: 978-0-8261-0609-4

10 11 12 13 / 5 4 3 2 1

Library of Congress Cataloging-in-Publication Data

Earleywine, Mitchell.
Humor 101 / Mitch Earleywine.
     p. cm.
  Includes index.
  ISBN 978-0-8261-0608-7 — ISBN 978-0-8261-0609-4 (ebook)
  1. Wit and humor—History and criticism. 2. Comic, The.   I. Title.
PN6147.E26 2011
809.7—dc22   2010046119

Printed in the United States of America by Hamilton Printing

Contents

Preface

t all started with a cymbal crash. As I put in my ear-plugs while preparing a psychology lecture during the University of Southern California Marching Band's practice, I was in a bit of a funk. Like most newly tenured associate professors, I had severe workaholic habits. My few remaining friends—both of them—were constantly ribbing me, telling me to have more fun and develop some skill at taking my leisure. I was reworking a lecture about anxiety, trying to find something witty to say about panic and trauma. I searched the Web for jokes and came across a stand-up workshop that sounded splendid. "It's probably in Manhattan or something," I thought. But it was less than a half hour from my house. In Los Angeles, that's right next door. I ended up in a class with comedy teacher extraordinaire Greg Dean and some of the funniest people I'd ever met outside a mental hospital. Greg explained his unique twist on Attardo's model of humor, got us all to loosen up in front of a crowd, and taught us the intricacies of joke structure.

The next thing I knew, I was onstage at The Comedy Store, relishing the crowd's laughter. Fifteen months of regular performing and I made my way to "the big room"—this stage that serves as the mecca of comedy, where greats like Lewis Black, George Carlin, Steve Martin, Paula Poundstone, Richard Pryor, and Rita Rudner stood at one time. The humor spread to other facets of my life. Enrollment in one of my undergraduate classes spiked to 330 (and then 460 after my move to Albany). I had to change my phone message to say, "There's no room in my class. It doesn't matter if your parent is a trustee." The teaching awards started piling up, too. I finally understood what everyone had been yelling about: Leisure is important. It sounds ridiculously self-evident, but humor is fun.

This book is an academic's attempt at spreading the word. Humor is indeed fun, and here are the data. Although it's not a manual for doing stand-up, writing a sitcom, making memorable presentations, or getting a date, this book can certainly help you in all of those tasks. Getting a handle on how humor works makes generating funnier days a bit easier. Understanding all of the benefits that humor brings to relationships, work, physical health, and happiness can motivate almost anyone to add a bit of wit to life. These topics all get plenty of attention in the pages ahead. In fact, I haven't devoted any space to the academic hair-splitting that regular folks don't care about. Few people are up all night trying to distinguish spoof from satire. (But hundreds of journal pages are devoted to the topic, with no sense of irony.) Instead, I've focused on big questions: What makes something funny? Can a joke help sell a product or negotiate a bargain? Could a witty story ease tension on the job? Can comedies prevent the common cold or spread a good mood? Can humor find you a partner for life, or at least for the night?

I've had the pleasure to work with some amazing comics who tagged my shows and brought me bliss in the hard days of fighting tooth and nail for stage time, and they included Brett Siddell, Derrick Jackson, Rob Smith, Michael Buzzelli, and Henry Senecal. Greg Dean taught me everything I know about comedy that's worth knowing. Their influences appear on every page. I can't thank James Kaufman enough for inviting me to do this project. It's hard to imagine him editing the Psych 101 Series, when some of my best memories include seeing him as a spunky undergraduate wowing the faculty at USC. His comments, flexibility, and encouragement have been divine. My fervent thanks to Nancy Hale at Springer for all her extraordinary critiques, tolerance, and tactful prompts, too.

My in-laws, David Gordis and Felice Gordis, read every word here and literally thousands of others that didn't make the cut. No one retires to Albany, New York, thinking that they'll have to wade through hundreds of pages on humor to get access to their grandchildren. I thank them heartily with love and affection. My dad, Bob Earleywine, tweaked multiple chapters and provided considerate support. Brad Armour-Garb put in countless hours helping me improve the precision of my language ("Do you mean 'jokes' here or 'humor'?"), organize thoughts in compelling and comprehensible ways, think through the intricacies of the humor literature, and take time for welcome distractions; I hope I get the chance to return the favor. Stuart Daman critiqued multiple chapters with his usual wit. Tony DeBlasi, Nicholas Van Dam, Elisa Albert, and Elana Gordis each commented on chapters in supportive and helpful ways. Several people labored throughout the years in an effort to get me to write well. It took a while for it to dawn on me that they were actually trying to get me to think well. They include Ian Frederick, John Houghton, Paul McNeil, Adina Cimet, Kenneth Koch, Harry Mathews, Peter Finn, and Richard David Young. Saskia Smeele, Stacey Farmer, and Michelle Stiles gave me wonderful comments and worked assiduously on my references. Folks from my usual support team whom I haven't already mentioned deserve unusual praise: Joe Earleywine, Clark and Suzy Van Scoyk, Russ Bellville, Karri Gallaugher, the NORML PodCast listeners, The Musketeers, Amy Griffin, Danny Goodwin, James and Sharon Danoff-Burg, Beth Deangelis, Lisa Wallock, Ed Schwartzchild, Jack Huntington, and Domenico Scarlatti. My effusive gratitude to all. My daughters, Dahlia and Maya, went about the world in their witty ways while I hid in the study when I should have played with them more. I thank them with love for their tolerance. As usual, I dedicate this book to my wife, Elana Gordis. I'll thank her more later.

Reviewing the humor literature as a trained social scientist and a comic, but with no investment in a specific theory or approach, provides a few advantages. I can take a fresh eye to the research without worrying that I'll insult someone big in the field who'll torpedo my career. That said, I want to extend my special thanks to all of the authors cited in the References. Only the bravest and most spirited writers can endure the criticism fired at anyone who devotes time to such a controversial topic. Without their hard work, I would have had nothing to write about. I'm sure they'll all feel that they should have written this book, instead of me, but it's been a great process. I look forward to the next cymbal crash in my life.

Models and Mechanisms— Funny in Theory

magine you're in charge of advertising an odd snack. It's allegedly salty enough to make your heart beat in your ears, with enough fat to clog a fire hose. It's also a snap to cook it, if you can call it cooking. You add boiling water to its plastic cup to unleash the delicate flavors of the dehydrated pasta, soy pieces, spice powder, and desiccated vegetables. It's manufactured in the United Kingdom—the land of, to put it politely, unparalleled chefs. In addition, the product goes by the oh-so-appealing moniker "Pot Noodles." It tastes great, but admitting you eat it is like getting caught picking your nose. What do you do?

Humor might help, as I'll explain later. For now, let's define humor as anything that might make people laugh because they think it's funny. We could go around in circles about what is

1

funny, but let's not waste the time. Let's leave this open and see if we can refine a definition as we go along. In this chapter, we'll sift through some ways to classify jokes into categories, discuss some theories about what makes something funny, and get into the caveats about why this work can be so difficult. This information can lay the groundwork for humor's role in communication, personality, health, thought, and the like.

There's a strategy that every good stand-up comic learns. It's named "calling the room." When the audience isn't laughing at a comedian's show, some comics just plow on through their list of jokes. But a good comic will say something. Johnny Carson was the king of calling the room. A joke of his would bomb and he'd say, "Tough crowd" or, "It's late in the week," and then the audience would often get back on his side. Jay Leno has jokingly berated one of his writers in front of the audience if a monologue of his was dying. Calling the room lets the audience know that the performer is with them, thinking and aware, not simply spouting memorized lines. As humorist John Vorhaus (1994) says, comedy is truth plus pain. Speak the truth and you're halfway to being funny.

I once played a show at The Comedy Store in Los Angeles, and had the poor luck of going on after a guy who was much more experienced and delightfully less cerebral than I was, and he was astoundingly funny. He went on to run the Ha Ha Café in North Hollywood. There's an old Yiddish saying: "Always follow a schmuck." I had clearly failed to take this advice. My opening jokes, which usually killed, were falling flat. The grumbling made it clear that the audience would soon turn on me. Although I always doubted the tales about the fear of public speaking surpassing the fear of death, I would have preferred to crawl into a coffin than get booed off the stage. I'd seen enough performers go into a tailspin in this situation. I knew that I needed to do something quickly. I could have walked through the rest of my prepared material and taken my beating. I could have put down the microphone and fled. Instead, I decided that I had nothing to lose.

I said, "Oh! So I'm not as funny as Dave?" Everyone looked up at that. I started repeating some of his jokes in a dumb voice and got a few chuckles. Then I pointed out crazy things he should have said but didn't, and riffed about how great it must be to be so funny. Suddenly the crowd was on my side. Calling the room, speaking the truth, seemed to help. I segued into my regular material and now it was working. I finished to applause and went home happy. Tragedy averted.

Pot Noodles essentially did the same. The company called the room; they told it like it is. You've read this far, so you can guess what the company did. When all else fails, get funny with the truth. They know that a cup of dried starch isn't a healthy gourmet feast, just as a comic knows when the show is bombing. Instead of pretending that the product was pheasant under glass, the promoters faced its reputation as an embarrassing fast food. They compared it to other popular but seedy habits. One commercial shows the character Desperate Dan skulking around sordid, neon-lit neighborhoods. He enters various dives and asks in a whisper for Pot Noodles, but gets slapped across the face again and again. Finally a leather-clad lady tells him to meet her around the back. In the next scene, the two of them grunt and groan on a motel bed, forks flying from their little plastic cups as they bounce suggestively. "That felt so wrong and yet it felt so right!" Dan blurts out. The ads were a huge hit. Nearly everyone in the United Kingdom recognized the memorable campaign. It helped Pot Noodles grab market share and profits. The company's Web site claims that the British eat 155 million of its snacks a year, which is nearly five per second. Tragedy averted.

I prefer to love and study humor for its own sake, but comedy does have applications. Humor can help us even if we're not stand-up comics or advertisers. Comedy alters mood, thought, stress, and pain. Jokes and laughter may play an important role in health, mental illness, marital bliss, education, and psychotherapy. Some humor transcends time and culture. It can also get you a date, or more. With all this potential, comedy seemed destined to fall beneath the microscope of scientists. Surely a few years of concerted contemplation and experimentation ought to uncover the grand secret of what makes someone funny. Surely science can make everyone as merry a joker as possible. After all, we developed antibiotics, put a man on the moon, and perfected the pork rind.

HUMOR RESEARCH TO THE RESCUE?

Many folks believe that humor research isn't a worthwhile pursuit. Any overarching attempt to investigate humor does run into problems. It may simply be too complicated to explain all at once. Part of the problem might arise because the word "humor" refers to too many phenomena. Funny things may have little in common other than being funny. Psychologists and other cynics often suggest that humor can't be studied at all. They lump a funny thing in with strange bedfellows like love and pornography. They know what's funny when they see it, but it can't be pinned down. Although a comprehensive model that explains every funny thing in the world would be quite complicated, humor definitely lends itself to study. Cynicism aside, experiments on comedy and mirth have generated amazing insights in the arts and sciences, leading to new ways to recognize, generate, and use funny material. These same studies have also uncovered a great deal about how we think, feel, and communicate. Devoted researchers can investigate humor, and the work pays off.

The cynics may be right, however, if they assert that humor cannot be studied in ways that are a laugh a minute. E.B. White, the author of *Charlotte's Web* and *The Elements of Style*, made this point with great fervor: "Humor can be dissected as a frog can, but the thing dies in the process and the innards are discouraging to any but the pure scientific mind" (White, 1941/2000). With a name like Elwyn Brooks White, he had to go by his initials. And he had to get funny. Otherwise, the other kids on the playground would have beaten him up. It looks like he was right about picking humor apart. I once sat with three comics at the Los Angeles Comedy Store as we watched one of the popular new acts—a guy who later went on to a 7-year stint on television. We'd all just learned a model of humor from the phenomenal Greg Dean's Stand-up Workshop. We sat in complete silence while the rest of the crowd guffawed with gusto. At the end, one of us said, "Great show." We all recognized that the jokes were funny, but none of us laughed. We were still so new to this way of thinking about humor that we couldn't help analyzing each joke as we heard it. Picking them apart messed up the mirth. This reaction to learning about humor happens often. Fortunately, the laughter returns. Once our thoughts about the model became more automatic, we could understand the underpinnings of the material and still enjoy it. We got to have our jokes and kill them, too.

People often ask if the study of mirth is a worthwhile pursuit. Humor seems rather minor compared to cheery topics like global thermonuclear war or leukemia. Even within the social sciences, a lot of work focuses on the phenomena that frighten taxpayers the most, like skull bashers or psychotics. But positive psychology, a relatively new branch of study, challenges this focus on negative topics. Much of psychology focuses on mental illness, impairment, or other aspects of the mind gone awry. Positive psychology addresses ways for people to thrive (Peterson, 2006). It emphasizes human talents like leadership, creativity, and even humor. A keen understanding of what is funny actually could improve the process of negotiation and decrease the threat of global thermonuclear war. It might also help folks handle the cumbersome aspects of leukemia treatment. It can diffuse conflict before skulls get bashed. I don't know about psychosis, though. Hearing voices, and other aspects of the disorder, probably respond best to medication. Nevertheless, I had one client who joked with his voices to keep them from getting him down until he got his monthly shot. One study suggests that showing comedy films in the psychiatric ward makes psychotic people less angry, too (Gelkopf, Gonen, Kurs, Melamed, & Bleich, 2006).

The other problem with the study of humor is the tacit assumption that the research ought to be hilarious. It's an odd idea. Few people expect a textbook on sex to be a turn-on. Nobody thinks that a cookbook should actually taste good. Journal articles like "Perception of humor in patients with localized brain lesions" are rarely knee slappers. (Yeah, that's a real title. It's actually a great article [Koviazina & Kogan, 2008]). Truth be told, a lot of academic stuff is, well, too academic. Books and articles on the topic definitely could benefit by cutting the jargon and technicalities. But lightening up on the details can make the ideas hard to follow. Subtle distinctions—which humor is all about, really—get lost without the unfunny particulars. Surely, no one can expect a book on humor to read like the script of the movie *Airplane*. In addition, extensive joking can make books seem less persuasive and less credible (Bryant, Brown, Silberberg, & Elliot, 1981). I hope it doesn't work against me. It's a little hard to take investigators seriously if they're wearing clown noses or repeating moan-worthy puns.

Despite how much everyone thinks they know about humor, much of the popular lore is dead wrong. The relevant research covers everything from brainwaves to politics, so there's a lot to learn that's extremely interesting. But it's not always comical. Plenty of things worth knowing aren't easy to learn. Studying humor can help uncover important information about thoughts, feelings, and actions. As we figure out what makes us laugh, we discover more about ourselves, each other, and our own happiness. That's a valuable process, but it doesn't always tickle. In addition, few can help wondering if studying wit might actually make people wittier. Given the impact of humor on persuasion, health, attractiveness, leadership, and personality, the curiosity makes sense. The answer, in a word, is: Maybe. Motivated people who are willing to take a playful attitude, learn the structure of jokes, and spend time in lighthearted practice find more and more humor in their daily lives. It might not happen in an instant, but it will happen.

HUMOR AND OX EATING:
THE ELUSIVE GRAND THEORY OF HUMOR

As ubiquitous and intuitive as comedy seems to be, the grand theory and explanation of all humor remain elusive. In fact, most of the models of humor are weak. Some theories rely on vague ideas that are hard to define. Others require multiple postulates illustrated with more targets and arrows than you'd find in an archery shop. No single model has clinched universal acceptance. Every kindergartner or senator can think of counter-examples for almost every theory of humor. Perhaps we expect too much. Humor is delicate and complicated. A small shift in wording or vocal inflection can kill a great joke. But then again, other sciences aren't perfect, either. Popular economic models don't account for the price of every cotton ball in Kathmandu. Computerized weather prediction is still all wet. So it's no surprise that humor theorists can't predict every time Chris Rock or your baby sister will get a giggle.

We seem to know humor, or an attempt at it, when we see it. Formal definitions are about as useful as golf clubs for a snail. Most dictionaries run a series of synonyms together. "Amusement", "hilarity", "comic", and "laughter" appear in most explanations of the word. None of these are going to help anyone who doesn't know funny. At first thought, it seems like the best way to identify funny would require gauging laughter. But relying on laughs alone to determine what is humorous remains problematic. Some laughs reflect amusement while others stem from nervousness. One revealing, recurring theme present in most formal definitions involves a focus on the *stimulus*—the joke, phrase, gesture, cartoon, gag, or tale. For brevity's sake, let's call all of these things jokes. Note that jokes are a little easier to study than all of humor. Let's think of them as any stimulus designed to elicit laughter, or its associated emotion, mirth. This emphasis on humor residing in the joke, as if what makes something funny is inherent in the thing itself, seems rampant. Many people think jokes are inherently funny or not, independent of the listener. But other definitions leap from the stimulus to emphasize the role of the perceiver—the person who finds amusement in the joke. This interaction of the perceiver and the perceived is essential. Shakespeare put it nicely: "A jest's prosperity lies in the ear of him that hears it, never in the tongue of him that makes it" (*Love's Labour's Lost*, 5, 2). Sorry about the sexist use of "him." Hey, it was the 1590s.

Humor is really a combination of who, what, when, where, and how—there are the folks who hear the joke, the joke itself, the moment they hear it, the context, and how it's told. We'll get into the various aspects of audiences and the delivery of jokes, but it seems like it would be a lot easier if we had a definition of humor. Unfortunately, we don't. Often when we know something when we see it, but can't quite define it, we benefit from a process known as "bootstrapping" (Crobach & Meehl, 1955). Bootstrapping is a way to make subjective ideas more objective, or turn rough approximations into more exact measures. For example, there was a time when we had no definition of temperature. You can imagine that cave dwellers could all agree that huddling around the fire felt hotter than rolling in the snow. When multiple people agree about what's hot and what's not, we say that our measure of temperature is "reliable." But this was still a pretty subjective process. A couple of ancient geniuses noticed that air in a container would expand when it was hot and contract when it was cold. Another mastermind noted that mercury in a tube would rise in hotter environments and fall in colder ones. It was easy to put a ruler beside the tube with precise markings. "Hot" might mean 90 millimeters of mercury or more in the tube; cold might mean 30 or less. Now a subjective sense of temperature became a more objective one. Later theories helped us define temperature as the average kinetic energy in molecules. We essentially pulled the idea of temperature up by its own bootstraps. (Philo, Hero of Alexandria, Galileo, Biancani, Fahrenheit, and Celsius all get credit for this work [Chang, 2004]).

So why not do the same with humor? The problem, of course, is in that first step—reliably identifying what's comical. People agree on what's warm and what's cold a lot more easily than they agree on what's funny. Dead baby jokes, observational humor, and shaggy-dog stories delight some but not others. A comedian friend of mine had a whole set of jokes about death. These killed in local clubs in Hollywood, leaving the crowds laughing uproariously. Then he made a trip to a hotel in the Catskills. The audience of senior citizens nearly wept him off the stage; death was not a funny topic to this crowd. His humor obviously wasn't some inherent quality of the jokes alone, but a combination of the setting and the content. Wisecracks about mortality simply lacked any hilarity in a room full of elders who had lost their loved ones while facing the Grim Reaper. Some of the same people might have laughed at the same jokes if they'd been part of a different crowd in a different environment.

What's funny varies in different eras, too. An acquaintance of mine had a routine about Middle Eastern folks that worked incredibly well until the attacks on September 11, 2001. He had to quit using those jokes, but he dusted them off in 2010 and got laughs once more. Imitations of Gerald Ford's pratfalls made audiences squeal in 1976. They may never be funny again, except to old fogies who remember watching him spill out of a helicopter onto his presidential noggin. Humor is an intricate interaction between the perceiver and the perceived. That's what makes it so individualized. But the fact leads to a nice conclusion: You are already an expert on humor. The universal indicator of what is and what isn't funny is already yours. The planets really have to align to crack folks up. This is what makes humor not only hard to define but also delightful. With all these contributors to laughter, it's easy to see why any model designed to account for all of comedy would have to be extensive, complicated, or impossible. Perhaps it's just too grand a task. When puzzles grow too big and complicated, sometimes it helps to break them down into smaller pieces. That's one way to eat an ox. So let's begin with the idea that humor is anything that someone deems funny.

SORTS OF SILLINESS AND PLATYPI

If a single theory can't explain all of humor, maybe different models could work for different types. We need a way to arrange the funny stuff. Dividing humor into types makes it easier to talk about, and also reveals how important it really is. Human language probably wouldn't have all these words for different kinds of humor if it didn't matter. The fact that we have so many of these terms supports the idea that humor's not just one thing. There are anecdotes, wisecracks, witticisms, parodies, cartoons, and comics. There's sarcasm, irony, parody, caricature, and mockery. There's banter and joking and repartee and teasing and wordplay and Sneezy and Dopey. This is serious business.

Hair-splitting definitions of everything from the jocular to the ludicrous exist, but they often only lead to fights among linguists, psychologists, and drunks. A simple set of categories of humor, however, can make a nice shorthand for discussion. A first distinction that might prove helpful involves separating jokes from wit. The definition of wit has changed over eons, making this distinction particularly important. A joke is a form of humor that is deliberate and self-contained. That is, people tell them to get a laugh. They don't require a ton of explanation or context. Jokes tend to involve a setup and a punch line (or "punch," for those in the know). Ideally, the setup and punch are enough to get the laugh. Many have a recognizable format that immediately communicates that they're jokes: "How many teamsters does it take to put in a lightbulb?" "Ten. You got a problem with that?"

Wit, in contrast, leads to amusement in the context of a conversation. At one time, wit implied an elite, hostile mockery inherent in aristocratic games of one-upmanship. The French film *Ridicule* documents the phenomenon nicely as each character tries to outdo the other with putdowns and affronts. Even in Freud's time, wit had more aggressive connotations than humor (Freud, 1905). Today, wit has lost its antagonistic connotations and simply means that something is funny in a given setting. Wit is less portable than jokes. A witty remark can break up a room but might require too much explanation to repeat in another environment. I've been having witty lunches with the same crew of academics for years, but retelling any of the wisecracks to my wife at dinner would be a waste of breath. Invariably, I'd have to respond to her stunned silence by saying, "Guess you had to be there." That's no way to stay married for long.

Given their self-contained, portable, repeatable nature, jokes lend themselves to easier divisions. Well, easier study anyway. What makes a good set of categories for jokes? It depends on what the categories are for. Lots of categories differ depending upon their use. In junior high school, I had two kinds of jokes: those I could tell my girlfriend's mom, and those that were funny. These sorts of classification systems, or taxonomies, can genuinely help communication, even if the one I used in junior high didn't. It's best, of course, if the taxonomy fits reality somehow. If you invent a category of humor that doesn't contain any jokes, it's no use. The goal for humor researchers has often been to provide categories that could describe all sorts of comedy efficiently.

One of the best known taxonomies is Carolus Linnaeus's categories in biology. Linnaeus (1751) put every living thing into a kingdom, phylum, class, order, family, genus, and species. It wasn't a perfect arrangement; there were always the platypuses of life. But the categories seemed to reflect what was out there. They helped people group living things in interesting ways. Anytime someone discovered a new species, there was a way to see where it would fit. Although simpler categories of living things fit most people's needs (friendly versus not, tasty versus not, etc.), this one provided a way to communicate about

11

narrow types or large groups with ease. This system also had one, and only one, category for each species, so we could call it "monothetic." The categories are mutually exclusive. No animals are both rats and humans—even lawyers. Each category has defining characteristics, the attributes that are necessary and sufficient. For example, a mammal is warm blooded and gives birth to live young. Alternatively, some systems can be called "polythetic." Members of the category share plenty of attributes, but may not have a specific one in common. Games, for example, don't seem to have a defining quality. Some are played on a board, others on a field, and others on a court. They aren't all competitive. (Burn through an afternoon playing Prui sometime. This game was designed to be noncompetitive and ends with everyone holding hands—how quaint.) They aren't all played for fun. (Watch a televised tennis match and look at all the joy and playfulness.) They aren't all physical. (Tiddlywinks? Care to argue for the fitness benefits of bowling?) But they're all games. Humor might require a polythetic set of categories.

FUNNY FACTOR ANALYSIS

A taxonomy of humor as elaborate as Linnaeus's might prove a little unwieldy, but identifying the general kingdoms sounds like a grand idea. Getting a bunch of comedians to generate some different categories might seem like a good way to start, but there's no way to know if these categories genuinely reflect reality. This approach might not be very efficient, either. (When comics get together in groups, they tend to do little work and lots of wit-waving.) Instead, researchers took literally hundreds of jokes and cartoons that appeared to represent all types of humor. Then huge groups of people rated how funny all this stuff appeared. I have to have a little sympathy for people asked to rate jokes, cartoons, and stories as part of an experiment. Advertisements attempt humor every second. The Internet

Movie Data Base has a list of more than 113,000 comedies. Stand-up comics are only a YouTube away. All this humor seems to dwarf a captioned drawing or a few lines of text. How funny can squiggles and words be when there's so much humor available? Nevertheless, written jokes and cartoons still get laughs.

Getting folks to say what's funny in the laboratory has its own quirks. Fortunately, people seem candid about what they do, and do not, find funny if the environment is right. If their answers are reasonably anonymous, the ratings correlate with smiling and laughter in response to the joke, suggesting that we can trust their reports (Ruch, 1995). Without anonymity, answers might not be as valid. When participants in a research study report what they think the experimenter wants to hear, rather than how they genuinely feel, we call it "response bias." If undergraduates were forced to evaluate an instructor's puns as the instructor looked on, we might expect the scores to be a bit inflated. Rating Viagra jokes in front of their mothers might also lead to biased scores, though my mom would probably laugh. This kind of response bias is troublesome in research on all kinds of topics, ranging from AIDS to zoophilia. Sidestepping response bias is essential. For this reason, the best laboratory studies of humor use anonymous questionnaires in comfortable settings. Researchers then analyze the ratings in an attempt to see if they can reduce the categories of jokes and cartoons from hundreds to only a few factors. This approach can help identify types of humor without a lot of the researchers' preconceived notions creeping into the interpretation, too.

The statistical technique for identifying these factors is an aptly named procedure called factor analysis. Factor analysis takes a whole lot of variables and helps explain how they fluctuate by reducing them to just a handful of key factors. It's really just a fancy way to see if people tend to rate some of the jokes very similarly, but meaningfully differently from the way that they rate other jokes. In a sense, some jokes would go together to form a factor of their own that is distinctly separate from another factor formed by other jokes. I won't go into the math involved;

it requires Greek letters that sound like cat noises. But the factors wouldn't have to fall into obvious categories like "funny" and "not funny," especially because what's hilarious to one person is idiotic to the next. Each factor would simply contain jokes that each person rated similarly, whether or not the rater thought that all the jokes on the factor were sidesplitting or idiotic. In the end, instead of hundreds of joke ratings, a factor analysis might be able to explain the ratings with three or four key ideas.

One superb line of research started with 600 jokes or cartoons, and had all different kinds of people serving as raters (Ruch, 1992). This approach is a great one because the jokes were numerous and varied—many were simply selected at random from magazines and books. A more focused, less randomized selection would not provide results that could apply across a lot of different domains of humor. For example, if raters had only examined knock-knock jokes, the derived factors might not apply to Shakespeare's comedies. (Although, see *Macbeth*, act 2, scene 3, for some knock-knock jokes from the Bard of Avon.) In addition, the raters included all different kinds of people. They were young and old, came from everywhere from Australia to Zurich, and had a variety of economic and educational backgrounds. This approach helps create results that apply to a more diverse array of people than if the researchers only focused on the folks they could grab most easily: college students. If all the raters come from the Introductory Psychology class at an American Ivy League school or at Frankfort University of Central Kentucky, their ratings might differ markedly from each other and from everybody else in the world.

In addition, participants not only rated how funny they thought the joke was, they also rated how aversive or harsh it seemed. Note that these two ratings could be independent of each other. Aversive jokes might still be funny to some people. In memory of my Uncle Chuck, I should mention one that he told often despite its aversiveness.

"What's yellow and tastes like bananas?"

"Monkey spit."

But people might see some jokes as being funny without being aversive. A trendy example from a groovier era was:

"How many hipsters does it take to change a lightbulb?"

"What! You don't know?"

Other jokes might strike raters as aversive but not funny. My wife's grandmother, who caught the last train out of Vienna as World War II was heating up, does not want to guess what Hitler called his boogers (Snotzies).

Ruch and his colleagues found three factors that accounted for a lot of the variation in perceptions of humor and aversiveness. One factor, much to the delight of many and the dismay of some, had to do with the actual content of the joke or cartoon. This factor relied on the joke's topic rather than the structure of how it worked. The subject matter, that universal theme across languages, cultures, ages, economic backgrounds, and education was—drum roll, please—sex. In fact, comparable work has suggested a sex factor of humor for more than 65 years (Eysenck, 1942). This result was no stunning surprise. Sex jokes have quite the history. Aristophanes' comedic play *Lysistrata*, where the women withhold sex until the men agree to stop an unpopular war, came out in 411 B.C.E. (I hope comparable steps might work today.) We've had sex jokes for at least that long. People's reactions are reasonably consistent when they rate material that has anything to do with double entendre, nakedness, or Rabelais's legendary game (1524/1973) of the beast with two backs. In addition to sex, the sole content factor, two other factors arose, but these seemed unrelated to content. They had more to do with the way that the joke worked than with what it was about. One was labeled "incongruity resolution" and the other was called "nonsense."

Mechanisms of Mayhem: The Incongruity-Resolution Theory of Humor

Incongruity resolution is at the heart of many explanations of comedy, so it's no surprise that Ruch's results revealed it as an underlying factor in jokes. One of the more accessible theories of humor is Suls's intuitively named incongruity-resolution model (1972). A simplified version of the model appears in Figure 1.1. Incongruity arises when a joke or story generates an expectation but then adds new information that violates it. Legendary comic Emo Philips often says, "My grandfather died peacefully in his sleep, but the kids on his bus were screaming."

This example can help illustrate the incongruity-resolution model. Suls suggests that the setup of any comedic material leads a person to generate a prediction—an expected meaning. The comment "My grandfather died peacefully in his sleep" provides most of us with an image of the old guy lying tranquilly in bed. Suls emphasizes that the punch line of the joke has to differ from our prediction or we won't find it funny (i.e., you could see it coming). The punch line has to violate one of

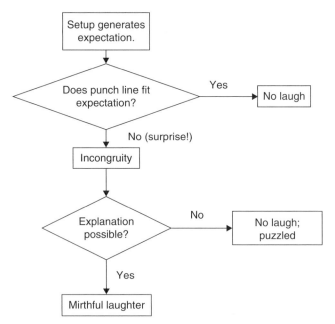

FIGURE 1.1 This is a simplified version of Suls's incongruity-resolution model.

our assumptions about what's going on and lead to a surprise. Comics often call this aspect of the punch "the reveal." The reveal surprises the audience by pointing out that a previous expectation was incorrect. No surprise; no laughter (at least in Suls's model). If you say, "My grandfather died peacefully in his sleep and everyone cried," it fits the initial prediction, offers no surprise, and wouldn't be funny even if you knew Emo Philips's grandfather. If you say, "Everyone cried when my grandfather died," it is even less funny, if that's possible. There's simply no incongruity. A comparable model, the script-based semantic theory of humor, from the linguistics literature, suggests that any joke must initially be compatible with two different scripts or meanings. These two meanings must be incompatible and run counter to each other somehow (Attardo, 1994; Attardo & Raskin, 1991). Elaborations on this idea appear in the General Theory of Verbal Humor (Attardo, 2008), a model with a name too serious for its subject matter. But in a sense, anything that can be seen two different ways can serve as the foundation of a joke, as we'll see in the last chapter of this book.

The next step involved in the incongruity-resolution model relies on how we handle the surprise. Suls (1972) asserts that humans tend to try to make sense of the world. (Perhaps he doesn't know too many politicians.) We deal with the surprise in the punch line the same way we tackle other surprises, with an attempt to solve the problem that it creates. We search for some rule, some explanation, that might make sense of this new information. We try to find some way to look at it to resolve the incongruity. The punch line "...but the kids on his bus were screaming" clearly defies the image of a gray-haired old man snug in his covers. We rack our brains for some way to get the punch line's information to follow from the setup's content. The idea that the grandfather fell asleep at the wheel while working at his job as a bus driver offers a reasonable explanation. This new view resolves the incongruity. According to the model, a structure like this one gives the joke the potential to be funny. If a punch line presents information that is

17

incongruous with assumptions generated by the setup, and a moment's thought resolves this incongruity by changing that assumption, we find it funny. It won't create nervous laughter or polite smiling; it will create genuine mirth. Comprehending and appreciating the joke require solving a problem of sorts, but it pays off with delight. Of course, all this brain racking happens rapidly, but the model suggests that it has to happen so as to elicit a chuckle. And, as Elwyn Brooks White and the cynics warned, dissecting the joke in this much detail makes it about as funny as crabs.

Ruch's series of studies revealed that incongruity resolution helped explain a lot of the variation in the ratings of the jokes and cartoons. Incongruity resolution seems ubiquitous in comedy. Note that incongruity resolution need not require words. Charlie Chaplin's silent films are filled with examples. In a legendary scene in *The Immigrant* (Chaplin, 1917), the camera shows bedraggled, weary refugees enduring a rocky boat ride. Charlie's character hangs over the railing, his back turned to the audience, feet flopping off the ground, and back arching as if he is fatally seasick. When he turns to face the camera, we notice quite the incongruous sight: a fish on a line. What does this fish have to do with Chaplin's nauseated ride? We realize that the character was fishing, not retching—resolving the incongruity with an alternative explanation for all his odd movements.

The incongruity-resolution model says that this aspect gives the scene the potential to create laughter. We get a setup from the view of all the refugees on a swaying ship and Charlie's odd motions when his back is turned to us. We get a moment of incongruity when he turns with a fish, but it's resolved in an instant when we see what he's been doing. Other models of humor focus on different aspects of content and structure, but most modern theories include incongruity as an important component. Alternative models jump through hoops while explaining why they don't include incongruity, and methinks sometimes they protest too much (see Latta, 1998).

Keeping Surprise to a Minimum

Suls's original incongruity-resolution model emphasizes that the surprise of the incongruity can get us started in our search for the resolution and our appreciation of the joke. Nevertheless, data suggest that there shouldn't be too much surprise. Plenty of jokes told in everyday life begin with, "Have you heard the one about...?" They keep the surprise to a minimum. Most punch lines in incongruity-resolution jokes aren't astonishing bombshells. One study asked people to rate the predictability of punch lines in jokes, and then asked other people to rate how funny the jokes seemed (Kenny, 1955). Surely enough, the predictable punch lines were generally funnier. Another study emphasized that the folks in Kenny's (1955) work had already heard the punch lines when they rated them, potentially altering their claims of predictability (Pollio & Mers, 1974). As an alternative, these guys played tapes of stand-up routines and stopped them right before each punch line. Participants then wrote down what they thought the punch line would be. Trained raters then coded whether or not the punch lines matched what these participants guessed, assessing their predictability. These predictability ratings correlated significantly with how much people laughed in response to the jokes. Both of these studies suggest that predictable, rather than surprising, punch lines can be funnier. These data belie other models that rest on the violation of expectancies as inherent in humor, too.

Nonsense: Incongruity With No Resolution

The other factor that appeared in Ruch's examinations of jokes was nonsense—incongruity with no resolution. Like incongruity resolution and unlike sex, this factor focuses on structure rather than content. Part of the beauty of nonsense is that it can involve any topic at all—even multiple, outrageously unrelated topics. Football might meet up with sponge diving. Rappers might zoom to Mars in tuxedos made of bacon. These jokes tend to appear completely nutty and bizarre. They contain the incompatible, surprising aspects that are central to the incongruity-resolution model, but the resolution is incomplete. The search for the new rule that makes sense of the incongruity never quite succeeds. Suls's model suggests that this situation should lead to a puzzled reaction rather than laughter. Many times, for many people, it does. Some folks find jokes that use this structure hilarious; others truly despise them. It may say quite a bit about Shakespeare's "ear of him that hears it."

It's hard to explain why some unresolved or partially resolved incongruities seem funny while others leave folks scratching their heads. This problem with nonsense becomes a challenge for models of humor. Gary Larson's infamous *Far Side* cartoon "Cow Tools" shows a heifer standing on two legs beside a workbench covered with instruments that look completely useless and vaguely udder-like. Even a Troglodyte would have ridiculed these gadgets. The incongruity is definitely there—we don't expect cows to have any tools at all. And there's certainly something of a surprise in the appearance of this gear. But the view that can resolve it all is hard to find. The work seems to suggest something about our stereotypes of early instruments. Perhaps those who denigrate primitive human tools should cut our ancestors some slack, particularly given how unsophisticated the inventions of other animals would be. Nevertheless, this view doesn't quite explain this bizarre scene. The drawing generated so much mail that the cartoonist had to issue a press release in an attempt to explain that there was nothing to explain (Larson, 1989).

These two structural factors, incongruity resolution and nonsense, were not completely independent of the content-oriented sex factor. Some jokes on sexual topics work by resolving incongruities. One joke that won't make my publisher wince comes from an academic article (Long & Graesser, 1988).

A man invites his date back to his apartment, opens a bottle of bourbon, and begins pouring it into a glass for her.

"Say when," he says.

"Right after this drink."

The punch line is an incongruous, unexpected answer to a question about how much bourbon this woman wants. But the incongruity is resolved if we view her statement as the response to a more pressing inquiry. There is sexual content within an incongruity-resolution structure.

Other sex jokes weigh largely on the nonsense factor. These have sexual content and work via an incongruity that is not resolved. The animated television show *Family Guy*, a notorious source of this kind of humor, provides an example of a sex joke that works partly via nonsense. In the episode "The Road to Germany," Brian explains to Stewie that failing to use his time machine to rescue Mort would be an egregious error. "That'd be more irresponsible than silent movie porn," he states. Suddenly the scene cuts to a grainy, black and white film of a man and a woman, in bed, who are accompanied by piano music. Via the silent-movie-style intertitles, the woman asks if the man has rubbers. He reveals his rain boots. The incongruity of showing the rain boots in the discussion about rubbers is resolved. Thanks to the knowledge that rubbers can mean either condoms or rainwear, this joke makes sense. But Brian's initial, incongruous expression "That'd be more irresponsible than silent movie porn," never quite gets resolved. The cut away may imply that porn from the silent era was irresponsible because it depicted unsafe sex, but this point isn't communicated exactly. The scene then returns to Brian and Stewie as if nothing ever happened, adding to the sense of nonsense. The sexual content and non-sense components would suggest that this scene would weigh largely on both factors.

Making Sense of Nonsense

Ruch's three factors may not fit everyone's preconceptions about humor, particularly for folks who are accustomed to focusing on content. After all, where are the fart jokes? But they provide a great shorthand for talking about humor and a nice framework for helping to explain it. The nonsense factor actually presents a challenge to the incongruity-resolution model because a complete resolution is not essential to this form of humor. Sometimes, in the right environment, incongruity may be all that it takes. Odd events that never make sense can still be funny, for both children and adults (Pien & Rothbart, 1976). Critics of the incongruity-resolution model suggest that one line of laboratory findings supports the idea that resolution may not be essential to humor.

This research began with a crafty study by Nerhardt (1970) that used a weight judgment paradigm. These experiments typically ask people to close their eyes and lift a small, round weight, often about a pound. This initial weight serves as a reference. Participants first lift this reference weight and then lift a comparison weight to estimate if the second one is lighter or heavier than the first. The first 10 comparison weights are within a couple of ounces of the 1-pound reference weight. Most participants work assiduously in their judgments. They lift each weight multiple times and mark their answers with great care. The last weight is then dramatically lighter (by 14 ounces) or heavier (by 6 pounds) than the reference weight and all the previous comparison weights, creating a drastic incongruity. Lifting this last weight often makes people crack a smile. They report that they find lifting the deviant weight funny or amusing. As psychology researchers are wont to do, they altered all kinds of other aspects of the experiment and asked participants a plethora of other questions in doing additional work. The results suggested that the smiles didn't stem only from surprise, embarrassment, tension, or anger. Several researchers assert that this result means that resolution is not essential to humor (Deckers, 1993).

Supporters of the incongruity-resolution model argue that the weight judgment paradigm actually does have a resolution. They assert that participants lift the last weight, recognize the incongruity, and resolve it with the idea that this last weight is some sort of joke. This explanation seems to go a bit beyond the way the model was initially proposed. Now it's not as if the punch line creates and resolves an incongruity, but it's as if it communicates that the expectation of the experiment is out of whack. Lifting the disparate weight is an incongruity resolved by the realization that the situation is really a joke. The result clearly suggests that broadening the scope of the incongruity-resolution model could help explain more examples of humor. It might even help us handle the nonsense problem (Wyer, 2004; Wyer & Collins, 1992). Suls, perhaps feeling cornered, emphasized that he designed the incongruity-resolution model to explain humor comprehension, not humor appreciation (Suls, 1983). Additions from other theorists helped. These new theories added more conditions for specifying what's funny and when it's funny.

Playful Perspectives and Diminished Punch Lines

As part of a more general framework of motivation called "reversal theory," Apter (1982) suggested that humor requires important conditions besides an incongruity, whether they are resolved or not. First, humor is part of play, so its appreciation requires a playful mental state. Apter's periods of play are distinctly separate from the goal-directed, serious, "real world" mindset of moments while on a mission. Everyone has stretches of each. It's a bit like the distinction between focusing on a journey or focusing on a destination. A leisurely drive through hillsides has no goal other than the enjoyment of the ride. In contrast, as an ambulance speeds to the emergency room, there's no time to smell the asphalt. Apter calls the goal-directed mindset the "telic" state. *Telos* is Greek for "purpose" or "goal." The playful mental state is "paratelic," meaning "alongside the goal state." The paratelic conditions would be more mellow, oriented in the present, and spontaneous. The chance of laughter is a lot higher.

The point may seem obvious, but it's essential. If Nerhardt had done the original weight judgment task using identical suitcases of disparate weights, lifted by people who had just stepped off a train, few would have found a markedly heavier or a dramatically lighter suitcase to be much of a giggle. They probably would have preferred to get home already. One formal experiment offers support for the influence of a paratelic state. Participants read stories that either did or did not have a punch line. Some were told to read the stories as they would any magazine or novel—more paratelic instructions. Others were asked to read the story in order to provide important, formal ratings of its level of humor—a more telic, goal-oriented condition. Of course, everyone rated the stories with punch lines as funnier, but the impact of the punch lines was greater in the paratelic condition than in the telic (Wyer & Collins, 1992). I bet that a group instructed to search the stories for typos would find the punch lines even duller. I'm sure that my copy editor would agree.

Apter continues by asserting that in addition to requiring a playful, paratelic setting, each joke itself must have certain qualities, including a punch line that leads to diminishment. Essentially, the setup suggests a serious predicament that the punch line reveals as less serious—it's diminished. Herbert Spencer (1860) first alluded to this notion, calling it a "descending incongruity." It's a bit like discovering that a telic situation is actually a paratelic one, which can certainly prove enjoyable, if not funny outright. A *New Yorker* Caption Contest winner provides a good example of diminishment. In cartoon number 124, over a dozen people crawl among the cacti under a fierce sun in a dehydrating desert. Apparently they will all soon die from thirst. One turns to another and states, "I don't know about you, but I'd be willing to pitch in for a new contact lens." The potentially critical condition of imminent death is diminished to a mere search for a plastic disk.

The idea of diminishment seems important for identifying situations that may have incongruity and a resolution but no genuine mirth. Imagine if the scene in Chaplin's *The Immigrant* went from a less serious situation to a more serious one. Instead of panning across a bunch of nauseated faces, the camera might show lots of people fishing off the side of the boat. We would then see Charlie's feet flailing in the air and assume he was fishing. He might then turn with a hanky (or worse) across his mouth. The incongruity would be resolved when we realized he wasn't fishing; he was seasick. Though the incongruity is resolved, the second situation is not a diminished one. Seasickness seems more serious than fishing. Few would find this scene funny—even my Uncle Chuck. In fact, many horror stories work by resolving an incongruity in this opposite direction of diminishment, with the resolution suggesting a critically more serious situation than originally expected. The competitive ballet academy that turns out to be a coven of witches, an attractive date who is actually a vampire, or a pious clergyman unmasked as a child molester remain staples of the horror genre. Much of the laughter at horror movies is of a nervous nature rather than mirthful, too (Lewis, 2006).

Apter emphasizes that diminishment need not happen to the characters in a joke; the quality of the communication between the teller and the listeners could be diminished as well. This approach suggests that the punch line can work in two different ways: within the joke and above it. The punch line can reveal an incongruity based on a previous assumption within the story of the joke, as in Emo Philips's grandfather's dying in his sleep. Or it can communicate on another level, *above* the content of the joke, so to speak. Diminished punch lines that work above the joke send a message that the whole story and the telling of it require a less serious interpretation. An example comes from my Uncle Tom, Chuck's older brother.

A traveling salesman stops at a farmer's house to ask if he can stay the night.

"Sure, you can stay," says the farmer, "but you'll have to sleep with my three dogs."

"Dogs!" the salesman exclaims. "I must be in the wrong joke."

The punch line communicates to the listener that the whole story is a bit of a scam, violating assumptions about the way a joke is told rather than an assumption within the words of the joke.

Any comment that undermines the formality of a conversation can diminish the situation and potentially generate a smirk or two. This kind of diminishment can help explain everyday examples of wit that might not fit standard incongruity-resolution models. Nonsense jokes may create this kind of situation. Their punch lines often communicate the thought that "this ought to make sense but it doesn't; so don't take it so seriously." This kind of diminishment has helped students endure some astoundingly dull lectures and brought me some teaching awards, too.

Shaggy and Diminished Dogs

Shaggy-dog stories can work via this form of diminishment, when they work at all. These convoluted tales begin like important parables, but they subsequently end with some absurd conclusion. The punch line reveals that the content of the story itself is diminished, which may explain the humor in this format. My dad takes 40 minutes to tell the original story, which involves a man who owns a disheveled mutt. Everyone raves about her supreme shagginess and encourages him to drag the canine to the queen to receive the substantial cash prize for having the shaggiest dog. At every turn, new characters confirm that this hound definitely will win the award. When the man reaches the throne, the queen states flatly, "That dog's not shaggy."

Apter's model suggests that our usual view of social interactions that involve stories of this length creates an expectation of an important message. The punch line diminishes the content. How a yarn like this generated a whole category of jokes remains a mystery, but many shaggy-dog stories reveal the diminishment of their content via a punch line that involves a pun. Puns, which Samuel Johnson allegedly called the lowest form of humor, rely on words or phrases that sound similar but have different meanings. My stepdad tells a shaggy-dog story that involves a man who offers to pay his friend Arthur to strangle his wife for him. Arthur has no experience with murder, so he agrees to commit the crime for two rolls of pennies. The murder is successful but the butler and the maid catch Arthur in the act, forcing him to kill them as well. The next day's headline reads, "Artie Chokes Three for a Dollar." Again, the punch line suggests that a potentially serious news story is not news at all. It's not the content of the story that is reinterpreted, as in an incongruity-resolution joke, but it's the context of the storytelling that is diminished. This view of diminishment can explain how these stories work. Unfortunately, it does not explain how my mother married two such storytellers.

Slapping Sticks, Aggression, and Superiority

Note that diminishment might also provide a novel account of the appeal of another form of humor: slapstick. The hallmark of slapstick is exaggerated aggression that causes inordinately little harm. The original slapping stick itself—two boards connected so that one smacked loudly against the other without applying much force—had diminishment built into it. Actors could bop each other and generate plenty of noise without injuries. Each whack suggested a serious situation, but each reaction revealed a harmless, diminished one. Aggressive humor like this inspired a lot of early theories of comedy, including an aside from Plato (360 B.C.E.). Up to a point at least, gags that are more hostile also appear funnier (Bryant, 1977; Zillmann, Bryant, & Cantor, 1974). (Increased hostility can backfire if it's too severe. The comedy instructor extraordinaire Greg Dean tells a story of a crafty slapstick routine where he whacks a partner with a mop. When the two got so good at it that they could make the smack seem particularly hard, audiences actually gasped, instead of laughing [Dean, 2000]). Freud (1905), the father of psychoanalysis himself, viewed jokes as an opportunity to enjoy repressed sexual and hostile impulses without upsetting internalized standards of propriety. They allow us to let our own sexual, violent urges eke out in an acceptable way.

What often makes these urges acceptable is the diminished status of the joke.

Others assert that humor involves a feeling of superiority. These theorists even depict benign wordplay as a sort of dominating trickery. They view pun-induced groans as declarations of defeat (Gruner, 1997). This approach is hard to disprove. If each incongruity that could lead to a laugh essentially pulls a fast one on the perceiver, there's no way to have a joke without a smidgen of hostility. Larson's "Cow Tools" becomes bovine aggression; Chaplin's fishing scene in *The Immigrant* chides viewers for thinking that he wasn't fishing.

The notion of superiority as an essential requirement for humor seems unlikely, given the innumerable comics who ridicule themselves for laughs. But superiority theorists claim that self-deprecating humor becomes a domination of who we were before now. The self-deprecating comics of the present moment are proving themselves superior to their former selves. A friend of mine tells a story of how he once had a headache and so his mother gave him an aspirin. He had no idea how an aspirin worked, so he stuck it in his bellybutton. Superiority theorists suggest that even though my friend is seen as the butt of his own joke, the story involves his current self, at age 40, poking fun at his previous self, when he was only 21. With this kind of time lag, perhaps the superiority of the current self over the former self makes some kind of sense.

Nevertheless, a host of comics mock themselves in their current state and at the current time. These jokes make this interpretation of superiority seem a bit odd. Louie Anderson, a stand-up talent whose weight is dramatically above average for his height, calls the room about his size when he comes on the stage. He moves the thin microphone stand and says, "I'll get this out of the way, so you can see me." This opener invariably gets a laugh. The only way that Louie could genuinely think that he could hide behind a thin metal rod would require an IQ below freezing. By making himself seem both fat and dumb in the current moment, Louie is hardly dominating anyone, including any previous versions of himself. Perhaps the superiority aspect comes from the audience's feeling both thinner and smarter than the comic, but the idea of diminishment may offer a reasonable alternative explanation. Louie's incongruous comment suggests that a serious, taboo topic (his weight), is not so serious because he's well aware of the issue.

Although aggressive jokes certainly disparage their subjects, diminishment doesn't have to be negative. Apter's diminishment approach can help humorists generate punch lines with a broader scope than can mere domination, too. No one need be harmed or ridiculed. Each punch line can move a joke from a serious topic to a less serious one without violence. Moe Howard, of Three Stooges fame, need not have bashed his brothers, Curly and Shemp, to get a laugh. Humorists can make a topic funny by making it seem mundane; the poke in the eye is optional.

Diminishment in the Laboratory

Although diminishment seems common in a range of humor, only an experiment could support the idea that it actually makes things funny. Some artful work in the laboratory has taken some steps in this direction. Nevertheless, the work is not perfect. Researchers started with ambiguous stories. One story sounded like two people planning to kill someone, but an ending sentence revealed that they were actually trying to open a jar of pickles. Participants came to the lab and read different versions of the story. Some read the version that included the revealing punch line, shifting the tale from the murderous to the mundane. Those who read the alternative version, which sounded like a threatening plot throughout, found the story significantly less funny. The version that included diminishment was funnier, potentially supporting the theory (Wyer & Collins, 1992). Unfortunately, as far as I can tell, the unfunny version lacked incongruity as well as diminishment, making the results hard to interpret. The ratings might have dropped from a lack of incongruity rather than a lack of diminishment. This study actually needed a third condition—one that had incongruity but lacked diminishment. If the story seemed to be about murder but in the end had an incongruous sentence that made readers realize it was actually about a nuclear holocaust, then that would have done the trick, although I still suspect that the pickle version would be rated funniest.

In another experiment, researchers told participants that they would have to handle a large, white lab rat. Some learned that they would need to lift the rodent and hold it; others were told that they would have to take a blood sample from the red-eyed rascal. The experimenters provided a lab coat, elaborate cages, and detailed instructions in an effort to make the situation as credible as possible. Once the participants reached the rat, however, they saw that it was rubber. Most found the fact funny. Those who had expected to draw blood rated the experience as significantly more amusing (Shurcliff, 1968). These results might have arisen for many reasons, but a greater diminishment led to greater humor. Apter's work is particularly sensitive to the context of the joke. The punch line must reduce importance in a specific setting. This predicament with the rat would not be funny in other contexts. Imagine a doctoral candidate who must experiment on one more rat to finish a dissertation. When she reaches in the last cage to find Shurcliff's rubber rodent, she is not amused. This situation is not diminished in seriousness in relation to the expectation. It's potentially a complete drag.

Nevertheless, one counterexample may reveal that the definition of diminishment in context might grow slippery—or, perhaps, suggest that no single theory of humor can account for everything that is funny. Recall, again, Emo Philips's joke, "My grandfather died peacefully in his sleep, but the kids on his bus were screaming." We walked through the resolution of incongruity in this joke previously. The question remains: Is the situation described in the punch line diminished in relation to the original expectation? A bus squealing down the road, filled with shrieking children and a lifeless driver, seems a tad grimmer than an old fellow meeting his Maker in bed. Fans of the idea of diminishment might emphasize that the communication itself is diminished in this case, as it is in a shaggy-dog story. It seems unlikely that Emo would tell the tale in this manner if his grandfather had actually expired while in this predicament. He must be kidding. This interpretation emphasizes that either type of diminishment can contribute to the humor in the punch line—a diminished situation within the joke or as part of the communication. As a thought experiment, let's change one word of the punch line to alter the diminishment within the joke itself: "My grandfather died peacefully in his sleep, but the kids on his bus *died* screaming." Compared to the original version, this punch line is markedly less diminished. It also seems less droll.

LAUGHTER: AROUSAL AND RELIEF

Although Apter's theory emphasizes that diminishment is important for humor, he never precisely explains why. Intuition would suggest that when a punch line reveals that a potentially serious situation is not serious, anyone would experience a bit of relief. Theories of humor that rely on relief have a long history (Kant, 1790; Spencer, 1860), and never quite seem to die out (Latta, 1998). They suggest that laughter dissipates pent-up energy. If a setup sounds menacing but a punch line reveals it's innocuous, the initial angst disappears. Andy Kaufman's disheveled, snot-nosed appearance on David Letterman's show in 1980 generated astounding discomfort and raucous laughter. It's unclear who was, or who wasn't, experiencing genuine mirth related to humor. Letterman looked downright infuriated. Years later, Crispin Glover and Joaquin Phoenix pulled the same trick on Dave, who must be getting pretty weary from it. Shurcliff's (1968) work with the rodents revealed that those who were most anxious in the beginning found the rubber rat the funniest.

Nevertheless, plenty of humorous situations begin with a signal that menace is limited. These signs make these relief theories seem problematic. How anxious can a listener get when a tale begins with, "Have you heard the one about the...?"

Other research suggests that the notion of relief may be irrelevant. Instead, arousal makes things funnier, and funnier things increase arousal. Folks who are more stimulated view jokes as more humorous than folks who are less stimulated. A favorite professor of mine performed the classic experiment on this topic (Schachter & Wheeler, 1962). The participants were randomly assigned to one of three conditions. One group received an injection of adrenaline, the source of the body's "3F" response, which inspires fleeing, fighting, and mating. This shot aroused them considerably. A second group received a sedating drug. A third got an injection of saltwater. Participants then watched a slapstick flick. An experiment like this one would never get past an ethics committee today, but this was back in what Schachter often referred to as "the good old days." The people who received the arousing drug rated the film as funnier. They smiled and laughed more, too. Those who got the sedative scored the lowest on all measures; the saline group fell between the other two. Further work revealed that almost any kind of arousal—positive, negative, or otherwise—can make jokes hilarious. For example, researchers had participants read sexy or gruesome stories before rating jokes. They found that either form of arousal made the gags seem funnier (Cantor, Bryant, & Zillmann, 1974). This result reminds me of a time when I saw a rising comic have a bad set, lose his cool, and start yelling at the audience. It was a shocking, dreadful experience, but the woman who went on next had the best show of her life. The crowd's arousal from the first comic's uncontrolled outburst might have worked to her benefit. Since then, I've always wondered if paying the previous performer to flip out might make an act go better.

Folks who are more aroused appear to think that things are funnier, at least up to a point. But it doesn't look as if relief from arousal is the sole explanation for why diminishment works. In fact, monkeyshines enhance stimulation, rather than dissipating it. Jocular films, jokes, and cartoons increase stress hormones, skin conductance (essentially a measure of sweating), muscle tension, blood pressure, and heart rate (Hubert, Möller, & de Jong-Meyer, 1993; McGhee, 1983). Humor certainly relates to arousal; it may be an emotional response of its own. This seems to be one explanation for how diminishment might be important even if it's associated with an increase in arousal. Reducing a topic's importance doesn't require reducing an audience's stimulation. In fact, the diminishment that leads to laughter also increases arousal.

Thus far, jokes appear to contain a topic that can be seen two different ways, and a setup that creates certain expectations about what's going on (Attardo, 2008). The punch line adds new, potentially surprising information that is incongruent with the expectations inherent in the setup. This incongruity might or might not be resolved. The punch line should provide clues to an alternative way to view the information in the setup, so that it is consistent with the punch line, solving the incongruity and potentially leading to a guffaw or two. If the incongruity is not resolved, the whole communication is diminished. The perceiver changes perspective from viewing the material, the story itself, as potentially serious to viewing it as mundane.

THE IMPOSSIBLE DREAM: A COMPREHENSIVE THEORY OF HUMOR

Humor appears in many types. A comprehensive theory of every type may prove impossible, perhaps because the various forms don't all share a single, defining quality. One form of humor may differ completely from another in every way, save for making someone giggle. Dividing humor into jokes (including cartoons, visual gags, or spoken words) and spontaneous wit (the happy banter that occurs in conversation) helps focus the theories. It also suggests that perhaps no single theory can account for all of humor. Self-contained jokes and everyday wit might work in varied but comparable ways. In addition, some types of jokes might work differently than other types, and some types of wit might work differently from other types of wit, too.

Jokes appear to involve a single topic that can be seen in two different ways. Many rely on setups and punch lines. Setups tend to create an expectation. The punch line tends to violate the expectation in a special manner. The punch line often provides new information that seems incongruous with the expectation created by the setup. Comics have a name for the components of the punch line that uncover the incongruity: "the reveal." The reveal may create a feeling of surprise, but astonishment doesn't seem essential to the humor. Some jokes have a reveal that leads an audience to come up with a reasonable explanation for how their initial expectation went awry. The explanation often includes the realization that something they thought was serious is markedly less so. This explanation resolves the incongruity and leads to laughter. These incongruity-resolution jokes are common and popular. Other jokes seem to work on a different level. Instead of offering a genuine resolution of the incongruity within the joke's story, the punch line communicates that the whole tale is in jest. This nonsense generates laughs, but it's hard to predict when it will work and when it won't. Spontaneous wit has proven more difficult to study because it's hard to bring it into the laboratory. The banter that appears in everyday conversation seems to fit the structure and topics found in jokes. Catalogs based on forms of humor and content are numerous and varied, but they reveal a lot about the commonalities of funny subject matter.

All these different forms of gags and banter provide a quick way of discussing diverse types of humor. Questions remain. So far, the various categories of humor seem to miss its inherently playful, social aspects. Laughter seems important for forming new friendships, maintaining close ones, communicating interest and appeal, and attracting a date or three. Few people write one-liners for themselves alone. No one makes wisecracks to the refrigerator. But jokes and banter can form a two-edged sword. With humor, we can share our joy with others, show off our own wit, or discuss tough topics with less fear of offending. But we can also disparage ourselves, others, the world, and the future. Still, better a double-edged sword than no sword at all. Without humor, we may all find ourselves sitting around with a steaming cup of Pot Noodles and no one to share them with. Let's look in the next chapter at humor's interpersonal aspects.

Laughing Together: Interpersonal Humor

ashionable, young Anna Maria Italiano, a television regular and a 2-time Tony award winner, had played the beauty opposite macho heroes in three Hollywood flicks. She would soon appear as the definitive seductress in *The Graduate*, a movie that defined a generation. One night she sat in a trendy restaurant, and who happened by but the frumpy, down-on-his-luck Melvin Kaminsky. She had met the short, talkative, quirky writer on the set of a variety show earlier that day. Rumor suggests that he had bribed the show's staff to learn where she would be dining. That way he could appear to run into her by chance. He had also hounded a mutual friend to introduce them a million times. She had dated many who were markedly more famous, rich, and handsome. But she allegedly confided in her therapist the very next day that she knew she had met the man she would marry (Parish, 2008). What would bring a bright, rising star to fall for such an oddball nebbish? Well, let's examine how comedy might bring two such people together.

WHO LAUGHS ALONE?

Comedy is inherently interactive. If an oak falls in the forest and no one sees it, it's not funny. If one person sees it, it might be. If two people see it, there's an even better chance that they'll laugh. The words "social" and "amusing" relate in intriguing ways. Think of a business luncheon as opposed to a social luncheon, for example. The social one seems to have a lot more potential for fun. In this chapter, we'll look at the social psychology of humor, starting with a walk through how the presence of other people can make things seem funnier. We'll note how humor can have a positive or a negative tone and it can focus on ourselves or on those around us. Then we'll see how humor can function to maintain the status quo. When it comes to hierarchies, getting a feel for who's cracking jokes and laughing can communicate who's top dog. We'll move to gender differences (and the lack thereof), and then see how humor contributes to developing friendships, finding a date, and maintaining an intimate relationship. This literature connects to some big ideas in social psychology and has more than its share of controversy (and applications).

We laugh more with others than by ourselves (e.g., see Robbins & Vandree, 2009). In fact, we laugh 30 times more with others than by ourselves (Provine, 2000). Sometimes the other people are in our heads, but not in a psychotic, you're-hearing-voices sense. Solo laughter often entails imagined social interaction—we envision others talking or listening as we chuckle on our own. Solo laughter can also involve indirect communication via books, cartoons, or television shows. But laughing alone is the exception rather than the rule. People often ask me why I'd rather teach 400 students than 100, but the bigger the crowd, the bigger the laughs (Morrison, 1940).

We're more likely to chortle if others are around, particularly if they're chuckling, too. It's not crystal clear why we laugh more in groups. We seem to take cues from others about what is and isn't funny. Other folks might increase our general arousal, too, which might be part of what makes the laughter louder. As we saw in Chapter 1, arousal increases the giggles (Cantor, Bryant, & Zillman, 1974). But there seems to be something more social and interactive at play.

Arousal is not the whole story behind increased laughter in the presence of others. Even an inanimate gizmo can make us guffaw or grin if it emits repeated chuckles. I doubt that the mechanical cackle actually raises arousal, but it's a reliable source of amusement in the lab. As long as the poor participants don't have to hear the machine over and over, it'll leave people with a smile. The sound of laughter may cue us that it's not only okay, but actually appropriate, to chuckle and snort. This contagious aspect of laughter suggests that our brains might have evolved somehow to detect and replicate chuckles, for reasons that may be hard to glean (Provine, 1992). Tickling and laughing together supports the bond between infant and caregiver (Provine, 2000). The chuckles of children make them just cute enough to keep their financially strapped, sleep-deprived, and emotionally overwrought parents from killing them.

Even among adults, if everyone else is laughing, it's hard not to laugh, too. Television's dreaded laugh track relies on this phenomenon. Research reveals that prerecorded chuckles lead viewers to find the frolicking characters much funnier. After all, the sound track suggests that others think they're funny, too. The scripts are often embarrassingly predictable. One character invariably delivers a simple setup before the fanciful reply from another character. A third feigns surprise and gives the obligatory, exaggerated double-take. A television editor I know claimed that he could add laughter to Spanish sitcoms, despite having no knowledge of the language, simply because this format was so ubiquitous. Even if he didn't understand the joke, he certainly recognized the cues for when to laugh.

A few brave shows have dropped the canned laughter. They might be more generally ironic, rather than being arranged around punch lines. *The Office* has no laugh track, for example. The writers and producers might have avoided the recordings for ethical reasons, too. (See Woody Allen's movie *Annie Hall* for an indictment of the laugh track as a deceitful device.) These shows without laugh tracks also may not attract the viewers who would respond to prerecorded chuckles. In fact, canned laughter works, but only if we think that the people laughing are similar to ourselves. If we explicitly learn that the audience is a group unlike us, we laugh much less (Platow et al., 2005). Nevertheless, dishonest or not, shows that plant shills or the sound of their laughter make us laugh more—even leading us to rate material as funnier. (See Martin [2007] for a review.) Hell may be other people (Sartre, 1944), but comedy seems to involve others, too.

HOW WE USE HUMOR: FOUR HUMOR STYLES

The presence of others, or at least their chuckles, seems to increase our own guffaws. But interactions with people are much more complicated than simply laughing near each other or even tickling that goes back and forth. We saw in Chapter 1 that dividing jokes and wit by content or structure provides insights into what might make something funny. Again, we haven't quite pinned down exactly what "funny" or "humor" means. But we've got plenty of stimuli designed to make people laugh because they're feeling mirthful and amused. (We don't want those uncomfortable laughs in your boss's office to count.) To take humor more into the personal and interpersonal realms, we can look at how we use it by ourselves and with others. What does humor seem to do for us, our buddies, and our acquaintances? This line of work has focused more on the sorts of humor people claim to generate and enjoy. A lot of this research relates to humor's impact on health, which we'll detail in a later chapter. But the bottom line, as an astute theorist emphasized, is that some forms of humor may prove healthier than other types.

Suggesting that some types of humor have a different impact than others requires defining the forms. The proposed categories include four humor styles that are assessed with the use of the aptly named Humor Styles Questionnaire (Martin, et al., 2003). This survey asks folks about the kind of humor they use and enjoy, in an effort to establish how likely they are to use various humor styles. The styles include humor that helps you (1) cheer yourself up and stay lighthearted (self-enhancing humor); (2) make and enjoy friends (affiliative humor); (3) denigrate yourself (self-defeating humor); or (4) show hostility toward others (aggressive humor). Note that two are focused on the self (self-enhancing and self-deprecating) and two are focused on others (affiliative and aggressive). Two are positive (self-enhancing and affiliative) and two are negative (self-defeating and aggressive). Martin and his colleagues didn't see these styles as a conscious decision. They are more a set of habits that reflect people's experience of the humor around them or their intentions when cracking jokes. These terms have a lot of baggage that may need unpacking.

The Positive Humor Styles

Self-enhancing humor, the kind that you can use to help you see the lighter side of things, stems from an amused outlook, an appreciation for the world's folly, and a good attitude about the inane. A revealing item from the self-enhancing scale is, "Even when I'm by myself, I'm often amused by the absurdities of life." It's not about putting yourself above others; it's about catching life's little jokes. Self-enhancing humor makes stress tolerable. It can keep folks from viewing minor annoyances as unbearable disasters. People who report using self-enhancing humor show less anxiety, neuroticism, and depression; better psychological well-being and self-esteem, and more extraversion, optimism, and openness to experience.

An intriguing aspect of the Humor Styles Questionnaire (and lots of other good assessment devices) concerns its items that are scored backwards. Some questions ask what you do; other questions ask what you do not do. What you don't find funny might be as important as what you do. Most questions on a survey like this require that people state the humor that they find or generate. But some items ask about the opposite—things you don't find funny or never joke about. Many questionnaires use this approach to help sidestep several problems. These reverse-scored items can help researchers toss out answers from inattentive schmucks who mindlessly circle the same number for every question. Those who pick the number 5 on a 1–5 scale for both "I'm funny" and "I'm *not* funny" are probably confused, distracted, or worse. Their data aren't going to help science.

In addition, having a sense of humor is a socially desirable thing—there seems to be a big advantage to saying that you have it. (Just check the Personal ads!) We all would like to claim that we're hilarious, even if we aren't. In fact, most folks think of themselves as funnier than most others (Allport, 1961; Lefcourt & Martin, 1986). People tend to claim that they behave in socially desirable ways in a lot of different domains. They often report that they never lie, cheat, steal, use drugs, or have unsafe sex (LaBrie & Earleywine, 2000). So they're certainly going to claim that they crack jokes and slap knees. Therefore, some questions address moments specifically *not* spent exchanging witticisms or blurting out puns. These items give participants the opportunity to acknowledge that humor is not a priority, but without forcing them to confess that they're not funny. One reverse-scored item from the self-enhancing subscale reads, "If I am feeling sad or upset, I usually lose my sense of humor." A high score on this item would mean a low score on self-enhancing humor. Note that respondents could endorse this item without claiming that they're sticks in the mud; it's just that once in a while, they aren't the world's greatest comedians. Both types of items are used in the self-enhancing scale to get a feel for how well people claim to use humor to improve their own outlook.

The other positive style focuses on other people and is labeled "affiliative." Affiliative humor enhances connections among us. A typical item from the affiliative humor subscale of the Humor Style Questionnaire reads, "I enjoy making people laugh." A reverse-scored item from this scale is, "I don't often joke around with my friends." Those who use this style relay jokes to entertain others. They exchange banter in a sociable way. Their wisecracks bring people together or diffuse uncomfortable situations. This style is about pleasant companionship. Multiple studies reveal a lot about folks who use it. They are less stern and more cheerful, outgoing, and open. Like those who use self-enhancing humor, they're also less depressed, less anxious, and higher in self-esteem. Their friends and family are likely to note that they tell jokes and have an amused attitude. Romantic partners of people who use this type of humor report more satisfaction with the relationship (Campbell, Martin, & Ward, 2008). Although some who use affiliative humor make themselves the butt of their own jokes, these jests focus on not taking oneself too seriously. It's not the disparaging of one's own self or others that is present in the negative styles. A sense of self-acceptance remains in an effort to join with others.

The Negative Humor Styles

The negative humor styles—self-deprecating and aggressive— are the dark side of the positives. Those who use self-defeating humor turn their own jokes on themselves. They frequently belittle themselves in the hope of getting a laugh. The jokes often reflect low self-esteem, a denial of problems, or poor coping. Using this style may require generating jokes that cast the joker in a bad light. Even worse, it often includes letting others continue with the ridicule in a maladaptive or hurtful way. A characteristic item reads, "When I am with friends or family, I often seem to be the one that other people make fun of or joke about." A reverse-scored item is, "I don't often say funny things to put myself down." Note that people who use this style can still be quite comical, but in a way that maligns them. Many class clowns spent their childhoods entertaining a room full of peers before they were sent to the principal's office for a reprimand (or to my office for therapy). Folks who use this style report more anxiety, depression, aggression, hostility, and bad moods. They are less conscientious and agreeable. Their romantic partners do not report that they are likely to tell jokes or have a jocular attitude. Their partners do, however, claim that these jesters go overboard in putting themselves down when they try to be funny (Campbell et al., 2008). Let's hope that they don't do the same in the bedroom.

Aggressive humor is exactly the sort of disparaging, hostile, controlling ridicule that its name suggests. The style relies on using laughter at someone else's expense. Typical racist, sexist, homophobic, classist, anti-intellectual, and elitist jokes are the bread and margarine of this style. The manipulative, threatening aspects of this type of humor are paramount. In addition, the authors of the scale emphasize an uncontrolled, blurting aspect to this humor. It's not always thoughtful insults so much as angry slurs. Folks who employ this style seem unable to resist uttering these caustic jabs. Their reports on other questionnaires suggest that they are more hostile, belligerent, and stereotypically masculine. They are also less agreeable and conscientious than others. Their romantic partners recognize their use of aggressive humor. I bet their partners must try to stay out of the line of fire. The style seems unrelated to depression, anxiety, other psychological symptoms, and even optimism. Surprisingly, the style is independent of the joker's own reports of perceived intimacy and social support. Nevertheless, these are their own views of intimacy and social support, not the opinions of friends, family, or partners. Subsequent work with heterosexual couples has shown that relationship satisfaction goes up as a partner's use of aggressive humor goes down, as I'll detail below (Campbell et al., 2008). A sample item from this subscale states, "If someone makes a mistake, I will often tease them (sic) about it." A reverse-scored item reads, "People are never offended or hurt by my sense of humor." Clearly, dividing humor into types in this way is useful in our study of how people interact and stay happy.

THE HUMOR HIERARCHY

Laughter can communicate that it's appropriate to giggle and encourage others to do so. It can also reveal who is on top, and who is not, in social settings. It says a bit about domination. I need to offer a word of caution as we get into this research. This work rarely depicts humans in the nicest light, as we'll see in more detail later. Given what we know about affiliative humor, we need to interpret these experiments with about three grains of salt. It's easy to see all this work and think that everything from puns to punch lines is all about one-upmanship. Teasing and jokes may communicate who's the boss, but comedy has other uses, too. Part of what makes this work so negative is its initial theoretical framework—one that focuses on hostility in jokes.

Early studies on how humor establishes hierarchies rest on aggressiveness and disparagement theories. One of the first of these theories focused on psychodynamic interpretations of jokes as a way to release pent-up hostility (Freud, 1905). Gruner (1997), one of the most outspoken, modern devotees of aggressiveness theories of humor, suggests that every joke is hostile in one way or another. As Mel Brooks's character, The 2,000 Year Old Man, said, before he met Anne Bancroft (as described at the beginning of this chapter): "Tragedy is when I cut my finger. Comedy is when you fall into an open sewer and die" (Reiner & Brooks, 1961). Many jokes suggest that the in-group dominates

45

an out-group, be they blonde-haired people, Jews, academics, those who can't count, or all three. Any group that has a genre of jokes devoted to ridiculing them undoubtedly has a low spot on a totem pole. It's sad but true.

Even humor that is not overtly violent, racist, or sexist can reveal who is in charge. Knowing who laughs when, how much, and in response to whom can tell a lot about status. Adolescents claim that telling jokes can be a key to establishing a top dog (Fuhr, 2001). Folks with more money are less likely to laugh when meeting a stranger, but their poorer peers tend to meet someone new with at least a chuckle or two (Kraus & Keltner, 2009). High-status presenters get more audience laughs than low-status presenters (Kane, Suls, & Tedeschi, 1977), leading many full professors to think that they're funnier than they really are. High-status folks also seem to get away with self-deprecating humor in ways that low-status people cannot. For example, high-status people can look more attractive when they poke fun at themselves, but it doesn't help low-status folks one whit (Greengross & Miller, 2009).

Spontaneous humor in groups also reveals the status effect. An intriguing study looked at groups of six people each. They came to the lab to solve a problem together. Close examinations of the transcripts from laboratory interactions proved telling. First, the contagiousness of humor was obvious: Participants were more likely to get laughs once someone in the group had already inspired a few. Perhaps the first witty comments let everyone know that it's okay to joke. Second, the status of participants predicted humor quite well. The researchers suggested that those who interrupted others were higher in status, an idea that previous work supports. These high-status folks cracked jokes and made others snigger more often than group members of lower status did. The high-status folks spoke more, but that's what we'd expect, given all their interrupting. The researchers controlled for the amount of speaking and got the same results—more jokes per turn speaking for those in higher standing (Robinson & Smith-Lovin, 2001). Men interrupted more, made more jokes, and got more laughs. Women made markedly more jokes in groups that had no men, perhaps because they weren't interrupted. These gender differences may say something about status or reveal different styles and choices in humor for men and women.

GENDER DIFFERENCES

The literature on gender differences in psychology is enormous (Tannen, 2001). Questions about gender differences rest on certain assumptions about the sexes—usually that they are worlds apart. Men and women are actually more similar than different, no matter how delightful those differences may seem. In addition, lumping all men into one category and all women into another misses huge variations in both groups (Crawford, 2003). Nevertheless, gender differences have an undeniable appeal and remain astoundingly popular in psychological research—even more popular than humor. For example, PsycINFO, a source for research in the field, shows over 140,000 publications that mention gender or sex differences. In contrast, humor, comedy, or jokes appear in a mere 9,500. Making sense of this research on differences between men and women requires a careful look at how preconceived notions about the sexes might creep into the interpretation of results.

Early work in the humor literature was consistent with stereotypes of its era, suggesting that women had no wit. Some publications went so far as to recommend that research should focus exclusively on male participants, implying that women's responses were too irregular to predict (Middleton & Moland, 1959; Williams, 1946). Most of this research depicted men as happy jesters and women as an approving audience. Progress from there was embarrassingly slow. Studies from the days of the second wave of feminism, when women could vote but few held paying jobs, focused primarily on humor appreciation.

Publications in the 1940s and 1950s suggested that men liked aggressive and sexual jokes but that women didn't, and that women liked nonsense. But a close look at the stimuli revealed that the aggressive and sexual jokes often belittled women. They weren't just hostile in general, or just sexual, they were downright sexist. It's no wonder women didn't like them much, though at least two studies suggested that they liked these sexist gags more than jokes that disparaged men (Cantor, 1976; Losco & Epstein, 1975). I guess that back in the 1970s, it was more acceptable to ridicule women even to women. A couple of decades later, studies showed that each gender viewed jokes that ribbed the opposite sex as more amusing than jokes aimed at their own sex. Men liked making fun of women and women liked making fun of men. In addition, ratings of sexual jokes that weren't sexist actually showed no gender differences in appreciation (Hemmasi, Graf, & Russ, 1994). Gee, women have great senses of humor if only we stop degrading them. A review of over 40 publications across 26 years suggests that tolerance for sexist jokes has dropped. Comedy that questions traditional gender roles has grown more popular, too (Lampert & Ervin-Tripp, 1998). A cartoon that shows a man cooking and a woman chopping wood could appear funny today but might have been shocking 50 years ago.

Jokes and cartoons remain an incredibly minor part of humor in daily life, so gender differences in other domains may be more important. When it comes to everyday quips and titters, the sexes are more similar than they are different. When men and women track laughter in daily diaries, women laugh more when talking to men than men laugh when talking to women (Provine, 2000). But throughout the day, both laugh with the same frequency and show similar numbers of chuckles in response to media reports, jokes, and anecdotes. Women did report laughing more in social settings. As we've seen before, everyone thought that they were funnier than the average person. But in these data, men rated their own senses of humor as higher than women rated their own. Participants rated men and women as equally funny on average. A look at 10 different aspects of humor found gender differences in only a handful. Men were more likely to claim that they tell jokes, enjoy slapstick, and laugh at hostile humor. Women relayed witty, personal stories more often than men did (Martin & Kuiper, 1999).

Despite rating men and women as equally funny, both men and women, when asked to write a paragraph about a particularly funny person, were more likely to write about a man. Of course, the effect was greater in men. Men wrote about a man 5 times more often; women wrote about a man only twice as often. This result might suggest that we all think of a man when we think of a witty person. After all, it is still true that most comedians are men. But I wonder if there may be less here than meets the eye. There was no control task. Everyone wrote about a particularly funny person and nothing else. I would like to have seen participants also write about a particularly healthy person, or a person performing some innocuous task like making a sandwich. If participants wrote about men more often in tasks like these, we might conclude that people spontaneously tend to write about men regardless of stereotypes about humor (Crawford & Gressley, 1991). Finally, men use disparaging, aggressive humor more often than women do (Greengross & Miller, 2009; Martin et al., 2003). This fact may not come as much of a surprise, but it seems to undermine one of humor's most intriguing potential uses: making friends.

LAUGHTER, LIKING, AND TOGETHERNESS

Saying that friendship is important belabors the obvious. People want friends, but they particularly want friends who have a good sense of humor. In one study, it was as important to have funny friends as it was to have witty romantic partners, with ratings of the desired sense of humor averaging almost 8 on a scale that only went up to 9 (Sprecher & Regan, 2002). The importance of wit plays out in relationships almost immediately. A crafty experiment revealed that people who laugh a lot when they first meet feel closer than those who have an equally enjoyable time but don't actually laugh. The researchers invited same-sex pairs of participants (who had never met before) to come to the lab. One group did tasks designed to elicit giggles. They played a game that was a variation on charades, other games that required odd uses of straws and blindfolds (but no handcuffs), and acted out TV commercials in imaginary languages. The other group played comparable games that were less funny, and reported having an equally enjoyable time. Nevertheless, the folks who had laughed ended up feeling closer at the end of the experiment.

The results of this work suggest that part of humor's effect came from distracting folks from the discomfort of an initial meeting. In addition, the closeness appeared to arise from what the authors called "self-expansion"—the feeling that folks got a new perspective and a greater sense of awareness due to their partner. The idea that humor is all about one thing that is seen two ways (Attardo, 2008) might help explain the new perspective. Participants often come to the laboratory with a certain set of expectations. Many experiments require a full hour of staring at a computer screen and pressing buttons when an X moves, or answering questionnaires about dropping acid with your mother. Researchers do everything they can to keep participants from tuning out, but it's not easy. In contrast, once the laugh-inducing games began in this experiment, participants must have realized that it had the potential to be a lot more fun. The games could let them use their own creativity as they thought up ways to make the tasks particularly humorous. Each realization of a punch line or a witty way to play must have felt like a nice solution to a little problem. When two people share these "ah-ha" cognitive snaps together, it might make them feel more connected. Suddenly the moments are worth attending to. They could be filled with surprise and delight. I find these results especially captivating in the light of other research on how being mindful of the current moment makes people delighted and content (Kabat-Zinn, 2003).

Something about joking and laughing may bring people back to the present. Rather than feeling guilty about the past or worried about the future, they can attend to the current moment. They may be less lost in their regular ruminations about the distractions of the day, making them more attentive to each other and the environment. Some of the changes in brain waves that occur in response to a punch line are comparable to those found whenever we notice some rare, intriguing event that captures our attention (Derks, Gillikin, Bartolome-Rull, & Bogart, 1997). Becoming pals with someone who creates this kind of experience sounds like fun. In fact, under the right circumstances, who wouldn't want to sign up for a lifetime of these experiences? Perhaps the idea contributes to how people find their partners. The literature on dating and humor is a genuine hoot—it makes more sense if we first review a few caveats on dating and mating.

EVOLUTIONARY PSYCHOLOGY: FINDING MATES AND MAKING BABIES

Explaining how people partner can be an impossible task. Some of us are better off assuming that our spouses are irrational and counting our blessings. Intricate guesses about mate selection come from evolutionary psychology, an interdisciplinary look at how our actions may arise from the strategies that we use to find chromosomes to intermingle with our own. Some genes, in some circumstances, make having more kids more likely. These genes will become more common in the population. No one suggests that this process is particularly conscious or divine. It's just a statistical fact. Few people are speed dating with the explicit intention of altering the world population's gene pool. But any trait that correlates with having more children will end up in us having more children. That trait will get more common in each new generation until it no longer has an impact on the number of children someone has (or on their chances of having children, too). Unfortunately, misunderstandings can make evolutionary psychology sound as if it stereotypes everyone as being on the prowl. It's as if we're all consciously eager to pump out ample numbers of ankle-biters as quickly as possible. Evolutionary psychology attempts to explain trends in huge populations over multiple generations, not every one-night stand. We're talking about small but significant effects among millions of people over millennia. We're all alive today because of inherited chromosomes that made it possible. Genes that allow someone to have plenty of kids will become more common because they end up in plenty of kids. It is especially true if the kids also get to have plenty of kids themselves. This is what evolutionary fitness is all about.

Many findings that support evolutionary psychology take a hearty ribbing in the media, too. My former Columbia classmate Geoffrey Miller's data come to mind. He showed that lap dancers make more tips when they're in the most fertile part of their menstrual cycles. This finding supports the idea that attraction might increase when the chance of conception is high, which evolutionary psychology would predict. Of course, anyone who has ever menstruated or had PMS could point out good alternative reasons for why it might not lead a woman to do her best bump and grind (Miller, Tybar, & Jordan, 2007). Evolutionary theory also accounts for many findings in regard to how people attract each other. They might shed some light, for example, on why Anne Bancroft married Mel Brooks or on how Sacha Baron Cohen got Isla Fisher to tie the knot. (Okay, he might be cuter than Mel Brooks.)

Choosy Mothers Choose Mates

A few facts about differences in the sexes are hard to dispute, even for the most egalitarian of us. Women can give birth only so many times. Occasionally a woman with 15 children gets her picture in the paper, but the rarity of such events is what makes them newsworthy. Men could have many more of the little darlings, particularly if they didn't let distractions like monogamy and child-rearing get in their way. This potential inequality in parental investment suggests that the genes of heterosexual men and women will appear in more people if they find certain kinds of mates. People who have partners who can help their children reproduce will end up with their genes becoming more common in the population.

Since women can have only a few kids, they have to be choosy. Actually, they don't *have* to be choosy, which has made some men feel particularly lucky. Nevertheless, genes that lead them to be choosy will end up in more offspring, making the children of choosy mothers more numerous. The impact of a potential father's willingness and ability to provide care and resources can be dramatic for women. This is especially true in societies where men monopolize stuff and the opportunity to get it, like everywhere on the planet Earth for the past 2.6 million years. Women who choose partners who have the material goods that can make their offspring thrive will end up with more of their genes in the population. Generations ago, anyone out gathering berries for their wee ones could benefit from a partner who could put a little extra yellow-cheeked vole on the fire. Not that women can't do this on their own today, but a little help never hurts.

In contrast, men's genes can become more common in the population under different circumstances. Genes that provide men with a propensity for finding fertile mates will appear in more offspring. Genes that encourage men to take care of a few kids particularly well, so that they get the opportunity to mate, could become more common, too. Alternatively, genes that lead men to seduce all the women around, and impregnate them, could also show increased fitness. This second strategy need not require a big investment in finding women with a maximum of material goods. Nevertheless, the quest for women who look fertile would continue. It's easy to imagine how this approach might have worked in days of yore, back when *Homo erectus* tromped around in the Pleistocene Epoch.

A Funny Thing Happened Back in the Old Stone Age

As fun as mating undoubtedly must have been at the time of our ancient ancestors, playing a game of the beast with two backs didn't put one in the ideal position to fight off Paleolithic predators. Each coupling had its potential for danger back then (though I don't want to minimize today's dangers). Men would want to find the most fecund female available during her most fertile time. Well, I don't know what they *wanted* to find— probably central heating and a cold six-pack. But those with genes that made them more likely to find fecund females at fertile times got to have more kids, who would likely do the same eventually. Remnants of these different preferences for mates remain. Women's ratings of the importance of a partner who is a good financial prospect exceed men's ratings of the same. It's not just a quirk about the materialistic Western world; it's true in countries of all sorts. Of course, nobody really rates good financial prospects in a mate as a bad thing, but women rated it higher.

In contrast, men's ratings tend to exceed women's on youth and physical attractiveness—two indices of potential fertility (Buss, 1989). Men also find women more attractive if their hips are wider than their waists in a proportion that suggests easy conception (Swami, Jones, Einon, & Furnham, 2009). The theory, at its worst, tends to make men look like sociopathic skirt-chasers and women look like conniving gold-diggers. We all have our moments. But it doesn't mean that every mom and dad who ever lived behaved exactly this way. The counterexamples of couples who walk out of bars each evening don't mean that the theory is wrong. My wife has more money than I have. That doesn't make Darwin a liar. People who choose warm, kind, genuine partners give their kids a leg up in the world, too, but that research rarely gets as much press (Giosan & Wyka 2009).

Funny Sexual Selection

But what about how humor relates to choosy mothers choosing partners? Yucking it up in the ice-free lands of the Old World probably didn't help our ancestors bring home the mastodon. Instead of playing a straightforward role in natural selection, in the standard, survival-of-the-fittest sense, humor might be more important in sexual selection. Darwin (1871) emphasized that many behaviors are designed to attract mates even if they don't lead directly to creating more viable offspring. The peacock's tail remains the classic example. Miller (2009) has emphasized that this sexual selection might contribute to the development of wit. (Yes, he is the same guy who studied the lap dancers—well, gathered data from them.) Almost everyone claims to want a good sense of humor in a partner, particularly a long-term mate. In some studies, a good sense of humor outranks physical attractiveness. Humor, musical talent, and creativity might all be decent predictors of resistance to the mutations and parasites that could impair these brainy abilities. And who wants to bed some mutant filled with parasites?

Several facts are consistent with the idea that humor relates to sexual selection. A few studies suggest that we find the trait more important in romantic partners than in friends. Women, the generally choosier selectors of partners, value humor production in a partner more than men do. Men, in contrast, value humor appreciation. A quick look at the Personal ads reveals that heterosexual women want men who make them laugh; heterosexual men want women who laugh at their jokes (De Backer, Braeckman, & Farinpour, 2008). A good sense of humor is indeed important enough to have its own abbreviation in the Personals: GSOH. Perhaps men figure that women who laugh at their jokes would be more likely to date, mate, and breed. Notorious guides for attracting women emphasize humor consistently (e.g., Strauss,

2007). Why, then, would women value humor production? Perhaps because it's a decent correlate of intelligence.

Wits and the Witty

Lab studies show that producing humor correlates significantly with IQ. For example, smarter folks fashioned e-mails and drawings that were more comical, suggesting that wit genuinely requires wits (Howrigan & MacDonald, 2008). Though many of my academic pals would swear otherwise, women do perceive smarter men as more attractive (Prokosch, Cross, Scheib, & Blozis, 2009). A craftier parent could help offspring in several ways. High IQ actually correlates with better sperm quality, so a smart guy may have a better chance of creating offspring in the first place (Arden, Gottfredson, Miller, & Pierce, 2009). The kids of smarter parents are more likely to be smart, which ought to help them flourish. It also ought to make them more fun to raise. (Though if mine are any indicator, they do get sarcastic awfully young.) Smart parents should be better providers and caretakers, too. (See Kaufman et al. [2008] for an engaging review.) So what might men do to show off intellect? Perhaps they could crack a few jokes to get women breathing heavily with laughter. If women genuinely look for smarter partners, and humor correlates with IQ, then it seems like an intriguing choice. A heterosexual woman could grab a funny fellow, assume he's smart and fit, and get busy. This idea makes a wonderful tale, but a close look at available data reveals that it may not be the whole story.

GENES WITHOUT INTEREST: A DAY WITHOUT SUNSHINE

Clearly, humor is more than just a technique for attracting sexual partners. For one thing, humor in the lab and humor in life might be two very different things. What passes for humor in daily life isn't the stuff that appears on the standard tests of humor production that correlate with IQ. When people mention which of their peers are humorous, those identified as funny don't do any better on these humor production tests than folks who aren't considered hilarious (Babad, 1974). It's great to fashion snarky captions for cartoons or draw droll doodles, but most laughter occurs after statements that are astoundingly mundane. At least 85% of guffaws in natural settings follow humdrum statements like, "It was nice meeting you, too" and "How are you, Mr. Wilson?" (Provine, 1993). Even sitcoms can't get away with this sort of drivel, no matter how loud the laugh track. I doubt it would have worked for Mel Brooks, either.

In addition, the sweet nothings that romantic partners murmur, even the funny ones, would bore or nauseate almost anyone other than the love-struck pair. I'd share a few from my own marriage, but I don't want to spend the rest of my life sleeping on the couch. Documented cases include the following: "We went to see *The Nutcracker* and he started calling me his little sugarplum fairy." (See Bippus [2000] if you have the pancreas for this sort of thing. I think that this one might be a lot funnier if it didn't come from a heterosexual woman.) Researchers have yet to administer humor production and IQ tests and then follow participants around to see how they entertain their pals or whisper wished-for words to their lovers. Nevertheless, the expressions that elicit everyday chuckles in partners may require as much from the Three Stooges as from Albert Einstein. If humor indicates intelligence and fitness, it must be doing a lot of other work in relationships as well.

Unfortunately for some of us, and for some interpretations of sexual selection women don't always think that funny guys are smart. One study showed that comical folks seemed less intellectual (Lundy, Tan, & Cunningham, 1998). Subsequent work confirmed this finding and showed that funnier people also seemed less trustworthy—another trait that women looking for serious romance might appreciate. Nevertheless, women still rated these funny guys as better potential partners

(Bressler & Balshine, 2006). Could something be more important than IQ or trustworthiness? Funny folks who occasionally fall down in the genius and trust departments might take a little solace from the idea. A sense of humor may remain a nice index of resistance to disease, absence of stupidity, and a distinct lack of head injury. In addition, it may also indicate interest. Joking around can help people gauge a conversationalist's level of intrigue with the chat, a sort of purring of invisible antennae. These signals may be how we let each other know that we're romantically inclined. They can at least suggest that we're having a good time. This may explain why men search for women who laugh at their jokes, too. It's the only way we know if things are going well.

Examining Humor as an Index of Interest

Examining humor as an index of interest is intriguing. First, a sad note for those of us who get laughs but still fall below the mean on attractiveness. Heterosexual women found men who used humor more desirable than men who were more mundane, but only if they were good looking. For unattractive guys, even an hour's worth of pumping out the punch lines may be no help (Lundy et al., 1998). Fortunately, attractiveness ratings vary enough among women to leave us all hope. As George Borrow (1893) said, "Every dog has his day." I guess Mel Brooks was cute enough to get Anne Bancroft to let the laughs reach her. But more importantly, the humor can set the tone for the dialogue. Decades ago, researchers asked men to rate some sexual and some aggressive cartoons. The men had to write the ratings down or say them aloud to a female laboratory assistant who was either attractive or unattractive. The highest ratings went to sexual cartoons the men rated aloud to the pretty woman. It was as if the guys were attempting to send her a message. Consciously or not, the men in the experiment may have rated the sex jokes higher in an effort to communicate that the whole idea of sex was a good one (Davis & Farina, 1970).

A more recent example of comedy as a communication of interest compared joking to everyday conversation in different situations (Li et al., 2009). First, the researchers asked participants about meeting someone new. Participants imagined meeting someone whom they found attractive as well as someone whom they didn't find good looking. In these "hot versus not" comparisons, people claimed that if they were meeting someone unattractive, they were significantly more likely to initiate mundane conversation than humor. In contrast, if they were meeting someone they found romantically appealing, they were significantly more likely to initiate humor than everyday chitchat.

The researchers also asked about humor in an imagined long-term relationship. Participants imagined that they were in a long-term relationship that they felt either satisfied or unsatisfied about. The authors of the paper predicted that the distinction between humor and general conversation might be less important in a long-term relationship than in an initial encounter—at least from a strict, sexual selection, "Let-me-show-you-my-stellar-genes" perspective. Participants might not need to advertise the chromosomes of comedy once a long-term relationship is already established. In contrast, if humor indicates interest as well as fitness, the preference for humor, particularly in satisfied relationships, should still exist. Indeed, it did. When imagining themselves in a satisfied relationship, participants reported that they were more likely to turn to humor than to everyday conversation. When they imagined an unsatisfying relationship, they claimed that they would be more likely to stick to everyday conversation rather than to humor. The results were essentially the same as in "hot versus not" conditions of meeting someone new. They seem to run counter to the idea that humor is more important in the initial seduction than in the maintenance of a long-term partnership.

I think that many evolutionary psychologists (and anyone who has ever tried to stay both happy and monogamous) would take issue with the initial prediction that humor should wane in the long term. The issue stems from one simple fact: Those of us lucky enough to have desirable partners often see potential competitors checking them out. The world is filled with mate poaching—hooking up with somebody else's spouse or partner. This form of poaching means stealing something that belongs to someone else. (Although my wife has made it clear that the alternative definition of poaching—simmering mercilessly for hours and hours in hot water—is not completely irrelevant here.) Sadly but truthfully, a percentage of allegedly monogamous partners dally on the side. The percentage ranges from 10 to 75%, depending upon the era, the anonymity of the question, and several other caveats. (See Schmitt [2004] for an eye-popping analysis.) Concerns about mate poaching are justified. We do plenty more than crack jokes to keep outsiders from encroaching on our partners, including everything from the wildly romantic to the counterproductively violent (Platek & Shackelford, 2006). Thus, plenty of us might try to keep our mates chuckling in the long run to ward off poachers.

But Would You Laugh?

In addition to asking about initiating humor, the researchers (Li et al., 2009) also asked about receptiveness to the other person's humor. It's one thing to tell a few jokes yourself, but another to grin at someone else's. This give-and-take of initiating and responding to humor can reveal a lot about its function as a sign of interest. Participants claimed that they would be more positive about the other person's humor if they were attracted. This result isn't a stunning surprise to those of us who have been shut down while trying to flirt with someone new. The uninterested simply don't respond, even to the best material. This result also replicates a delightful set of observations of patrons trying to pick up servers at a diner. Waitresses were quick to disapprove of jokes, particularly sexual ones, if they came from unwanted patrons (Walle, 1977). Receptiveness to another person's humor was comparable in the long-term and "we-just-met" conditions. If someone new was attractive, or if a long-term partner was satisfying, participants were receptive to humor. Otherwise, no deal.

MORE GENDER DIFFERENCES (OR NONE)

The sex differences in these responses, or the lack thereof, were again illuminating. From a strictly evolutionary perspective, one might predict that the sexes would differ in some of these effects of attractiveness and length of the relationship. Women searching for the fit and wise might be more concerned about wit than conversation in initial meetings, but this concern would decrease once the selection process has turned into a serious connection. Perhaps once a woman has used humor to make an initial pick of a partner, it might be less important. But both women and men claimed that they would crack jokes often (or be receptive to them) in the same circumstances—when meeting someone hot or while in a satisfying long-term relationship. Let these results be a lesson to us all, regardless of race, creed, sexual orientation, or your favorite French philosopher. If your partner no longer jokes around or laughs at your jokes, something is clearly awry in the relationship. Every marital therapist I've ever known emphasizes that clients come in too late. Many couples don't arrive for treatment until they already hate each other. Perhaps if they intervened earlier, as soon as the laughter stopped, divorce rates might drop. I can see the public service announcement now.

It's all fine and good to ask folks what they think they would do when they first meet or when they are in a long-term relationship. Nevertheless, we all can be pretty bad at guessing what we'll actually do in a situation. We might think that finding the right person will make us dance, sing, and cook waffles every day. Reality reveals that even the best relationships are as much about mopping and laundry as moonlight and roses. Data from couples who are actually dating or married might provide better evidence for humor's import than questionnaires about what we think we'll do. Is humor genuinely important to dating or not? The answer to this question is the same as the answer to nearly all the research questions on humor (and perhaps all the big questions in the social sciences): It depends.

Happy Dates

So what does humor's effect depend upon in real dating couples? In this case, the impact depends on the humor's type. Some types of humor may help partners while other types may hurt. Early work on couples who were dating suggested that a similar sense of humor, based on ratings of cartoons and jokes, went along with stated love and a desire to get married (Murstein & Brust, 1985). Appreciating the same jokes seemed a nice source of fun that could help partners communicate similarity and joy. But subsequent work with married couples failed to find comparable results. The link between their ratings of cartoons and marital satisfaction was essentially zero (Priest & Thein, 2003). Appreciating the same jokes might help dating couples get that initial warm and cuddly feeling, but it didn't do enough to keep a marriage happy. It seems that finer distinctions about humor might be necessary to explain its import for married couples.

In this case, the finer distinctions may involve humor styles again (Martin et al., 2003). An intriguing study looked at couples who had been dating for at least 3 months (Campbell et al., 2008). Three months of dating might not sound like much of a relationship, but the authors gathered these data in Texas, where the average age at first marriage is one of the lowest (23–25 years old). Dating in college can be much more serious there than in states like New York or Massachusetts, where age at first marriage is about 4 years older (U.S. Census Bureau, 2005). The couples who participated had actually been dating for an average of almost a year and a half, so these had the potential to be very serious relationships. When I lived in Hollywood, I saw marriages that didn't last half that long.

The researchers had couples come to the lab to discuss a conflict that they had not resolved. This task can reveal how couples attempt to solve a problem that might be intractable. It's a standard in couples research. It can lead to a lot of clashing and quarreling. The occasional couple cannot even agree on what to discuss, which can make for some informative fireworks. The couples in this study tended to mirror each other in their use of different styles of humor. Each partner was more likely to make a humorous comment if the other partner had just made one. Thus, an affiliative joke from one person led to an affiliative joke from the other. Tossing an aggressive barb tended to lead the other person to retaliate.

The affiliative and aggressive styles also related to satisfaction with the relationship and with feelings about the resolution of the conflict. Folks who were satisfied with the relationship had partners who used more affiliative humor and less aggressive humor while chatting about the chosen problem. Those with partners who used more aggressive humor and less affiliative humor were less satisfied. Oddly enough, a person's satisfaction had little to do with his or her own use of humor in the lab. In a sense, even if you are the most hostile teaser in the world, if your partner responds with jokes designed to decrease tension and bring the two of you together, you stay satisfied. At least this is true in dating couples. Over time, though, the more aggressive humor you use, the more likely your partner will use aggressive humor, too. The data showed that aggressive humor from one partner led to the same from the other. This hostility will make each of you less and less satisfied eventually. This initial look at humor styles in couples appears to have a lot of promise. A close look at humor styles in married couples might confirm these results found in dating couples. Unfortunately, a lot of other work on how partners chuckle together was performed before the distinctions among humor styles became popular. Marriage is its own little mystery.

And Happy Marriages

Those of us who have racked up some double-digit anniversaries can say in complete honesty that marriage and dating aren't in the same ballpark. They're not even the same sport. Nevertheless, humor remains important in ways that may be more complicated. Couples who have been married more than 50 years claim that laughing together is important to staying together (Lauer, Lauer & Kerr, 1990). Early work on this topic confirmed that folks who are happily married appreciate their partner's sense of humor, even if they don't laugh at the same jokes (Rust & Goldstein, 1989; Ziv & Gaddish, 1989). Trust me—it's true. In addition, research that used the laboratory discussion technique described above showed a lot about marriage. Happily married couples showed a lot more laughter and humor than others (Carstensen, Gottman, & Levenson, 1995). Although the category of affiliative humor hadn't been identified at that time, the happily married couples showed more friendly banter while the unhappy couples resorted to sarcastic sneering when they showed any humor at all.

These results are certainly warm and fuzzy but don't say much about humor actually helping out in a marriage. Like any correlation, the one between humor and marital bliss can arise for several reasons. The most likely reason may be a halo effect: If you think that your partner is an angel, you think everything about him or her is great. People tend to view each other (and plenty of things) as essentially good or essentially bad. When it comes to making fine distinctions between strengths and weaknesses, we stink. It's easier to assume that if people are good in one domain, they're probably good in lots of them. This can be a blessing for those of us who are less than perfect, but a curse for those whose bad points stick out.

For example, we tend to think that political candidates are trustworthy and competent if they also happen to be good looking (Surawski & Ossoff, 2006). The contrapositive is true, too. So if we think one aspect of something is bad, we tend to think that the whole thing must reek. Many call this satanic bias the negative halo or the forked-tail effect. For example, people think that overweight kids are also lazy and dumb (Thiel, Alizadeh, Giel, & Zipfel, 2008). Instructors always get lower teacher ratings if a course involves math (Steiner, Holley, Gerdes, & Campbell, 2006). These halos and forked tails apply in couples, too. Folks who genuinely like their partners might find them funny out of a general feeling of love, even if their sense of humor is nothing to laugh at. Others might think that their partners' jokes fall flat simply because no other aspect of the relationship gives them a rise.

A better look at humor's impact on marriage requires longitudinal work. The only way to find out if humor actually makes marriages better is to follow the funny. These studies bring couples to the lab to assess their humor, then contact them again years later to see who has grown closer and who has grown bitter. In one of the first studies along these lines, humor in a 15-minute discussion did not predict who would divorce four years later (Gottman & Levenson, 1999a). This result made humor seem unimportant, but using divorce as the outcome has its quirks. Many couples realize that their marriages were a mistake. They divorce quickly and stay happy on their own. This sort of divorce might prove better than hanging on for decades to exasperate each other to death. But the focus of this work is really on the health of the marriage, not on the happiness of the individuals. So those who have divorced have certainly had a negative outcome, even if some of the folks who stayed married are still distressed. I should emphasize that this work preceded some of the categorizing of humor, especially the affiliative and aggressive styles (Martin et al., 2003). The aggressive style of humor has some overlap with one of the most important predictors of a couple's chances of staying together. It's the one emotion that seems to poison marriages like no other: contempt.

Contempt predicts later divorce and distress better than just about anything (Gottman & Levenson, 1999b). Contempt involves an insulting criticism from a disgusted person. It not only denigrates whatever the partner did, it also adds a pinch of character assassination. "Please take out the garbage" is a simple request. "I'm upset because you didn't take out the garbage" is a simple complaint. Criticism involves a simple complaint but assumes that the criticized act stems from some inherent negative trait in the partner. It's not about a specific act; it becomes about the person. Critics never give their partners the benefit of the doubt. They can't imagine that forgetting the trash might have stemmed from being too busy—it must arise from some personal flaw. Thus, criticism would be: "You're too lazy to take out the garbage." Contempt adds insult to that injury: "You idiot! You're just too lazy to take out the garbage, aren't you?" (Add eye rolling here.) Contempt often includes sarcasm, hostile humor, and mockery. Imagine contempt like the following: "Everyone's a brilliant feminist theorist until it's time to take out the garbage" or "Think that when you're done ogling the anorexics on TV, you could deign to take out the garbage?" Once a couple starts showing contempt like this, a few guffaws can't save the relationship. Even marital therapy has a rough time if couples wait this long before intervening. As I mentioned, they should have gotten help when the laughs first ended.

And Happy Marriages II: The Sequel

Studies showing more humor in happy couples inspired an initial longitudinal study that found little impact of comic interactions in the long run. Further research showed humor does have some impact if you look at additional variables. As before, it depends. There's a giant gap in this literature. Unfortunately, humor's role in the happiness of gays and lesbians is pretty much unknown. In heterosexual marriages, the husband's humor and the wife's humor appear to serve different functions. One study found that humor might not predict their staying married directly, but it altered how stressful life events led to divorce. For couples who had a lot of stress, if the husbands used a lot of humor in the laboratory discussion of problems, they were more likely to be divorced 18 months later. It's not clear exactly what these guys were joking about or what style of humor they used. Nevertheless, if they were making light of their wives' stressors or using humor to avoid solving their troubles, divorce was on the horizon. It's no wonder that they ended up alone in their underwear, eating Pot Noodles in front of the TV (Cohan & Bradbury, 1997).

In case those results aren't complicated enough, another study found that wives' humor during the problem discussion predicted the couples' staying together 6 years later, but only when it soothed the husbands at the time. In this case, soothing the husband meant decreasing his heart rate (Gottman, Coan, Carrere, & Swanson, 1998). In a sense, the wives seemed to use humor to calm their husbands so that they could continue working on the problem. This arrangement probably sounds a little odd, but all of these kinds of studies show that the conflict discussions drive men bananas. Men are often more reactive to conflict on physiological measures, whether it's heart rate, hormones, or sweating. The whole "we-need-to-talk" thing is more than most of us guys can manage. Our arousal tends to increase like we're preparing for a beating.

Not to sound patently Pleistocene, but guys tend to think that we didn't really evolve to solve problems by sitting and talking. Surely there's some smilodon to smash or a football game to watch until everyone feels better. An astute wife who sees her husband is starting to get too amped up has only a few options. Though humor may not be the average husband's first choice for how his wife should decrease his arousal, it's probably an appropriate pick for a discussion in the laboratory. (It's probably the best option during a picnic with the kids, too.) The two studies above suggest that husbands who can discuss troubles without making light of stressors in inappropriate ways, and wives who can soothe their husbands through these discussions, are more likely to stay married.

WHAT'S IT ALL FOR?

Humor and laughter appear inherently interactive. The presence of others, or even the sound of their chuckles, increases our own amusement. Much of the banter that occurs in groups wouldn't look funny on paper, but we can use it to affirm or denigrate ourselves or those around us. Keeping an eye on who's joking and who's laughing can reveal a lot about status within a group, and various yarns and quips seem to maintain hierarchies. Research from the previous century made women look humorless and witless. Studies that use less sexist stimuli showed more similarities than difference across the genders. Men and women vary in humor appreciation and production in ways that are consistent with evolutionary theory, suggesting that the slapstick of the Pleistocene era might have helped us become who we are today. But other work shows that witty repartee between men and women may have more to do with communicating their interest and satisfaction than simply showing off wits. Giggling enhances our liking of each other in initial meetings. Affiliative humor seems to delight dating couples. Men who avoid teasing their wives, and women who use jokes to soothe their husbands, can make it through a conflict without a call to the divorce lawyer. You'll note a big absence of data on same-sex couples in this literature. I hope researchers will soon fill this gap.

Emphasizing the role of others in humor makes it clear that a lot of laughter relies on the setting, not on the comedian. There are funny situations, not just funny people. Nevertheless, some people seem better at understanding and generating quips than others do. Unfortunately, people seem to overestimate their own sense of humor. A stunning 94% of people rate their own sense of humor as average or above average (Allport, 1961)—a manifestation of the Lake Wobegon effect. (Garrison Keillor's mythical town by this name has children who are all above average.) Obviously, this is statistically impossible. It's also completely infuriating to the truly funny. The question itself assumes that a sense of humor is something we all carry around with us from one spot to the next. The appreciation of humor might be distinct from choosing to repeat jokes or produce one's own. Producing jokes seems like it ought to be a teachable skill, while training people to understand humor sounds like a formidable task. The notion that funny folks are either born or made generates plenty of debate, too. Is this an accident of birth, something in the genes, or the result of a strict diet of Pot Noodles? Let's investigate.

Funny Folks: Linking Sense of Humor to Personality

ot long after World War II, veteran psychologist Dr. Bertram Forer ran into a nightclub graphologist—a man who claimed to read people's personalities from their handwriting. The entertainer offered to interpret Forer's penmanship. The psychologist declined. The man persisted, emphasizing that his insights into the human psyche were uncannily accurate. "How do you know?" Forer asked. "My clients all tell me," the performer reported. Dr. Forer sent him on his way. But their interaction started cogs turning. Dr. Forer had an intriguing idea for a demonstration for his Introductory Psychology class.

This chapter links facets of personality, and other individual differences among people, to aspects of their sense of humor, including the way that they use comedy in their lives and the kinds of jokes they generate and appreciate. The study of personality back in the 1940s had grown quite convoluted. It had started in ancient times, when Hippocrates, of the legendary oath, proposed four temperaments. Unfortunately, they were also called "four humors." He thought that personality arose from different proportions of fluids in the body, creating a popular link between personality and physiology. A model with that kind of simplicity would be ideal, but these four temperaments failed to account for important aspects of the way people behave. Unfortunately, theorists went from the extremely simple to the extremely complicated. Famous philosophers, including Descartes, Locke, Hume, and Kant, all elaborated on the Hippocratic humors in an attempt to explain human dispositions. By the late 1800s, Sir Francis Galton, brilliant half-cousin of Charles Darwin and noted polymath, reasoned that any important aspect of personality ought to make it into the language. He fashioned a taxonomy based on a dictionary (Caprara & Cervone, 2000).

Gordon Allport, the same guy who showed that we all think we're funnier than average, identified almost 18,000 words in the English language that described people. At least 4,000 referred to personality traits (Allport & Odbert, 1936). Organizing all of these words into manageable groups was generating a ton of debate. One researcher's mathematical wizardry condensed the thousands of terms into 16 factors that had the potential to describe everyone (Cattell, 1946). This feat has adherents today. Sadly, 16 factors lack the simplicity that would make them as helpful as possible. Further, the model doesn't always fit data. It's great for trait words, but when people report on their own behaviors, the 16 factors don't quite fit. The quest for a simpler approach continued, but Dr. Forer and others could see trouble ahead.

Meanwhile, the thought that one's sense of humor and personality must be related retained its intuitive appeal. It seems obvious that people who laugh often, tell jokes, and generate witty remarks must differ from those who don't. Goethe (1920/2000) said, "Men show their characters in nothing more clearly than in what they think laughable." A few theorists even suggested that asking clients about their favorite jokes or their interpretations of cartoons might help psychological diagnosis and treatment (Strother, Barnett, & Apostolakos, 1954; Zwerling, 1955). Fortunately, we have more reliable and valid techniques. A handful of researchers have done in-depth personality assessments of professional comedians, comedy writers, and humorists of various sorts. The most common personality profile for these successful comics appears below. It may seem remarkably detailed, but research of this type often consists of questionnaires and interviews that include hundreds of questions and hours of probing. As an experiment, see if this personality profile applies to you.

AN ASSESSMENT REPORT FOR A SUCCESSFUL COMIC

You tend to show a calm, self-assured, serene kind of stability. This often masks an inner tumult. You are prone to a certain cynicism about being a part of a group. You even show a mild dislike of people who seem to prefer following the crowd. These feelings can be particularly strong when you notice a close friend trying to gain other people's approval. This inclination has led you to feel like an outsider in many situations, a role you find yourself taking more often than you had anticipated. On occasion, you defend this role even when it might not be in your best interest, sometimes leading you to consciously avoid being a part of groups, organizations, or institutions. At certain times, you have rebelled against authorities of one kind or another even when you knew they were correct. This role as an outsider can create long, private periods of self-examination.

These periods of self-examination and of having a strong sense for preferences have had an impact on your relationships. At times, you like to gossip a bit, but you are capable of keeping a secret. You are also an extremely attentive and sympathetic listener when you want to be. You are currently tempted by a dream that may not be very realistic, including fantasies about a perfect relationship, which can get in the way of your current happiness. It makes sense for you to acknowledge your attachment to a specific outcome. You can then work on making it less important by appreciating other domains where you are succeeding. Your relationships with your family can be conflicted and may be currently a bit strained.

You relish your time alone, despite moments of loneliness. This contrasts sharply with your remarkable ability to appear very engaged socially, which leads to times where you seem to be the life of the party, the person who keeps conversation flowing, or the one who holds a group together. This can sometimes feel like a façade. In fact, though you have many close acquaintances, the number of people whom you view as dear friends is relatively small. You have developed a dry sense of humor that seems to engage others and attract people. At times, this aspect of wit moves so quickly that you make jokes that go over other people's heads. Either these people are unappreciative of nuance or they do not have sufficient background information to understand your broad range of references. Nevertheless, you take considerable pleasure in this ability and often find yourself rehearsing remarks in an effort to seem spontaneous in your entertainment of others. Although you occasionally feel awkward when you catch yourself doing this sort of thing, it is consistent with your desires and aims and you rarely let it get out of hand or interfere with more important pursuits.

Personality and the Forer Effect

This extensive, detailed comedic profile reveals just how accurate these assessments can be. I think that most comics would find that it captures them quite well. You may see yourself in the description, too. But before you enroll in Clown College (if you aren't already in a clown college of sorts), the rest of Dr. Forer's story might be relevant. The mental health professional and instructor ditched the nightclub graphologist, but left the club with an intriguing idea in his mind. He bounced into his next Introductory Psychology class and began the lecture with a tale of a new personality scale, the Diagnostic Interest Blank. He explained how he had been developing the test for years and years. He noted how instructive and enlightening the device was, emphasizing its astounding precision, insight, and comprehensiveness. He mentioned how the scale had helped clients turn their lives around. Of course the students begged him to let them take it. Dr. Forer balked until they begged some more. He then agreed reluctantly. The next lecture began with a written version of the personality test, a series of queries about hang-ups, hobbies, and hopes. Dr. Forer gathered the responses and promised an individualized personality vignette to each student.

Attendance must have been excellent at the next class, where Dr. Forer emphasized the confidentiality of the results and requested that each student respect the privacy of classmates by refraining from examining the personality profiles of others. He asked students to rate the profile for accuracy on a 5-point scale, with 5 meaning "perfect." Most gave the description a 4; the average rating was between 4 and 5. Forer then unleashed his reveal. He read a line from one vignette aloud, and asked all whose profile contained the line to raise their hands. Every hand shot skyward with enthusiasm, until they saw how many others had also raised their hands. He read another line with the same request and got the same response. The students chuckled. Everyone had received the exact same profile (Forer, 1949). In fact, it was a lot like the one detailed above. Each sentence described everyone in the room, as all the students realized. I wish he had published his teacher ratings for the semester.

The assessment report discussed above does a good job of describing many of the most successful comics, comedy writers, and humorists. If it sounded like you, join the club. It sounds like virtually everybody. It's a more elaborate version than the one that Forer gave to his class, but the key ideas are the same. Despite their appearance of specificity and uniqueness, lists of traits like these apply to almost anyone. It's not that we're all easy to hoodwink; we're all just very much alike. The fact that these characteristics are nearly universal is misunderstood nearly universally. People especially like profiles that make them look great. When people receive assessments with common positive characteristics listed, they rate them as more accurate than when they receive profiles that contain equally common but negative traits. The bottom line is: Everyone loves to think they're great (Dickson & Kelly, 1985). I guess we're all impressed with the precision of a list of our positive personality traits, too, no matter how many other people share them. The Forer effect has been replicated numerous times, including data from years after the initial study. It's not that people were simply more gullible in the 1940s (Claridge, Clark, Powney, & Hassan, 2008). Even in the 21st century, British mentalist and magician Derren Brown demonstrated this effect quite dramatically on his TV show.

Barnum Statements

Paul Meehl, the same guy who detailed the bootstrapping discussed in the Chapter 1, rechristened Forer's results as the "The Barnum Effect." Purportedly, P. T. Barnum hawked his circus as having something for everybody. Meehl (1956) stressed that many cookbook assessments of personality could make the same claim. The profile cited above certainly has something for us all. These sorts of Barnum statements are common in the work of various fortune-tellers, psychics, channelers, and mediums. The film noir classic *Nightmare Alley* shows Tyrone Power fooling a local cop with a spirited set of these statements as part of his psychic act.

In fact, Forer fashioned his feedback to students from lines he picked up in an astrology text. I can't help wondering if

Meehl actually chose the name because Barnum had allegedly said that there was a sucker born every minute. There was a time, when I lived in Los Angeles, when you couldn't throw a rock without hitting someone who claimed to contact dead relatives, spirit guides, angels, or faeries. These charlatans, many of whom had convinced themselves of their own veracity, spewed one Barnum statement after another until someone in the audience burst into tears. They invariably said things that would apply to anyone, like "Someone close to you has recently experienced serious distress" and "Your life is about to take a major turn." They also offered advice that had all the specificity of an IKEA shelving unit: "Your dead grandfather says it's time to let go" or "The spirit guides say that you shouldn't take life so seriously." I shudder to think how many people shelled out hard-earned cash to hear this kind of malarkey. The fact that some of these hacks continue to tour the country and perform at prestigious events is mind-boggling.

Because so many statements apply to so many of us, I want to interpret any findings, about personality and about humor, with extreme caution. There really are detailed studies of the personality of comic performers, but we can't make much sense of them without looking at the personalities of other people. We have to compare comics to a control group. It means nothing to say that those with a sense of humor have struggled with their identities or sometimes doubt their abilities—we've all done that. The only way to get unique insights into the comic personality, if there is such a thing, is to point out how it differs from the personality of the average person who lives comparably but has less of a sense of humor. Any results from this kind of work will have to be more than mere Barnum-type statements if it's going to be informative.

In a detailed and entertaining project, Fisher and Fisher (1981) reported over 200 pages of material comparing stand-up comedians and circus clowns to other performers. Unfortunately, the temptation to lapse into Barnum-like statements might have been too great. They described comics as having "a style that resists demands to behave in a driven, methodical, machine-like fashion and instead focuses on the human side of life" (p. 203). Obviously, we all would resist demands to behave like machines. We all prefer to focus on our humanity, no matter how cheerful or sour we may be. Clearly, studies of one's sense of humor and one's personality will do better when we have accurate, informative measures of each. Like humor itself, both one's personality and sense of humor have nuanced, multifaceted components. Let's review relevant aspects of personality, then explore definitions of a sense of humor to see how they all fit together.

PERSONALITY: SWIMMING IN THE BIG FIVE OCEAN

There are probably as many theories of personality as there are people. The list of human traits goes on and on, as Allport showed from our language's multitude of terms. Reducing these to a reasonable number of clusters is no easy feat. Despite Cattell's plug for 16 factors, a lot of research suggests that human characteristics comprise five factors. This Five-Factor Model—or the Big Five—includes: Openness to experience, Conscientiousness, Extraversion, Agreeableness, and Neuroticism. Thus, the first letters of the five factors form the mnemonic OCEAN. "Openness to experience," or simply openness, involves a person's tendency to appreciate imaginative forms of art, a range of ideas, and novel adventures. People high in openness are intellectually curious, reflective, unconventional appreciators of beauty. Those who score low on the scale are often more traditional, straightforward, cautious types who prefer familiarity to novelty. Typical questions on an openness scale ask people if they see themselves as original, imaginative, and valuing the arts. A reverse-scored item (one that assesses the opposite of the trait) asks if they prefer work that is routine.

"Conscientiousness" is the domain of traits wherein a person is disciplined, dutiful, devoted. It's the goody two-shoes of personality. High scorers keep their noses to the grindstone. They know that a stitch in time does save nine. They plan their work and work their plan. They also show great attention to detail. As you'd guess, employers love their persistent, scheduled approach to a job well done. But extreme scorers seem like obsessive, perfectionistic workaholics as they whip out their protractors to rearrange their sock drawers. Low scorers are in no danger of compulsive achievement; they can, in fact, seem haphazard in their work and personal lives. Typical items ask if people are reliable workers, avid planners, and attentive to details. Reverse-scored items ask if they are distractible, lazy, or disorganized.

"Extraversion" refers to the tendency to behave in outgoing, boisterous, talkative ways. Extraverts, those who score high on the extraversion scale, are often the energetic, outspoken, attention-seeking lives of the party. Those on the very high end can seem like crass, blabbering backslappers. Introverts, the low scorers, seem less exuberant, more low-key and deliberate. Extreme introverts might appear like plodding, aloof loners. Typical items ask if the individual generates enthusiasm, speaks frequently, and tends to be assertive. Reverse-scored items ask if an individual is reserved, shy, or inhibited.

"Agreeableness" refers to a person's considerate, compassionate, friendly nature. Agreeable people get along with others, compromise, and make folks feel at ease. They tend to have a positive view of human nature and assume that most people are trustworthy, honest, and decent. Low scorers—the disagreeable—are more suspicious, interested in themselves, and uncooperative. They are more concerned about doing well themselves than about getting along with others. Typical items ask about behaving in kind, considerate, and cooperative ways. Reverse-scored items query about rude, quarrelsome, and fault-finding tendencies. Finding faults just never gets old for some of the disagreeable. Believe me, they are no fun to date and hell to live with.

Neuroticism involves a predisposition to negative emotions and moodiness. Some researchers call this trait "emotional instability." Their more optimistic colleagues focus on the flip side, "emotional stability." High scorers are often distressed, anxious, irritable, and sad. Neurotics appear sensitive to stress; they frequently view events in their worst light. These poor worrywarts fret over the trivial and unlikely, often turning the smallest decisions into bouts of agonized hand wringing. Austrian psychological theorist Alfred Adler described the neurotic man aptly: "He is nailed to the cross of his own fiction" (Adler, 1924). Low scorers are much more calm, mellow, and stable. Typical items from the neurotocism scale might read: "I see myself as someone who worries a lot" and "I get upset easily." Reverse-scored items might read: "I'm the kind of person who handles stress well" and "I'm seldom in a terrible mood."

Note that none of these traits apply to everybody the way that Barnum statements do. We aren't all open lovers of the arts, conscientious workaholics, extraverted loudmouths, agreeable well-wishers, or neurotic fussbuckets. Assessments of these traits are bound to reveal genuine differences among people, not uninformative universals. Links between these five traits and aspects of humor seem likely, but other personality characteristics are also important to many theories of the comic.

Beyond the OCEAN: Sensation Seekers, Authoritarians, and Religious Fundamentalists

Although the Big Five model accounts for a great deal of the data on differences in individual characteristics, several, more specific aspects of personality seem particularly relevant to humor. These involve sensation seekers, authoritarians, and religious fundamentalists. Sensation seeking includes a love for novelty, thrills, and adventure. If you've ever waited in an extra-long line to stick your head in the mouth of a lion, you're probably a sensation seeker. Variation in the trait may arise because some individuals are less aroused than others. In an effort to increase their arousal to an optimal level, these folks might prefer the complex, unfamiliar, and risky.

Sensation seekers like to taste exotic foods (Otis, 1984; Pliner & Melo, 1997), quaff alcohol by the liter (Earleywine, Finn, & Martin, 1990), and bring home lots of sexual partners (Kalichman, Simbayi, Jooste, Vermaak, & Cain, 2008). Typical items ask about a love of mountain climbing, shocking artwork, or visits to foreign lands. Reverse-scored items might ask participants about the joys of staying home at night, watching Aunt Gertrude's slide show of her trip to the wax museum, and rereading Aristotle's *Nicomacean Ethics*. As you might guess, many who score high in sensation seeking also score high on the extraversion factor of the Big Five. In a sense, sensation seeking may be one facet of extraversion (Aluja, Garcia, & Garcia, 2003). It's very much like risk taking, impulsivity, and susceptibility to boredom. One facet of the openness scale (actions) gets at the same ideas. Sensation seeking is the flip side of traits that mean the opposite, like harm avoidance, neophobia (fear of novelty), and inhibition. Folks low on these traits end up high in sensation seeking.

Authoritarianism emphasizes the importance of obedience, hard work, tradition, convention, and stereotypical family values. Authoritarians know that the world could be a much better place if we'd all just do what they think that we're supposed to. In their heart of hearts, they think that we should find courageous leaders and focus on productivity instead of frivolous pursuits like art, entertainment, and books about humor.

They believe that locking up the immoral, keeping a keen eye on the ill-bred, and silencing the rebellious will allow us all to thrive like never before. Obviously, try to avoid having an authoritarian for a boss. The originators of the idea of authoritarianism were no fan of it; they had all escaped Nazi Germany (Adorno, Frenkel-Brunswik, & Levinson, 1950). High scorers show a rigid attachment to strict rules and devote a lot of time to keeping the lint off their brown shirts. The most typical items ask about trust in the proper authorities of government and religion. Other items on the original scale emphasized the import of productivity. A personal favorite reads: "The businessman and the manufacturer are much more important to society than the artist and the professor." Every time I see that item, I wonder if I should go back to selling ice cream.

There were no reverse-scored items in the original scale—a fact that generated considerable criticism. For each item, agreeing meant more authoritarianism; disagreeing meant less. There is something intriguing about the idea that agreeing with every item leads to a high score on a scale that's supposed to measure obedience to authority. Perhaps high scorers were even obedient to the questions. But the lack of reverse-scored items confounded interpretations of the score. Did a high score mean you were an authoritarian, or just someone who agrees with everything? Researchers labeled this problem "acquiescence," or "yeah-saying," after the tendency simply to agree. Later versions of the scale remedied this acquiescence problem. Reverse-scored items ask participants to agree that atheists might be as good as churchgoers, or that the country benefits from free thinkers (Altemeyer, 2007).

Folks who score high in authoritarianism often score lower on the openness-to-experience scale from the Big Five and higher on the conscientiousness scale (Sibley & Duckitt, 2008). A number of comparable constructs remain popular in humor research. Measures of conservative attitudes overlap with authoritarianism. An index of religious fundamentalism taps some of the same ideas. Religious fundamentalism is more than just religiosity—delighting in a trip to a house of worship. High scorers on religious fundamentalism tend to think there is only one true religion. They also believe that those who behave immorally are more likely to act as lightning rods for heavenly rebuke. In fact, a big red guy with horns and a tail waits on every corner to tempt these folks into heinous crimes, too. These ideas tend to correlate highly with authoritarianism. One item reads: "When you get right down to it, there are only two kinds of people in the world: the righteous, who will be rewarded by

God; and the rest, who will not." You'd better make sure you're in the good group, folks say. A reverse-scored item is: "It is more important to be a good person than to believe in God and the right religion." Folks who agree with this item are missing the fundamentals of fundamentalism.

WHAT PEOPLE SENSE ABOUT THEIR SENSE OF HUMOR

Almost all of us claim that we have it, everyone believes it's great, and nobody knows what it is—that's a sense of humor. A majority of people think that their sense of humor is above average, which is nearly impossible (Allport, 1961; Lefcourt & Martin, 1986). In Allport's (1961) data, 94% of the people thought that their sense of humor was average or above average. One survey found that only 2% of people thought that their sense of humor was below average (see Cann & Calhoun, 2001). It's possible that definitions of humor vary enough that almost everyone is above average in one form or another, but it's unlikely. Perhaps everyone's idea of "average" is a little different. Or maybe we're all just bad at math.

What do we mean by a "sense of humor"? It's hard to tell, but apparently it isn't a single trait so much as a constellation of a bunch of related characteristics. There's no formal, scientific definition; it's more of an expression. I tend to think that I can identify people with a good sense of humor pretty reliably; they laugh at my jokes. But having a sense of humor could mean appreciating gags, remembering funny stories, making up good one-liners on the spot, or having a light-hearted approach to life. With this many definitions of such a fashionable quality, we need to get more specific. Otherwise, a sense of humor simply becomes another one of those Barnum expressions that applies to everyone. More than 70 years of research have revealed that we equate a sense of humor with almost any good trait. We view those with a sense of humor as smart, easygoing, and likable (Cann & Calhoun, 2001; Omwake, 1939). Whatever a sense of humor is, it's clearly good to have it.

Stereotypes About a Sense of Humor

There are plenty of things that you can't define, but you know them when you see them. Take genuineness, empathy, warmth, or pornography. We all know when people are being genuine, but we can't quite point to any specific behaviors that make them seem so. They might not be the same behaviors in the same people. Perhaps a sense of humor is comparable. If that's the case, maybe we could understand personality correlates of a sense of humor by asking participants to describe those who have it and those who don't. This approach could at least reveal what traits appear to go with our stereotypes about funny people. Cann and Calhoun (2001) asked undergraduates to think of three different sorts of people: a typical undergraduate; someone with a below-average sense of humor; and someone with a sense of humor well above average. Since almost all of us think we're average or above on our sense of humor, they emphasized that they wanted people to think of someone well above average, rather than just above average.

Participants then rated the typical undergraduates, the well-above-average ones, and the below-average ones on 36 different traits that varied in desirability. Some traits were the sorts of things that everyone would love to have—being reliable, clever, interesting. Others were the ones that no one wants to claim—being passive, vain, phony. The person with a sense of humor that was viewed as well above average was rated higher on all the good stuff. Participants considered them friendlier and smarter as well as more creative, intelligent, cooperative, pleasant, and even considerate. The funnier folks received lower ratings on all sorts of socially undesirable traits. Participants viewed them as less cold, complaining, shallow, passive, and troubled. They even thought that funny people would be less mean. In the only caveat, the funny folks were considered more boastful and restless—two traits that rarely make the list of the socially desirable. But positive traits tended to increase with having a sense of humor and negative traits tended to decrease.

Stereotypical Humor and the Big Five

Cann and Calhoun (2001) had another group of participants complete a measure of the Big Five traits, rating the personalities of the well-above-average funny person and the below-average funny person. The results showed that stereotypes about a sense of humor related to all five of the Big Five traits. Compared to the below-average funny person, the well-above-average funny person was rated as higher in openness to experience, agreeableness, and extraversion. This person was also considered lower in neuroticism and conscientiousness. Our stereotypes of funny folks suggest that they are outgoing, appreciative of the arts, and easy to get along with. They're not too moody, not particularly hardworking, or phenomenally attentive to detail. The sum of the two studies suggests that a sense of humor is a positive thing. But we know from the work on Barnum statements that simply saying that a sense of humor is positive is not enough. Fortunately, this work has results that are more specific. When people say that others have a good sense of humor, it implies a curious, unconventional, sociable type who rarely gets worked up but might not make the most meticulous accountant, for example. These traits don't apply to everyone off the street. Nevertheless, these only provide personality traits that go with stereotypes of the comedic. Stereotypes are a far cry from defining what a sense of humor actually is.

Professional Funny Folks

Any people whose paychecks depend on generating yucks essentially put their funny bits where their mouths are.

Professional stand-up comedians, writers for television shows, circus clowns, and humorists ought to reveal a great deal about personality and sense of humor. Nevertheless, these jobs require a lot more than wit. The perseverance alone is astounding. Stand-up comics and circus clowns have no union and none of the specialized degree programs available to other artists, like the master of fine arts (MFA). Many spend years driving from one small town to the next, living hand to mouth. The jobs require a certain hardiness. A friend of mine who played the West Coast circuit had a gig at a hotel club that put up all its mainliners in a special suite. Not exactly the presidential suite; more like the janitor's closet. He found a daunting bit of graffitti written beside the bed, which said, "Stand-up—nice career choice."

Comedians and clowns also lack the bronze trophies and crystal statuettes common to their mainstream counterparts—no Grammys or Emmys for comics or Academy Awards really. Some of the honors that they do have are not all that they're cracked up to be. One competitive contest in Hollywood boasts a first prize that includes a week as the opening comic at a well-known Las Vegas spot. A friend of mine whose quips and wisecracks earned her the coveted award braved the desert trek only to learn that she had to cut her act to 5 minutes. To add insult to injury, she also had to sell T-shirts and sweep up after the show. (I still wish I would have won.) Those who write regularly televised monologues for other performers often battle long hours and a capricious job market. A friend who was delighted when he received a 14-week deal writing for one of the late-night shows became deflated when the contract was not renewed. He was told: "You're funny, but you're not 'Dave' funny."

If we keep the vagaries of these jobs in mind, data from comedy professionals may say a bit about one's sense of humor and personality, but only if we compare them to people with equally grueling jobs that don't require wit. Actors endure some of the same tribulations but don't always need to generate laughs in the same way; they make a nice comparison group. Actors tend to score higher than average on extraversion, agreeableness, and openness (Nettle, 2006). Creative writers who are not explicitly humorists also have some of the same challenges as stand-up comics and humorists. These creative types often score higher in neuroticism and openness (Nowakowska, Strong, Santosa, Wang, & Ketter, 2005; Strong et al., 2007; also, see Kaufman, 2009).

EARLY APPROACHES TO RESEARCH ON COMEDIANS

Some of the first research on professional comedians (Janus, 1975; Janus, Bess, & Janus, 1978) relied on personality measures that have proven unreliable. Assessments and analyses of handwriting, dreams, and early memories don't provide data consistent enough to meet scientific standards. Comparable studies focused on family dynamics or other aspects of personality that are hard to pinpoint. Many of these are barely more specific than Barnum statements. These studies suggested that funny folks had mothers who were colder and fathers who were more passive. I uniformly hate these "refrigerator mother" tales. The cold-mommy theories began as an explanation for autism in the 1940s (Kanner, 1943) and continue to cause needless distress, despite compelling evidence for the disorder's strong genetic roots (Abrahams & Geschwind, 2008). The idea that kids start cracking jokes in an effort to pull a distant mommy closer always seemed a bit too pat. But a comparison of the parents of class clowns and controls suggests that the moms really are less kind and sympathetic and the dads more withdrawn (Fisher & Fisher, 1981). A comparable study had kids nominate the funniest student in the class. Those considered humorous had less cohesive families with greater conflict. They also appeared more distant from their dads (Prasinos & Tittler, 1981). It's not entirely clear how this contributes to a comic's personality and sense of humor, though. We needed better measures of personality.

Studying the Narcissistic Comic

An intriguing study from my old stomping grounds at the University of Southern California shed some light on personality in comedians by examining narcissism in celebrities. Though many stars live in a virtual fishbowl in this era of reality television, celebrities rarely provide systematic, anonymous data for research. About 200 Hollywood icons, including 20 comics, appeared on Dr. Drew Pinsky's radio show *Loveline* and completed the Narcissistic Personality Inventory (Young & Pinsky, 2006). "Narcissism," named after the Greek mythological figure who fell in love with his own reflection, is a potentially pathological form of vanity, conceit, and selfishness. This scale is more reliable than the early interviews on refrigerator mothers and the like. The study confirmed a couple of truths: Reality TV personalities are unbearable megalomaniacs, and musicians are the coolest, least narcissistic of all the celebrities. I know—big surprise. Comics' scores were higher than musicians' scores on many of the subscales of the narcissism measure. Comics scored even higher than actors on two subscales: superiority (the sense that you are extraordinary) and exploitativeness (finding others easy to manipulate).

The researchers also compared the celebrities to MBA students. I can hardly call budding MBAs normal controls. Their narcissism is above average in several studies and this one was performed in Los Angeles. The business school at USC was notorious for its leather couches imported from Italy. When I was in the psychology department there, we had one Naugahyde couch imported from Burbank. A close look at the data reveals that the comics scored higher than the MBAs on exhibitionism, a love for showing off and getting attention. (My favorite item on this subscale reads, "Modesty does not become me.") Narcissism appeared to be independent of the number of years that people had worked in entertainment professionally. This absence of a link with years in the business suggests that the comics might have been narcissistic before they hit it big, rather than growing more self-absorbed as their celebrity status increased. Given the demands of this profession, a glorified self-perception may be essential to success.

The Big Five in the Professionally Funny

The lone study of comedians that focused on the Big Five compared small samples of professionals, amateurs, and humor writers to a large sample of college students. The professionals and amateurs did not differ significantly from each other, which might suggest that those willing to stand in front of a crowd and tell jokes have some consistent traits. Nevertheless, the number of amateurs in the study (nine) was so small that the researchers could only detect huge differences between these groups. The problems that come from studying a small sample like this arise because of their low degree of statistical power. Researchers always need as big a sample as possible if they want to assume it represents the whole population. (You wouldn't want to draw conclusions about all men after dating only two of them, for example.) Personality scores from a couple of pro and amateur comics might say very little about every single pro and amateur in the world. But scores from thousands of pros and amateurs would probably average somewhere close to the average of every single pro and amateur around.

A bigger sample is thus more representative of the whole gang. When samples are small, one oddball can throw the average of the whole group off a lot. So researchers only consider small groups statistically different from each other if their average scores are tremendously disparate. That way the researchers seem less gullible—less likely to say that the groups differ when in reality they don't. When samples are larger, researchers are indeed more confident that the average of the sample is pretty close to the average for the whole population. They give these huge samples the benefit of the doubt and consider smaller differences significant.

So amateurs and pros didn't differ, but it might be because there weren't many amateurs included in this study.

Compared to the students, the pros were significantly higher on openness and significantly lower on conscientiousness. These results aren't a huge surprise. We'd expect comics to be more appreciative of the arts and more open to travel and novel ideas. We'd also assume that they aren't the best choice for alphabetizing your student loans by smell. The curious findings concerned neuroticism and extraversion. Despite the stereotypes of the overwrought kvetching common to many stage personae (think of Woody Allen or Richard Lewis), the comics were no more neurotic than anyone else. Let me repeat: Professional comics are no more neurotic than your average college student. The authors emphasize that a true neurotic would likely lack the emotional stability and courage to work diligently on material and perform it in front of a crowd. The extraversion results were also a surprise. Surely anybody who steps on a stage and gets a lot of laughs has to be more outgoing than your average undergraduate scholar, but that's not how it turned out. Students scored higher than professional comedians. The authors of the study mention that perhaps the comic's stage persona is a more extraverted mask to cover the person's real, introverted personality. This situation is certainly possible, but I can't help wondering if something else is going on.

I think that a professional comic might approach the personality questionnaire with a different perspective than would a college student. Professional comics, particularly those who know that they've been selected for the study because of their job, might answer questions about their extraversion relative to other professional comics rather than the population at large. When asked "Are you the life of the party?" or some comparable item, comedians might compare themselves to a different set of peers than the college students who answer the same questions. Sure, I'm an extravert, but compared to the screamer comics of the 1980s, like Sam Kinison, I'm a wallflower. Perhaps professional comics rate themselves as less extraverted because their reference group is not your average college sophomore, but Robin Williams on steroids. Although the study did not focus on comparisons between humor writers and college students, the writers were markedly higher on openness, a result that is common in creative people of all sorts (Greengross & Miller, 2009).

These studies shed some light on humor professionals. These folks might have grown up with distant moms and passive dads. Those who reach celebrity status have a touch of narcissism in them. One odd finding suggests that they may be lower in extraversion than the average college student. They also appear lower in conscientiousness and higher in openness to experience—results that are commonly found in artists and performers (Nowakowska et al., 2005). Links between these traits and other definitions of a sense of humor will help confirm which aspects of personality vary with what is whimsical.

HUMOR PRODUCTION

A comparable, intuitive approach to senses of humor that parallels looking at professionals involves the ability to generate funny material. Plenty of folks are capable of creating jokes and witticisms worthy of laughter. They're still funny even if they don't choose to go on a tour that takes them from Long Beach's Chuckle Hut to The Amarillo Possum Pouch. Tests for this ability have a straightforward logic. Participants can make up captions for cartoons, create monologues, or design bumper stickers, slogans, or remarks. Coders can then rate these responses for their funniness. A comparable approach is popular in the research on creativity (see Kaufman, 2009), but it requires expert raters.

Humor may lend itself to scoring by a wider range of researchers and their assistants. In a sense, we are all equally enlightened, or in the dark, about what's funny. So we're probably all comparably good at knowing it when we see it.

In one intriguing study participants made up jocular descriptions of photographs, answered serious questions in a funny way, and drew comical pictures of animals and people. Student coders showed a reasonable but imperfect degree of agreement on the humor ratings. The correlations among raters weren't terrible, but they could have been better. Agreement among raters is a form of reliability. Low reliability can make it harder for measures to correlate with the personality indices. For example, if one judge's ratings don't correlate well with another judge's ratings of the exact same cartoon, they're certainly not going to correlate with the personality of the guy who drew it. Essentially, low reliability means more error in the measure, like more noise in the signal. Despite a lot of chaff in the wheat, the humor production measures still correlated significantly with extraversion and openness (Howrigan & MacDonald, 2008). These two facets of personality appear to be a recurring theme in humor research. Comparable studies also show that extraverts produce funnier material than introverts craft (Köhler & Ruch, 1996; Thorson & Powell, 1993). Another study shows strong correlations between openness and the number, wittiness, and originality of the punch lines people created for cartoons (Ruch & Köhler, 1998). In addition, humor production was significantly related to intelligence and gender. Smarter folks showed more wit and men's answers were funnier than women's. The authors reasoned that humor's correlation with intelligence might explain why it's valued in sexual partners (Howrigan & MacDonald, 2008)—I discussed all of that in Chapter 2. I asked my wife why men would seem funnier than women. She said it had something to do with the way men get out of trouble for not paying attention, but I didn't quite follow the argument. But extraversion, openness, and IQ correlate with generating funny stuff.

HUMOR APPRECIATION

Although an examination of humor production is one way to approach who is funny, alternative approaches offer different perspectives on a sense of humor. I cited a couple of promising approaches in Chapter 1. Perhaps a sense of humor could be as simple as an appreciation of jokes. Ruch's (1995) work, where people rate different kinds of jokes for their funniness or aversiveness, relies on this perspective. People who like jokes must differ from those who don't. Ruch's series of studies found that jokes fell into categories based on their content or the way that they worked. The key content factor is sex. Sexual jokes all contain some sexy content—something about body parts or seduction or the act itself. For the structure of jokes, the way they worked tended to fall into the incongruity-resolution category or the nonsense category. The incongruity-resolution jokes had some kind of setup that created an ambiguity of sorts that the punch line resolved in a way that made sense. The nonsense jokes created an incongruity but didn't quite resolve it in the most straightforward, sensible way. It seems only natural that some folks would appreciate one type of joke more than other types, or that certain people would rate all jokes as childish while others would find them sidesplitting. The aversiveness ratings seemed like they should also add important information, with some personality traits correlating with aversiveness in ways that might not show up in the ratings of a joke's amusement.

As you might guess, extraverts generally liked all jokes more than introverts, and neurotics saw all jokes as more aversive (Ruch, 1992; Ruch & Hehl, 1998). Involvement in religious fundamentalism and in various forms of conservative orthodoxy also meant decreased overall ratings of humor (Ruch, McGhee & Hehl, 1990; Saroglou, 2003). Outgoing, nontraditional folks appear to see the world as a funnier place in general. Ruch and his colleagues hypothesized that the appreciation of different types of humor should relate differentially to these traits as well. First, sexual jokes aren't for everybody. Just take a look at the distribution of my teacher ratings on ratemyprofessor.com. Consistent links between personality and attitudes about sex suggested that reactions to sexual humor should vary among people with different traits. As measures of sexual satisfaction, libido, permissiveness, pleasure, and experience increase, so does a love of sex jokes. I wouldn't make too much of this finding, though. Sexually active people seem to like all sorts of humor, sexual or not, more than their less active peers (Prerost, 1984). Talk about putting a smile on your face. It could be that all of these sexually satisfied people are also extraverts. Extraverts like sexual humor more than their introverted pals do, a fact that previous work had established decades earlier (Eysenck, 1942). You'll also be stunned to learn that folks high in conservatism, authoritarianism, and religious fundamentalism likely don't want to learn jocular definitions of the word "penis." And, yes, guys like sex jokes more than women do (see Ruch, 1992).

Personality and Joke Structure

The personality correlates for enjoyment of different joke structures are particularly intriguing. Since incongruity-resolution jokes actually make sense, Ruch reasoned that folks who need traditional forms of closure should like them best. Those who appreciate structured, unambiguous stability in their lives would also appreciate incongruity-resolution jokes a great deal. In contrast, this same gang should show a distaste for nonsense humor and its unsettled, absurd, incomplete resolution. Sure enough, as neuroticism increases, the preference for incongruity-resolution jokes over nonsense humor increases, too. The anxious and emotional may find the relief of incongruity-resolution jokes more entertaining. They might dislike the fret-inducing loose ends of nonsense humor. In addition, conservative, authoritarian, law-and-order types who value religious fundamentalism, stereotypical family ideologies, and orthodox views rate incongruity-resolution jokes as funnier and nonsense jokes as more aversive.

Also consistent with Ruch's reasoning, as sensation seeking increases, funniness ratings for incongruity-resolution jokes decreased and ratings of nonsense increased. Those who love adventure, thrills, and excitement show less joyful appreciation for resolution jokes and more love for the novelty of nonsense humor. They appreciate the idea of the pope eating pizza with a monkey in diapers. Openness to experience, that index of appreciation for the unconventional and imaginative, also tends to decrease perceptions of funniness for incongruity resolution and increase them for nonsense. As an aside, a person's exclusive love of incongruity resolution predicts a lower level of intelligence, whereas an appreciation of nonsense has a small but significant link to higher intelligence (Galloway & Chirico, 2008; Ruch, 1992; Ruch, Busse, & Hehl, 1996). I'm not saying that conventional, unimaginative, tedious people are dumb. I'm just curious why they always end up as university administrators. Links between joke preferences and personality appear in Table 3.1.

Focusing on Situational Humor

Tests that focus on appreciating jokes or generating wit aren't the only approaches to the study of a sense of humor. Some

TABLE 3.1 **PREFERRED TYPE OF HUMOR FOR HIGH SCORERS ON THE BIG FIVE AND OTHER PERSONALITY TRAITS**

	O	C	E	A	N	Religious Fundamentalism	Authoritarianism	Sensation Seeking
Incongruity resolution				+		+	+	
Nonsense	+	+						+

of the best work on this topic varies its focus, depending upon relevant theories and phenomena of interest. Some researchers might focus more on the tendency to remember or reproduce funny material. Others might find a humorous approach to life more important. Researchers have examined people's perceptions of their own funny experiences in different ways. Historically, these self-reports of humor experiences developed after the completion of research on the humor appreciation tests like rating jokes. Researchers reasoned that simply saying a joke is funny doesn't tell enough about how much someone laughs in daily life. For example, scores on humor appreciation tests appear unrelated to how people or their peers rate what kind of appreciator, reproducer, or producer of humor they are (Babad, 1974). In an effort to understand comic aspects of everyday life and get a clear picture of how humor relates to personality, assessments had to have a different focus.

One form of a humor appreciation test focuses on hypothetical situations, instead of jokes or cartoons. Imagine that you stubbed your toe and inadvertently blurted out the "F" word at your niece's christening. What if you accidentally e-mailed a professor from your alternative address, homeworksux@hotmail.com? Would these events amuse you or irritate you? The Situational Humor Response Questionnaire (Martin & Lefcourt, 1984) describes a range of predicaments and asks respondents if they would have laughed under the circumstances involved. The situations have quite a dramatic range and don't fit most people's stereotypes of the comic. One item describes losing a dating partner to a rival. Another mentions riding in a car that takes a spin on sleet. A third refers to injuring yourself so badly that you have to spend a few days in bed. An intriguing line of research supports the validity of the questionnaire; it seems to measure what it purports to measure. For example, scores correlated well with how much people smiled and chuckled during an interview about pleasant experiences. A peer's rating of how much a person tended to laugh in a variety of situations also correlated with the situational humor responses. In addition, people with high scores generated funnier material in the laboratory when asked to make up a monologue or perform a creativity task (Martin, 1996).

These situational responses appear unrelated to the humor appreciation measures that focus on the funniness ratings of jokes, suggesting that they are tapping a different aspect of a sense of humor. People might enjoy all sorts of jokes and cartoons without necessarily finding humor in the events of their daily lives. A love for nonsense, sexual gags, or incongruity-resolution jokes may say little about your tendency to see, or not see, the humor in waking up in a full body cast to greetings from your partner and your best friend, who want to tell you they've fallen in love. Scores tend to increase with sensation-seeking scores (Deckers & Ruch, 1992). Who else would love driving doughnuts by the woods on a snowy evening? Extraverts also score higher, suggesting that the outgoing backslappers might find these awkward situations more of a chuckle (Ruch & Deckers, 1993).

Further work on the Situational Humor Questionnaire has stalled because of problems with the questions themselves. Like any other assessment device, this one is a product of its era. Some of the situations seem out of the ordinary. Others seem flagrantly unlikely for a broader audience of anyone but Canadian college students. For 14 years in Los Angeles, I never once skidded on the ice, so I might not have been able to say much about that situation. (Good thing I moved to Albany!) One bewhiskered item describes standing in line to get a computer problem fixed, a task that now would probably involve a phone call filled with accented English, rather than a walk to a software center.

Another item might show some gender bias that might have been worse in days of yore. It describes arriving at a party to find someone wearing a piece of clothing identical to the one you're wearing. There apparently was a time when showing up in the same dress was considered shameful for women and for anyone in drag. I have to admit I never thought twice about turning up somewhere in the same T-shirt and jeans (or black tuxedo) that all the other guys were wearing. Obviously, this item might create gender differences on the scale that really have nothing to do with humor. In addition, the responses to each item all focus on chuckles and guffaws, asking if the situation would have made the respondent laugh. People laugh for lots of reasons—not simply because they think something is funny. These limitations inspired the work on other aspects of a sense of humor and on other assessment devices.

Cheerfulness and Seriousness

Another approach to a person's sense of humor involves a generally jolly outlook. Anyone who can stay buoyant and bright in the face of hassles must have an optimistic approach to life that could include a good perspective on the absurd. Aspects of this sort of cheerfulness have a big impact in many domains. For example, a person's cheerfulness predicts what job satisfaction and salary will be 19 years later (Diener, Nickerson, Lucas, & Sandvik, 2002). That's a pretty amazing finding. I can't even predict what my height will be 19 years later. Ruch and his colleagues have looked at cheerfulness, bad mood, and seriousness in an effort to see how different states and traits might predict aspects of humor. Cheerful, happy, less serious conditions should enhance comedy, and those who are habitually in these states ought to enjoy, generate, and use humor. The most consistent results along these lines involve trait seriousness—the tendency to adopt a sober perspective. Serious people prefer to focus on the crucial and weighty, rather than on the lighthearted and entertaining. A revealing item from the trait seriousness scale reads, "One of my principles is: First work, then play."

One aspect of trait seriousness that is particularly relevant concerns an appreciation for straightforward talk—conversations without irony, sarcasm, or hyperbole. An illustrative item states, "I prefer people who communicate with deliberation and objectivity." Compared to those of us who prefer to communicate with cheeky fantasy, these folks don't create, love, or use jokes very much. High scorers on trait seriousness rate all jokes as more aversive, see nonsense jokes as less funny, and prefer incongruity-resolution jokes. They also appear to know fewer jokes. I guess that if you don't value jokes much, the riddles you learned as a kid will last a lifetime.

Cheerfulness and bad mood were unrelated to humor appreciation. In the production of humor, particularly tests that require making up a cartoon's caption, seriousness correlated negatively with their number, wittiness, and originality. Serious folks fail to generate captions for cartoons that are numerous, novel, or funny. Cheerfulness predicted the generating of wittier captions and a bad mood predicted less witty ones (Ruch & Köhler, 1999). These results and this approach tend to blur the distinction between personality and a sense of humor. In a way, trait seriousness is a sort of humorlessness—an inability to appreciate or generate humor. But the approach is very much about a temperament that goes beyond the sense of humor, including a preference for work (over play), straightforward communication, and earnest topics. All of these things are important, but it sounds as if some folks need to lighten up.

The Coping Humor Scale

As part of a large effort to examine humor's impact on health, Martin and Lefcourt (1983) developed the Coping Humor Scale. Instead of attempting to assess all the facets of funny, this device focuses on how people use wit to handle stress. "I can usually find something to laugh or joke about even in trying situations" is a typical item on the seven-question scale. People's reports on the scale correlate with what their friends say about them; the pals of those who score high say that they use humor in tough times and don't take themselves too seriously. In a study that asked people to make up comical monologues while watching films, high scorers created funnier responses to the stressful flick than their low-scoring peers did, but they were no funnier in response to a mellow movie. These results support the idea that the scale is genuinely tapping something about handling stress, not simply being funnier in general. A supportive study that is intriguingly titled "Joking Under the Drill" shows that high scorers facing dental surgery are more likely to yuck it up and chortle than low scorers. The scale correlates with Big Five constructs in ways that you would expect. As coping humor gets higher, extraversion increases and neuroticism decreases (Korotkov & Hannah, 1994). Optimism (a tendency to anticipate good outcomes) and self-esteem also increase with coping humor (Martin, 1996). All of these correlates of the Big Five appear in Table 3.2.

HUMOR STYLES REVISITED

We saw in Chapter 2 that people use humor in different ways in the discussion of Martin's work (Martin, Puhlik-Doris, Larsen, Gray, & Weir, 2003) on the four humor styles. Theses styles aren't about the content or the structure of the jokes that someone likes. Instead, they involve the general negative or positive tone of the humor and how it relates to ourselves and others. As I noted, there's the aggressive style—a biting, demeaning approach to jokes and teasing. The self-deprecating style makes one the butt of one's own jokes in a consistently pejorative, critical way. The self-enhancing style includes a bemused outlook on life, the universe, and everything. And the affiliative style emphasizes the friendly banter that brings people together. Exciting new work with twins in North America suggests that the positive styles have a large heritable, genetic component while the negative styles appear to arise from environmental contributors. Some investigators view these heritability data with optimism, reasoning that if negative styles don't seem genetic, they would likely prove easier to modify with an intervention (Vernon, Martin,

TABLE 3.2 ELEVATED (↑) OR DECREASED (↓) BIG FIVE PERSONALITY TRAITS IN PROFESSIONAL COMICS (PROS), ACTORS, AND PEOPLE WITH HIGH SCORES ON HUMOR PRODUCTION, HUMOR APPRECIATION, THE SITUATIONAL HUMOR QUESTIONNAIRE, TRAIT SERIOUSNESS, AND COPING HUMOR

	Openness	Conscientiousness	Extraversion	Agreeableness	Neuroticism
Pros	↑	↓	↑		
Actors	↑		↑	↓	
Production	↑		↑		
Appreciation	↑		↑		↓
Situational			↑		
Seriousness	↓		↑		
Coping			↑		

Schermer, & Mackie, 2008). I assume they mean the use of psychotherapy, but perhaps they have something else in mind.

An attempt to replicate this finding dampens the optimism about environmental contributors to negative styles while underlining key issues in humor and culture. Twins in the United Kingdom showed a high degree of heritability on all four humor styles, not just the positive ones (Vernon, Martin, Schermer, Cherkas, & Spector, 2008). These results may say more about cultural differences than about genetics. The authors point out that tolerance for aggressive humor seems greater among the citizens in the United Kingdom, where people aren't as politically correct and don't freak out the way United States citizens can. Perhaps changing negative styles will be more difficult for the Welsh, English, Northern Irish, and Scottish. At least they have Pot Noodles. Other links to humor styles are also revealing. Men consistently score higher on the aggressive style. This might stem from testosterone poisoning. The surgical intervention for them seems obvious. The self-enhancing and affiliative styles often correlate positively with psychological well-being; the self-deprecating style correlates negatively with well-being (Frewen, Brinker, Martin, & Dozois, 2008; Kazarian & Martin, 2004; Martin et al., 2003; Yip & Martin, 2006). At least one study suggests that folks of African or Caribbean descent report more affiliative humor (Romero, Alsua, Hinrichs, & Pearson, 2007). My experience with these folks suggests that they're more affiliative about everything, though, not just humor. These styles seem likely to vary with different personality traits, too.

The Big Five and Humor Styles

Some superb research on Big Five personality correlates of the humor styles has appeared recently. Although results differ a bit from study to study, several findings seem consistent. The negative styles, aggressive and self-defeating, tend to increase with neuroticism and decrease with agreeableness and conscientiousness. For the positive styles, the affiliative style increases as extraversion and openness increase. Self-enhancing increases with extraversion, openness, and agreeableness and it decreases with neuroticism. Folks who are more moody, uncooperative, and disorganized use cutting humor against themselves and others. Folks who are more outgoing, appreciative of new ideas, compassionate, and calm jest affably with pals and find the world amusing (Greven, Chamorro-Premuzic, Arteche, & Furnham, 2008; Martin et al., 2003; Vernon et al., 2008). The humor styles also relate to other traits in intuitively appealing ways. For the negative styles, the aggressive style increases with hostility. The self-defeating style increases with anxiety and hostility. The affiliative and self-enhancing styles decrease with anxiety and increase with self-esteem, social intimacy, and sociability. The self-enhancing style increases with optimism (Martin et al., 2003). These results suggest that personality traits can manifest themselves in the way that people use humor. The different styles actually relate to more of the Big Five traits than the humor appreciation and production measures do.

LINKS BETWEEN PERSONALITY AND SENSE OF HUMOR: WHAT'S IT ALL FOR?

The complicated links between one's personality and sense of humor reveal a few recurring themes. First, if personality itself has anything to offer the study of behavior, the personality measures must do better than standard Barnum statements that describe practically anyone. If a trait applies equally to everybody, it can't help us explain individual differences in humor or anything else interesting. In addition, "sense of humor" appears to be more of a folk concept than a scientific term. Everyone claims to have a sense of humor, even if no one can quite define it. Our stereotypes of those with a good sense of humor are all generally positive. In additon, one's sense of humor, whatever it is, clearly has different components. The appreciation and production of jokes and gags may say a lot about someone's sense of humor, but the two don't correlate with each other. A dispositional tendency to see the funny sides of things or a propensity toward cheerfulness, good mood, and seriousness may contribute to our view of jokes and the world, too. These might not, however, relate to appreciating and generating punch lines.

The way that people use humor relates to other important things that we think, say, feel, and do. Some people use comedy to deal with stress. Some make jokes to lash out at others or bring them together, build themselves up, or tear themselves down. These acts likely come from different people and create different worlds for all of them. Extraverted, sensation-seeking folks like humor of all types, including nonsense and sexual jokes. Authoritarian, fundamentalist, serious folks like humor less and prefer incongruity-resolution gags to nonsense jokes. Extraverted people who are open to experience seem to create funnier jokes. Professional stand-up comedians are particularly high in openness to experience, might be less extraverted than we think, and might not make the most conscientious bookkeepers. The jokes that make people chuckle, the ones that they tell, and the ones that they make up themselves might predict a lot about who they are and what they do.

But what's the point? Humor might predict a lot about us—how we spend our leisure time, create good work, attract mates, and stay healthy. But one's sense of humor correlates with important aspects of personality. With that in mind, we have to interpret any potential benefits of humor with caution. If we're all set to prove the wonders of wit, we have to make sure that any fortune and delight it might cause doesn't really arise from simpler aspects of personality. For example, intriguing studies of humor link it to personal ingenuity. Humor and creativity relate to each other in curious ways. But both are also correlated with extraversion and intelligence. Do these findings actually say something important about humor and creative work, or does personality really explain everything? Let's take a close look at this literature with these cautions in mind. Otherwise, we're back in Forer's classroom getting fooled by Barnum statements.

Practical Humor

Across the creaking floorboards of a stuffy attic, you find an odd abstract painting. The black and white enamel background looks familiar, as if someone famous had fashioned it. In the 1940s, the legendary abstract expressionist Willem de Kooning produced comparable works when he couldn't afford colored paints. But atop the background of the painting are green splashes, as if Jackson Pollock had paid de Kooning a besotted visit and spilled some crème de menthe on it. One splotch looks a bit rabbitlike and the others are little ovals. You head to the local gallery and tell the art dealer it's called "Easter on Mars." Bargaining with the dealer turns frustrating quickly, despite your assertions that this work is probably a groundbreaking one. You gesture toward the painting, cite a price, and say, "That's my last offer, but I'll throw in my pet frog." The dealer laughs and you leave with a pocket full of cash.

The gag that accompanied your final bid might have earned you a few more dollars than you'd otherwise have gotten. An experiment that had participants haggle with a confederate on the sale of a painting showed that this same frog joke (if you can call it a joke) led folks to shell out more for a painting than they paid in a jokeless situation (O'Quin & Aronoff, 1981). The participants were the buyers in this experiment, but the result was the same; a joke helped move the final price in the joker's direction. (I'd rather begin this chapter with an example of you making extra money with a quip than with an example of getting ripped off because of one.) A similar experiment conducted via e-mails revealed that beginning a negotiation with a bit of humor led to a more equitable deal in the end. In addition, the funny e-mails led to more trust in the other person and more satisfaction with the outcome (Kurtzberg, Naquin, & Belkin, 2009). Bargaining can be a stressful experience, but humor seems to create more pleasure about the final agreement. Extending this bargaining research to more general and diverse applications of humor has led to some intriguing findings. As this chapter reveals, this research provides a peek into the workings of negotiation, interactions on the job, persuasion, memory, education (the ultimate form of persuasion), and even creativity. But most of all, it tells us a lot about humor.

BARGAIN-BASEMENT HUMOR

Much of human life requires cooperation and compromise, which often means that few of us always get exactly what we desire but many manage to get something we want. The negotiation literature is huge, but the role of humor in this process is underinvestigated. Although we often play at give and take with spouses, children, friends and lovers, negotiating moments are particularly common in business. Studies of formal bargaining can reveal a lot about humor's function that might not appear in other contexts. Vendors often behave as if humor helps the entire process of their trade. Those who still hawk wares in open markets frequently rely on a witty patter to attract potential customers and make the final sale (Morgan & De Marchi, 1994). I shouted many a joke about butterfat and chocolate when I was an ice-cream man, and I don't know for sure if I sold more cones, but it definitely relieved my boredom. Advertising of various sorts can use humor for this first step of attracting buyers, as I'll discuss later in this chapter as a form of persuasion. In addition, humor can send the message that it's time to move from bringing a buyer and seller together to settling on a price. Humor frequently appears at times of transition like this in business meetings (Consalvo, 1989). Once the relevant buyers and sellers move to the negotiating stage of the interaction, humor can establish the parameters of the bargain, facilitate communication without confrontation, and diffuse tension.

Bargaining can be uncomfortable. It is one domain that often involves a delicate dance between affiliative and aggressive humor. A comedic offer can help negotiators fish for information about how far the other party might be willing to go in the process. Any such offer can be withdrawn as "just a joke" if the other person perceives it as an attempt to bargain outside the realm of the reasonable. Each joking comment can send a hidden message that could alter outcomes. Haggling over "Easter on Mars" might begin with a collegial quip that connects the people involved, as if to say, "We're just a couple of art lovers here. I'm sure we can find some common ground." But negotiation emerges from disagreement. Buyer and seller must start with different ideas or there would be no need to negotiate. Direct confrontation at this initial stage can blow the deal. In this part of the process, a joke might deride the painting or imply that someone isn't bargaining in good faith, but it has to do so indirectly. "My kid could paint that," a buyer might say with a grin, particularly about some modern art. A remark like this one implies that the work might not justify a high price. Playing this comment as a joke allows the statement to sound more like an attempt at wit than the beginning of a quarrel.

As the negotiators approach an agreement, jokes might diffuse tension by encouraging participants to notice how small the distance between them appears. The suggestion that a pet frog might seal the deal has a specific implication. What buyer and seller are offering is essentially the same. They're no farther apart than the price of a fly-eating amphibian. It's as if to say "We're very close here. Let's not worry about a few measly dollars." In some ways, this joke can communicate the fact that both parties have done a good job of negotiating. No one has lost face. In contrast, without the joke, negotiators might get drawn into a hostile competition. Once bargaining becomes more about domination and winning than compromising, there's often no deal. Neither participant can compromise, for fear of appearing like a pushover.

Qualitative studies confirm this pattern of using jokes and humor in negotiating. Qualitative research usually requires extensive, detailed data to gain insight into a process. Qualitative work of this type essentially asks why people use humor in negotiations and how they do so. It's great for getting a feel for what's going on, especially when a phenomenon is complex and multifaceted. As its name implies, qualitative research rarely reduces these interactions to numbers and statistical calculations, focusing instead on descriptors of complicated processes. In contrast, quantitative research focuses on a few variables that can reduce to numbers of some sort—hence the name. Quantitative work often relies on larger samples to find out when, and under what circumstances, humor might alter negotiations. It's great for testing if hypotheses generated from qualitative research hold up in bigger experiments.

The study of the frog joke is a quantitative one. Multiple participants each negotiated a dollar amount that's easily reducible to a number. One qualitative study of humor and negotiation examined tape recordings of business transactions, focusing on exchanges that ended in laughter (Adelsward & Oberg, 1998). These investigators found that joking and chuckles consistently signaled the transition from initial discussion to serious bargaining. Another qualitative study looked at videos of a salesperson and a potential buyer at a camera store

(Mulkay, Clark, & Pinch, 1993). These same two people met multiple times and repeatedly used humor to establish the parameters of the bargain, facilitate communication without arguing, and diffuse tension after they declined offers. Further work on this topic can help illuminate humor's role in setting the stage for bargaining and conducting negotiations. Each of these topics actually relates to many general issues of humor in the workplace.

HUMOR AT THE OFFICE

Humor consultants assert that joking on the job will soon have us all performing at 110% as we whiz around cubicles with our jet packs. These consultants frequently appear, clown nose prominently attached, as motivational speakers to big companies. They discourage the obviously troublesome gags—the sexist, racist, ageist, and hostile jokes. But they encourage a loosening of inhibitions via forced laughter, juggling, and balancing pennies on your forehead. (As if that's not hostile.) Their tacit assumptions include the idea that humor is some sort of tool to whip out as needed, like a portfolio of cartoons to share during breaks or a shaggy-dog story to tell over sandwiches. The thought that humor might actually point out the company's inconsistencies or foibles receives little, if any, attention. Humor consultants want employers to see comedy as an inexpensive enhancer of employees' motivation, morale, productivity, and satisfaction. After all, the employers pay the consultant's fee. I'm sure that employees don't mind a little time away from their everyday routine to watch some jokers spout the latest business jargon, especially if they do it while juggling between wholesome quips about bosses and paperwork. If these consultants can keep the promotion of their Web sites and newsletters to a minimum, the presentations will probably be more fun than a day full of cold calls and spreadsheets. The data on humor in the workplace, however, are a wee bit less impressive than these consultants often imply.

Some of the emphasis on humor in the workplace has appeared as part of attempts to make occupations more pleasant, a movement described as "the culture of fun." Lightening up the office certainly has potential benefits. Meetings could become more tolerable and repetitive tasks might appear less dull. But blurring the distinction between work and fun can come at a cost. If a naturally witty team of people happens to work together in an environment where they aren't too pressured, humor can give the day a little verve, help people communicate on difficult topics, and enhance creativity. Nevertheless, campy attempts to make work fun can have mixed results at best. One company with a team devoted to assisting an African airline decorated the walls in a jungle theme that included paintings of wild animals. Trainees sang a song by The Muppets and completed colorful crossword puzzles to learn the company's slogans and guidelines. On some days, employees were encouraged to dress up like superheroes. (I'm not making this up.) These activities generated an unsurprisingly large share of cynicism (Fleming, 2005). They also tempt me to attend faculty meetings in my Batman underwear. A look at this literature suggests that it is less definitive than some might believe, but humor clearly has a function in multiple domains of work.

Is Work Really Humorless?

Despite the concerns of humor consultants, even those of us who don't write for sitcoms still have fun at work. Not all jobs are a laugh a minute, but many are a laugh per every three or four minutes (Holmes & Marra, 2002a). In contrast, groups of friends generate humor about twice per minute (Hay, 2000). Work isn't as funny as a night with the pals, but it does have its moments of wit. The function of the wit, however, may be more varied at work than it is in our social lives. Some of it can maintain hierarchies or keep groups cohesive. Anecdotes, banter, and gentle teasing can be a great part of friendships. In the workplace, a lighthearted approach can help socialize new employees into the culture of the company (Vinton, 1989). Jokes on the job tend to pop up during transitional moments, when a group moves from one task to the next. These moments might be the only ones when a joke wouldn't interrupt the flow of work. Alternatively, humor and laughter at these times appear to say, "We're all in this together," as if to send a message to the team that everyone's on board (Consalvo, 1989).

But some jokes provide teams more of a whack with a board. A great deal of the humor at work is subversive, a socially acceptable way to challenge the hierarchy within a small team or an entire organization. These jokes often undermine status or threaten the values of the business, instead of signaling a supportive attitude for collegial relationships. Over 30% of the humor in meetings appears to be subversive, markedly more than what appeared in groups of friends (Holmes & Marra, 2002b). These jokes often deride working conditions, the skills of managers ("Here comes Captain Efficiency!"), or the capriciousness of regulations. Management often attempts to use jokes to divide their workers if they seem to be ganging up. Teasing comments also have a way of communicating unspoken norms about dress codes or other behavior without turning critiques into a full dressing-down (Collinson, 1988; Dwyer, 1991). ("Nice tie!")

OUR FEARLESS LEADER: HUMOR IN LEADERSHIP

The leadership literature is enormous, with literally thousands of studies published (see Mumford, 2010). Humor in leadership has also received a fair bit of research. Much of the work we've seen on humor in relationships also applies to leaders. People report that good leaders have a pleasant humor style (Priest &

Swain, 2002). A leader's positive humor correlates with other positive leadership characteristics, like intelligence and competence, as well as with greater job satisfaction in the workers (Decker, 1987). In contrast, negative humor, particularly aggressive jokes, leads workers to perceive their leaders as less capable and effective. These results seemed even larger for female leaders than for male leaders, with positive humor improving perceptions and negative humor decreasing impressions more for women than for men (Decker & Rotondo, 2001).

A lot of recent work focuses on transformational leadership, a style that contrasts with transactional leadership. I'm oversimplifying a bit, but transactional leadership involves a concrete focus on goals, dishing out rewards, and meting out punishments. Transactional leaders can be great at creating a clear set of expectations. Their subordinates know what goals to achieve, by what point in time, and what will happen if they succeed or fail. They often emphasize duty to the company as a source of motivation. In contrast, transformational leaders attempt to focus more on the individual needs of the employees, emphasizing some kind of intellectually stimulating way to look at tasks and goals in the hope of enhancing relationships and inspiring creativity. Transformational leaders tend to do these things by spending more time coaching and teaching employees, sharing a "big picture" vision, and getting workers to see problems from multiple viewpoints. As you might guess, the transformational approach leads to better job satisfaction and performance than does the standard carrot and stick. A dash of humor in these transformational leaders helps this style inspire more trust. The workers seem more willing to let these witty, transformational leaders make the big decisions, handle big tasks, and be in charge of their future in the company. The humorous transformational leaders also get more commitment to the organization from their workers. These workers feel more like they belong in the organization and express more dedication to their jobs (Hughes & Avey, 2009). These data suggest that humor plays a familiar and important role in leadership. It might also apply to one of a leader's key tasks: persuasion.

HUMOR AND PERSUASION

Everything from plugs for Pot Noodles to pleas for make-up tests can strain for comedy in an effort to persuade. In advertising, one of the most ubiquitous forms of persuasion, humor has had every conceivable impact. Some studies show it helps. Some show it hurts. Others find no effect at all (Weinberger & Gulas, 1992). Humor is clearly good at capturing attention, as research on television commercials confirms (Beard, 2007). It can make prospective buyers like a product more, too. Oddly enough, humor can alter our perception of a product without our knowing what's happening. We often can't articulate why we like certain merchandise, even if it has been paired with something delightful in our lives. Many folks leap from this idea to outrageous concerns about subliminal advertising, but that's another issue. In subliminal advertising, people can respond to an ad logo or a simple message presented outside their own awareness, but only if they are properly motivated for the product. Experiments on subliminal effects usually flash a word or image on a computer screen quickly—so fast that folks can't identify it. The logo alters behavior later, even in folks who can't recall seeing it. For example, people who saw the name of an iced tea preferred it to other drinks later in the experiment, but only if they were thirsty (Karremans, Stroebe, & Claus, 2006).

Humor's impact is a bit different, but it can also function outside awareness. Instead of a company flashing the name of a brand or product by itself, the product gets paired with something funny. In the everyday world outside the laboratory, advertisers place products next to almost anything alluring, even if it makes no sense that the two should be paired. How many beer commercials show bottles of brew and stereotypically glamorous women? Acquiring a feeling for something simply because it's been paired with something good (or bad) is known as "evaluative conditioning." For example, a product paired with our favorite music might acquire some of the good feelings that we have about the tune. At least one way that humor can persuade people involves this evaluative conditioning process. In one crafty study, experimenters designed their own online magazine. Amid all the articles, they placed images of products like energy drinks, pens, or scissors near witty cartoons or next to bland drawings. The cartoons had nothing to do with the products; they just happened to be close to them on the page. Participants consistently liked products paired with cartoons more than they liked products paired with the bland drawings. They even claimed that they'd prefer the product paired with a cartoon as a prize to take home (Strick, Holland, Van Baaren, & Van Knippenberg, 2009). This seems a curious effect given that the cartoon wasn't related in any way to the drinks, pens, or scissors. Perhaps advertisers will now pay extra to appear on pages near cartoons. Other mechanisms behind humor and influence are less automatic, but they're hard to understand without a more general model of persuasion.

A Comprehensive Theory of Persuasion

The impact of a persuasive communication depends on the audience as well as the message, much like the impact of jokes. One of the most comprehensive theories of persuasion is the Elaboration Likelihood Model (Petty & Cacioppo, 1986). As its name implies, it's all about the chance that someone will elaborate on a message, think about its content, and examine its logic. The model emphasizes that messages can persuade via two different routes: central and peripheral. Central processing concerns careful consideration of the rational argument behind a message. Motivated listeners who have an active interest in the topic and the desire (and ability) to weigh a message's points are most likely to engage in central processing. It usually includes more elaboration and thought, and can lead to stronger attitudes or dramatic changes in beliefs.

In contrast, peripheral processing is the default for those who aren't particularly interested in a topic, don't understand the message, or lack the motivation needed to examine the logic of an argument. In peripheral processing, people might rely more on an overall feeling rather than rational thought—going with the gut, in a sense. They might focus on their impression of the message sender's expertise rather than the form or content of the argument. In addition, during peripheral processing, listeners might react more based on how much they like the messengers, rather than on the points that they make. People can use each of these in different circumstances. If I'm going to purchase an expensive car, I'm motivated to get all the info, so I'll process messages centrally. I might check out *Consumer Reports* and weigh and measure different data extensively. I should arrive at a rational decision in this way. If I'm just picking a candy bar, I might not give it a lot of thought and end up choosing the one with the colorful wrapper or the catchy jingle.

Humor and Peripheral Processing

Humor alters persuasion via peripheral processing. Few of us say to ourselves, "I'm going to vote for new marijuana laws because of that hilarious radio spot," or even "I'm going to buy that brand of soda because the commercial was so funny." As we've seen before, humor can put people in a good mood, increase how much we like the humorist, and distract our attention. All of these provide opportunities for persuasion via the peripheral route. They don't do much for central processing of detailed arguments, though. A humor-induced good mood can persuade us in interesting ways. Generally, folks in a neutral mood will use central processing. They'll appreciate the quality of an argument, think it through, and come to a logical conclusion. They won't get distracted by the expertise of the arguer. In contrast, folks in a good mood tend to rely on peripheral processing. They'll pay less attention to the quality of an argument and, instead, rely on the arguer's degrees or qualifications. This approach can lead to fallacious conclusions. People who look like experts will seem more persuasive, even if their arguments are ridiculous.

Humor seems to work peripherally, perhaps by inducing a good mood (Mackie & Worth, 1989). In one experiment, participants either watched a witty clip from *Saturday Night Live* or a documentary film. Then they had about 1 minute to read a message about gun control. The message was either for or against gun control, but always the opposite of the participants' own views. (Participants who said that they wanted more gun control read arguments supporting less gun control, and vice versa.) The message contained arguments that were relatively weak or relatively strong, either for or against gun control. For example, a weaker argument against gun control might be that some people like to hunt. A weaker argument in support of gun control might be that guns are loud. A stronger argument against gun control would be that the second amendment guarantees the right to bear arms. A stronger argument in support of gun control would be that victims of crimes involving guns are more likely to die than if the perpetrator of the crime has another weapon.

In addition to varying the strength of the argument, the experimenters also varied the credibility of the person presenting the argument. He was either an expert (a legal scholar from a neighboring university) or an average Joe (a freshman from another town). Sure enough, attitudes of happy folks, the ones who had watched the comedy, changed with the prestige of the arguer, not with the strength of the argument. Happy participants who heard an argument from Dr. Big Shot changed their attitudes more than happy participants who heard an argument from Joe College. This result is exactly what we'd expect from peripheral processing. The attitude change for happy folks relied on the prestige of the arguer even if the arguments were weak. In contrast, those in a neutral mood, the ones who watched the documentary, responded to the quality of the argument, not the expertise of the arguer. This result is what we would expect if the participants used central processing. (See Table 4.1.) It didn't matter if Dr. Big Shot or Joe College made the points. The quality of the argument is what's important, as it should be.

It's possible that humor worked by improving mood. The experimenters measured mood; the folks who watched the funny film clip reported a more positive one. But there could still be something about comedy that altered persuasion that the experimenters simply didn't measure. Perhaps the cognitive changes associated with getting jokes altered processing of the subsequent messages. To buttress the argument that a good mood was the critical mechanism, Mackie and Worth (1989) did a follow-up experiment. Even when they manipulated mood another way, they still got comparable results. (Participants won a couple of bucks in a rigged lottery to make them happy.) This second experiment supports the idea that mood is clearly critical, even if it's not the only path from humor to persuasion. It also suggests that cognitive changes associated with humor probably aren't essential to persuasion. After all, winning a mini-lottery probably doesn't require resolving incongruities or appreciating puns. Other studies show that commercials

TABLE 4.1 **HUMOR LEADS TO PERIPHERAL PROCESSING ONLY WHEN PARTICIPANTS HAVE LITTLE TIME TO CONSIDER ARGUMENTS**

Rushed condition—1 minute to read the argument:	
Funny Flick First	**Documentary First**
Attitude change depends on the arguer's credibility (peripheral processing).	Attitude change depends on strength of argument (central processing).
Unrushed condition—Ample time to read the argument:	
Attitude change depends on strength of argument (central processing), regardless of film.	

that create a positive mood themselves can influence people's impressions about products—even getting underage kids to tell researchers about the beer they wish that they could buy (Chen, Grube, Bersamin, Waiters, & Keefe, 2005)

The results above, with central processing appearing during neutral moods and peripheral processing occurring during happy moods, arose when the participants had only about a minute to read the message on gun control. The experimenters also ran all of the same conditions with humor, message strength, and credibility of the arguer in a situation where the participants could read the message for as long as they wanted. (Again, see Table 4.1.) With more time to process the message, humor and the positive mood didn't lead participants into peripheral processing. Instead, the happy participants behaved more like folks in a neutral mood. Their attitudes changed with stronger arguments more than with weaker arguments. In addition, the prestige of the arguer had little impact. Unlike in the rushed, one-minute conditions, participants engaged in central processing rather than peripheral processing. In short, if you're happy and you need to make an important decision, take your time. In fact, taking your time may be a good idea for any important decision.

The fact that humor functions via peripheral processing can make it an ideal approach for changing attitudes about topics that people don't want to think about. A great deal of health psychology focuses on getting people to face facts about illnesses—I don't mean the common cold, but the spooky ones like cancer and AIDS. Discussions of these topics tend to make people shut down. They don't process the arguments and rarely do the things that might keep them from developing these dreaded diseases. An innovative study took advantage of humor's impact on peripheral processing to alter people's attitudes toward putting on sunscreen (to avoid skin cancer) and condoms (to avoid AIDS).

The researchers looked at how much people hated feelings of discomfort. They predicted that a humorous message would work better than a less humorous message for people who are averse to distress (Conway & Dube, 2002). In contrast, the humor of the message wouldn't matter for the people who could tolerate distress. The humorous message about sunscreen included a cartoon of a giant truck filled with the stuff. The humorous message about AIDS included a cartoon character that hummed and grinned as he walked along with his testicles and donned a condom. I'm not making this up. Results supported the hypothesis that humor worked peripherally and helped change attitudes in those who could not stand distress. What's funny was the measure of tolerance for feelings of distress: masculinity. Much as men like to think of themselves as butch and tough, people who claim that they're forceful, dominant, and aggressive (including women) can't stand discomfort. In these more masculine, distress-intolerant people, a funny message was more persuasive than a less funny one. In short, the absurd truck filled with sunscreen was more likely to get them to claim that they'd wear the stuff, and the cartoon penis got them to say they'd use a condom. For the less masculine folks, the humorous content didn't have any impact on the persuasiveness of the message. The truckload of sunscreen and the funny penis were unnecessary.

Another path leading from humor to persuasion involves how much an audience likes the persuader. On one hand, people like witty messengers, and the fact that they like them can alter their persuasiveness. On the other, if an audience views a funny messenger as "only joking" on a topic, they are likely to discount the argument and take it less seriously. So being funny makes people like you more, but it can also lead them to take your message less seriously. A nifty experiment on this topic took jokes from the popular comedians Bill Maher and Chris Rock (Nabi, Moyer-Guse, & Byrne, 2007). The researchers selected jokes from these comics that had specific, political messages. The researchers reworded some of their jokes to make them less funny. Some participants read the funny versions and some read the unfunny ones. They also either knew or didn't know that the messages were from these comedians. More humor increased the liking of the sender of the message. Nevertheless, any impact of this increased liking ended up getting washed out. Even though the humor made people like the messenger more, it also made participants discount the argument and take it less seriously. The impact of the humorous message reached statistical significance only when the participants reported their attitudes a week later. But immediately after the experimenters presented the message, attitudes hadn't changed. Clearly, it took time for humor's impact to kick in.

This gradual increase in attitude change over time is known as the "sleeper effect" (Hovland & Weiss, 1951). In most persuasion experiments, an argument changes attitudes at first, but then the attitudes drift back toward their original position. In the sleeper effect, people discount an argument for some reason and show little change in their attitude initially. After some time, though, they seem to forget the rationale for their discounting the argument and only remember the argument itself, leading to a greater attitude change later. Most studies of humor and persuasion have focused only on immediate attitude change; they missed the chance to see if humor increased persuasion days later. It's possible that humor's impact is greater than we realize but that it doesn't have much of an effect for a week or so. Further work on this idea seems warranted. Other applications of humor seem to rely on comparable effects on thought and action. A popular topic involves creativity.

HUMOR AND CREATIVITY

One aspect of humor that might have some practical implications concerns its link to creativity. Both comedy and creative ideas can rest on questioning assumptions, seeing things in multiple ways, or generating unique perspectives. Both can require a playful attitude and a propensity toward taking risks. Some theorists think of humor as a subtype of creativity (e.g., see Murdock & Ganim, 1993); others view them as distinct but overlapping ideas (O'Quin & Derks, 1997). Are funny people more creative? In a word, yes, but we have to keep all the cautions of the previous chapter in mind. A good sense of humor can correlate with creative flair, but both also vary with other aspects of personality and intelligence. Despite this correlation, we don't want to assume that humor causes creativity, or vice versa, until we rule out all of the alternative explanations for any link between the two.

The research on these topics gets a bit convoluted. Defining creativity may be even more difficult than defining humor. (At least humor tends to make people laugh.) What is creativity in the first place? Entire books are devoted to this question, and some damn good ones, too (Kaufman, 2009). Most researchers in the field agree that a novel, useful idea is a creative one. Some investigators focus on creativity as a skill or a trait that might be easy to measure in general. That is, creativity might be something we could assess independently from performance in the arts or sciences. Perhaps there's something that all creative folks have in common and that we could tap in a few simple laboratory tasks, a questionnaire, or an interview. These researchers might hope that the broad ability could apply in many domains.

Think of William Blake, the splendid poet and exquisite painter. Perhaps some test could show that Blake is outstandingly creative in the way that he thinks or solves problems. The test wouldn't rely on years of acquiring skill with a brush or a pen. Tests that aim to find creativity independent of the development of a technical skill often ask people to generate novel ideas or associations. One such test might ask people to list all of the things that they could do with a shoestring. High scorers generate more answers, answers that few other people provide, and answers that aren't the same idea over and over. So providing many answers tends to mean more creativity. Rare answers are also considered more creative. "I could use a shoestring to tie my shoes" is an answer that would score lower than the answer "I could shred a shoestring to make confetti." Answers that are essentially variations on the same theme would show up as less creative than lots of answers that are different. Thus, someone who listed only "I could use a shoestring to hang my brother" and "I could use a shoestring to strangle my least favorite aunt" might have a low score because these both are essentially the same idea. In contrast, someone who mentioned "I could stretch a shoestring and play it like an instrument" and "I could slip a shoestring into a plate of noodles to surprise a friend" would get a higher score because these two answers are so different from each other.

Generally, tests like these and tests that require generating humor correlate (see Kaufman, Kozbelt, Bromley, & Miller, 2008). For example, those who did well on paper-and-pencil tests of creativity also made up funnier captions for cartoons (Brodzinsky & Rubien, 1976; Treadwell, 1970). Self-reported humor also correlates with self-reported creativity. Folks who claim that they're innovative also report that they're particularly witty. A study of this type used the Situational Humor Response Questionnaire (Martin & Lefcourt, 1984), which asks about smiles and giggles in response to oddball situations like skidding harmlessly on ice or getting a drink spilled on you by a waiter. Folks who claimed to laugh and grin while in these predicaments viewed themselves as more creative (Wycoff and Pryor, 2003).

Note that none of this correlational work proves that chuckles enhance creativity or that ingenuity improves humor. We've seen that humor production correlates with extraversion and IQ before (Howrigan & MacDonald, 2008). At least in some studies, creativity does, too (see Kaufman, 2009). The correlations between trait measures of one's sense of humor and creativity might arise simply because each is also linked to intelligence or personality. That said, experimental work reveals that exposure to humor increases scores on creativity tests, suggesting that laughter leads to ingenuity. For example, high school students who listened to a popular comic scored higher on a subsequent test of their creativity than their peers who didn't listen to the comic (Ziv, 1976). Watching a funny film clip produced comparable results. College students who viewed five minutes of television bloopers did a better job of solving problems creatively than those who watched a film about math (Isen, Daubman, & Nowicki, 1987). Not that math isn't funny sometimes, but the bloopers led people to think of novel and interesting solutions more often. Simple instructions that encouraged students to answer in a funny way increased creativity scores, too (Ziv, 1983). The moral is: If you're ever asked to do a creativity test, think funny and you'll probably score higher.

Humor's impact on creativity might stem from its influence on mood. Happiness leads to more creativity, at least up to a point (see Davis, 2009). In a handful of situations, a positive mood can actually impair creative problem solving (Kaufmann & Vosburg, 1997). Generally, a mildly positive mood is a big help if you have to generate new ideas in a relatively unstructured task, like thinking up novel uses for shoestrings. It might be less helpful, though, if you have to find a specific solution to a specific problem, like how to decarboxylate an ester. Extreme moods are also less useful than mild ones. Unparalleled joy probably just makes people want to dance, shout, and open a bottle of champagne. Humor has not been applied to all of these tasks in all of these circumstances. When you've got a creative task ahead, a few minutes of humor or anything else that'll make you happy (and not impair your brain function!) can be a big plus.

HUMOR AND MEMORY

Much of humor's role in education, persuasion, and other applications could rest on its influence on one's memory. If funny material stays in people's heads longer, it has the potential for a greater impact. A ton of work in advertising and instruction relies on this idea. People definitely remember aspects of funny stuff better than less funny material, but only in certain contexts and with limited amounts of detail. Some of the results are inconsistent, so we're still figuring it all out. Our memories might only favor humorous material if it stands out—a saliency effect. When a mixture of funny sentences and less funny sentences appears in a list, participants remember the amusing sentences better than the dull ones. (The result where the same person sees both funny and unfunny statements in a mixed list is called a "within-subjects effect." The memory results for the funny and the unfunny come from *within* the same person. The investigator compares memory results from within the same person who saw both kinds of sentences.) Humor enhances memory for sentences within subjects. In contrast, if one group of people gets a list of sentences that are all pretty funny and another group gets a list of sentences that are all pretty mundane, both recall about the same. (This comparison is "between subjects." The memory results for the funny sentences come from one group of people and the results for the unfunny ones come from another group. The investigator looks at differences *between* the two groups.)

In addition, in the within-subjects conditions, where folks get the mixed list, enhanced recall of the funny sentences appears at the expense of the unfunny ones. Compared to the between-subjects conditions, where folks had lists that were either all funny or all unfunny, the mixed-list group generally did better on the funny material but worse on the unfunny sentences (Schmidt, 1994). Apparently, we remember witty material at the expense of routine information, and it happens only when both are present to create a bit of contrast. This selective memory for funny material at the expense of other material can undermine education and advertising. It's great to be a witty professor, but if students remember the jokes but not the material, that's a disappointment. Funny commercials can also capture attention, but if viewers don't remember the product, perhaps the ads are not helping to sell anything.

In addition, in the study of lists of sentences, humor enhanced people's memory for the general impressions of the sentences, but didn't help much for exact details. Folks could recognize the sentence if they saw it again, but didn't do a good job of recalling it word for word. This might be why people can have such a hard time retelling jokes even if they remember them. If humor only improves people's memory for the gist of a sentence but not for the details, people might form a memorable impression of the joke but forget the essential wording that makes it funny (Schmidt & Williams, 2001). My favorite example of this loss of details occurs during the credits of the movie *Diner*. Paul Riser's character begins a detailed yarn about a man in a bar. As he approaches the punch line, he realizes he has neglected to mention a critical point to the joke: the man is a quadriplegic.

In contrast to these results with funny statements, humor might improve memory for pictures with captions in both between- and within-subjects arrangements. One of these experiments used Gary Larson's *Far Side* cartoons as the funny material, and then wrecked their humor by making the caption a literal description of the picture. To get a feel for the stimuli, imagine another infamous Larson cartoon. This one shows three amphibious creatures immersed in the water at the edge of a pond. One holds a baseball bat while all three gawk at the ball that has landed on the ground just outside the water. The original caption reads, "Great moments in evolution." There's a bit of incongruity resolution when you catch Larson's implication that our ancestors made the transition from sea to land thanks to a frog's pop fly. The bastardized, unfunny caption might read, "Three fish lost their baseball." I don't think anyone will confuse that one with the funny original. One experiment using pictures like these replicated the results with the sentences; humor enhanced memory within subjects but not between subjects (Schmidt, 2002). This shouldn't be a huge surprise—the experiment was done in the same lab by the same researcher.

Another experiment using pictures found that humor enhanced memory even in the between-subjects conditions. This experiment used "droodles" as stimuli. Although they sound like drooling poodles, droodles are actually a combination of doodles and riddles—little designs that don't make much sense until you see the caption. Roger Price invented them (Price, 2000), the same guy who helped develop Mad Libs. Imagine you saw this: 000ME000.

It came either with the label "I work with a bunch of zeros" or the label "numbers and letters." Investigators manipulated the captions of comparable pictures to make funny and less funny versions. Participants remembered the funny droodles better than the less funny ones. This time the enhanced memory appeared both between and within subjects. Folks who saw a mixed bunch of droodles, some funny and some not, remembered the funny ones better. But folks who saw only funny ones remembered them better than those who saw only unfunny ones (Takahashi & Inoue 2009). It's unclear why the droodles didn't work the same way the Larson cartoons worked, but the authors suggest it might have something to do with the recall task. For the Larson cartoons, Schmidt (2002) had participants describe the picture and caption in the memory task. (What are they going to do, draw like Larson?) For the droodles, Takahashi and Inoue (2009) asked participants to scribble the squiggles and write the caption. Perhaps something about the differences in these tasks contributed to the different results.

Humor's impact also might vary with another aspect of context: foreknowledge of the memory test. In the droodles experiment, participants who looked at the pictures but didn't know they were going to be tested on them later showed humor-enhanced memory. In contrast, participants who were warned that they would be tested on the droodles didn't show better memory for the funny ones. Perhaps funny droodles naturally captured more attention or led to more rehearsal on the participants' part when they weren't expecting to have to recall them later, but the threat of a test got them to attend to or rehearse all the droodles, wiping out the humor-enhanced memory. We can keep these results in mind as we look at one of the biggest fields dependent on memory: education.

HUMOR IN EDUCATION

Many guides for instructors imply that comedic moments are the key to a joyous lecture. Some suggest that jokes will fill the classroom with the unparalleled motivation and creativity that will undoubtedly bring world peace, a cure for cancer, and better Pot Noodles. Most of these effusive endorsements of humorous instruction rest on anecdotes. I hate to let data get in the way of such enthusiasm. No one wants to see a return to the somber days of frightened students quaking in fear of an instructor's rap on the knuckles with a ruler. Nevertheless, the ubiquitous demand to make learning fun seems to undermine the idea that some material worth mastering actually requires effort. Although it's nice to see classrooms lighten up, I don't relish the thought that my neurosurgeon learned the order of the cranial nerves from a witty ditty (Simpson, Biernat, & Marcdante, 2002). It seems as if humor could make learning more fun. It's easy to hope that it could even increase learning. But what would motivate an instructor to increase the comedy of a class? Perhaps we should look at the dreaded teacher ratings.

Humor and Teacher Ratings

The brief evaluation forms that students complete at the end of each semester might be more important than many undergraduates realize. They can influence a professor's salary, promotion, and tenure; they definitely influence mood. One snarky comment can dishearten the best instructors more than a dozen positive ones can encourage them. These evaluations often contribute to decisions about teaching awards, too. I love to complain that few teaching awards include a cash prize, but they do influence raises. I recently received the Chancellor's Award for Excellence in Teaching, which supposedly marks me as a top teacher among all the instructors in the SUNY system. There was no check, but I did get a medal that looks remarkably like one I got for winning a wrestling tournament in junior high. As odd as it sounds, this silly decoration is actually a real source of pride and happiness, especially when research is going badly. And teaching rarely requires a headlock. If humor could help improve teacher ratings, most instructors would like to know about it.

End-of-the-semester teacher ratings correlate with a host of variables other than humor. The amount of research devoted to predicting these little numbers is staggering, until you remember that most of the researchers who publish this work also endure teaching evaluations every term. One of the most haunting findings in this literature relies on brief video clips—amounting to a mere 10 seconds or less of a lecture. Ratings from people who watch as little as 6 seconds of an instructor's lecture in the classroom correlate significantly with the ratings that teachers receive from students who have known them for a semester. This fact might mean that students make up their minds about a professor very early during the first lecture—a thought that fills some of us with dread. Clearly, a great deal of nonverbal and potentially unconscious behavior contributes to student evaluations. For example, fidgeting is the kiss of death for any teacher. Instructors with lower ratings made antsy hand motions, toyed with pens, and fumbled with chalk. They were also more likely to frown or sit down during lectures. In contrast, instructors with high teacher ratings were more likely to nod, laugh, and show warmth (Ambady & Rosenthal, 1993), but they had to do it without fidgeting.

The idea of warmth is important to psychotherapy, as we'll see in the chapter on psychological well-being. In the case of instruction, both humor and warmth appear to be part of what we call "immediacy." Immediacy involves that sense that a lecturer is right there with you, connected, following your understanding as the instruction progresses—the instructors indeed seem to be thinking along with the students as they progress through the material. There's no sense of a canned, memorized presentation. It's the difference between lecturing *at* students and lecturing *to* them. Immediacy might explain why university administrators haven't replaced all classes with videotaped lectures from experts—at least not yet. At first it seems as if a taped version of a lecture given by an award-winning teacher ought to be a great idea. In fact, a semester's worth of these lectures could show up on the Web somehow. Universities could use these over and over, even in a long-distance learning arrangement. These recorded presentations could generate lots of cash even after a professor has long been dead. They could also free up faculty members so that they could spend more time on research and the innumerable meetings devoted to vital decisions about general education requirements and paper clips.

But these taped lectures lack immediacy. Good teaching requires a relationship, not just a presentation. (Even a provost can understand that!) Measures of immediacy correlate with just about everything good. Immediacy increases teacher ratings as well as attitudes about the class and the topic of the course. It raises students' impressions of how much they think they've learned (Allen, Witt, & Wheeless, 2006), improves attendance (Rocca, 2004), and even makes professors look more attractive (Rocca & McCroskey, 1999). (Perhaps I should have my wife sit in on a lecture or two.) Most people believe that a clever presentation style is bound to improve teacher ratings, but it's not clear why. Several studies show that undergraduates' reports on a professor's use of humor correlated with course evaluations. As you'd guess, the type of humor is critical. Hostile and self-deprecating humor can hurt. Anything that appears clownish can undermine an instructor's credibility (Gruner, 1976). Affiliative humor helps (Gorham & Christophel, 1990). In addition, humor's impact seems to work indirectly through immediacy (Wanzer & Frymier,

1999). Instructors who can sprinkle discussions with a few ad lib jests must seem as if they are attending closely to students and making a personal connection. A joke in the moment can clarify that an instructor isn't simply regurgitating a memorized speech. This approach makes students claim to like the instructor and the material more. But how much do they actually learn?

HUMOR AND LEARNING

Improving teacher ratings is great, but increased learning would beat that with a stick. Anything that can get people to learn more and faster would be tremendously valuable. Early work on humor's impact on actual new knowledge was pretty discouraging. Adding jokes to a speech did little to enhance a listener's memory for content (Gruner, 1967). Reviews of studies that compared clever lectures to serious ones showed no meaningful effects, either (Gruner, 1976). Subsequent work with children showed more promise. Kids preferred educational TV programs if they included fast-paced jokes (Wakshlag, Day, & Zillmann, 1981). In addition, kids who watched instructional videos that contained witty cartoons remembered more information than peers who watched the same videos without the cartoons (Davies & Apter, 1980). These brief studies looked promising, but drew the ire of a prominent humor researcher who criticized their artificiality: Ziv (1988) emphasized that results like these would not generalize well to a situation where a real instructor teaches a semester-long course. Unlike most critics, Ziv actually proceeded to remedy the problem.

He trained an instructor to use three or four relevant cartoons, jokes, or stories to illustrate central ideas in a 14-week statistics class. This is no easy feat. (Hear the one about the binomial distribution?) Few undergraduates ever sign up for statistics classes because of an inherent love of hypothesis testing. Finding witty examples of mathematical concepts undoubtedly took a tremendous effort. The key here was that the humor was pertinent to the topic, consistent, and long-term. The same instructor taught the same course without these witty aids as well. Final-exam grades were almost 10 percentage points higher in the funny class—a difference that must have meant a lot to those who passed when they would have failed in the other situation. A replication of this experiment used two classes of Introductory Psychology (a course that instructors often dread almost as much as statistics) and found comparable results. These data offered compelling evidence that appropriate humor used over an entire semester genuinely could increase learning. They also imply that infrequent gags germane to the topic might be better than beginning every class with a funny tale or joking constantly with irrelevant asides. These results also seem consistent with the data on humor and memory, too.

Funny Exams

Many instructors attempt to fashion an amusing test in the hope of alleviating a bit of student anxiety. Unfortunately, professors may overestimate the magnitude of their wit, much like everyone else does (e.g., see Allport, 1961). (I once gave a test where all the response options were either "True," "False," or "Your mother." For one question, "Your mother" was actually the right answer, but many students missed it.) These purportedly funny exams can be hellish for international students who might not understand references to American pop culture. They aren't particularly funny to people who haven't studied for the exam, either. Many examinees find this approach distracting. In addition, humorous tests don't appear to improve scores even though many students claim to like them. One study found that funny directions improved scores on a subset of items, but only by 2% (Berk & Nanda, 2006). Most other studies on exam humor randomly assign students to one of two situations: a multiple-choice test with, or without, some droll options included (see McMorris, Boothroyd, & Pietrangelo, 1997). Scores on the funny versions rarely exceed those on the unfunny versions. I've tried this myself with over 600 students and found no improvement in grades, even when test takers laughed aloud or thanked me for the jocular items. One study of grade-school students showed that humorous math items actually made them perform worse (Terry & Woods, 1975). One experiment with eighth graders revealed that a funny test improved performance only if examinees actually thought that it was funny (Boothroyd, McMorris, & Kipp [in press; cited in McMorris et al., 1997]). This result might underscore the need to ensure that the humorous test is genuinely humorous. Of course, what students would think a test was funny if they had just failed it? Perhaps those who are confident about their test performance are in more of a paratelic state, one where they can appreciate the jokes.

Several investigators hypothesized that humor might improve performance for anxious test takers. A funny test question or two might lighten up the testing situation, decrease nervousness, and let an anxious examinee relax and focus. Although the idea is great, the data aren't compelling. One study (Smith, Ascough, Ettinger, & Nelson, 1971) found the predicted interaction: The humorous test led to higher test scores among anxious students. Two others found the exact opposite effect, with humor helping the less anxious students but not the more anxious ones (Brown & Itzig, 1976; Townsend & Mahoney, 1981). Four others found that humor's impact either didn't amount to much or didn't vary with students' test anxiety (Boothroyd, McMorris, & Kipp, in press; Deffenbacher, Deitz, & Hazaleus, 1981; Hedi, Held, & Weaver, 1981; McMorris, Urbach, & Connor, 1985). The effect does not seem robust enough to make it easy to identify the conditions necessary for humor to decrease test anxiety. There are probably more efficient ways to battle test anxiety than ending each multiple-choice question with the option "banana."

Funny Textbooks

Overdressed, chatty book reps knock on my door almost every day, trying to get me to switch from the texts I've already written my lectures for. Some occasionally mention that a new text is particularly engaging because of its humor. Hope springs eternal that a slick hardback, filled with witty comic strips, will captivate undergraduates so much that they will not only read each page, but also treasure the book too much to sell it back at the end of the term. Data suggest that this hope is probably a fantasy. Initial studies on the impact of humor in textbooks have shown such meager effects that few have attempted to replicate or extend this work.

Illustrations of key concepts can enhance learning under the right circumstances (Mayer, Bove, Bryman, Mars, & Tapangco, 1996)—a fact that most instructors knew implicitly since Pythagoras drew triangles in the sand. It seems only natural that a clever picture or two might help explain key concepts. Given the literature on humor and memory, one could hope that making these illustrations particularly funny might also help them stay with readers. Alas, no such luck. Readers of text chapters that contained cartoons found the witty chapters more appealing, but on a test of the content, they failed to outscore their peers who read an unfunny version of the chapter (Bryant, Brown, Silberberg, & Elliott, 1981). Those who read the funny texts did claim that they were more enjoyable, but they also found the funny chapter less persuasive. This finding seems to parallel the work on humor and persuasion, with jokes increasing the liking of the material but hurting the credibility. Perhaps the impact of the humor in the textbooks would show a sleeper effect of some sort, with those reading the witty chapters finding them more persuasive over time. Maybe even their memory for the content would decay less in a week or two, too. No one has yet published data on this possibility. A second study found that readers enjoyed humorous books more but did not think that they would inspire more reading, learning, or interest than a less humorous text (Klein, Bryant, & Zillman, 1982).

Despite these results, authors and reviewers continue to emphasize humor in textbooks. Statistics and introductory texts seem to harp on it the most, perhaps, as my editor mentions, in the hope of gaining more sales. Instructors might harbor some vague wish that a few panels of some familiar characters could make the book easier to open when the time has come for study. In fact, a better strategy might be to encourage students to recall the textbook information prior to trying to remember it for an exam. Once students have read a chapter thoroughly, they get little benefit from immediately rereading it (Callender & McDaniel, 2009). In contrast, they will recall it better for a test if they have attempted to recall it before (Butler & Roediger, 2007). Those who have written their own little summaries of sections or done other things to organize the material in their minds will flourish on the exams. Responding to short-answer questions about the material might help students learn better than all of the chuckles in the world.

SUCCESSFULLY APPLYING HUMOR

Folks in both education and business often turn to humor in an attempt to captivate, inform, and persuade. Despite effusive anecdotes, research shows that cartoons and gags help education and business only in some specific circumstances. Qualitative research and quantitative work reveal that humor appears frequently during bargaining. Quips often accompany transitions from initial discussions to serious negotiations. Banter can help establish the limits of offers. Continued teasing can communicate difficult ideas—like the thought that a product is not of supreme quality—without creating a quarrel. Comparable jolly gestures can soothe competitors as offers are declined. Jokes can often reveal that bargainers think they're approaching an agreement. They also seem to work in a jester's favor, leading to more money at the end of a negotiation.

Although many think of the workplace as supremely serious, organizational research confirms that plenty of jokes fly around in a business day. The humor in the office works the same way it does in bargaining or other interpersonal interactions. A droll story can ease tension and set a better mood. A gag can communicate that it's time to get down to business, without making anyone seem like an evil taskmaster. The occasional tease can communicate office norms, letting new workers know the rules, without requiring a big lecture. Good managers can use humor as part of a host of interpersonal skills. A witty style can increase the effectiveness of leaders who are willing to coach supervisees, share a vision with common goals for the employee and the company, and spend time encouraging innovation and creativity with more than bribes and beatings. Of course, the dark side of humor in the office is still evident. Prejudiced jibes and hostile wisecracks can undermine cohesiveness in a team. Banal or campy attempts to give a workplace a lighthearted feeling can make employees cynical and suspicious.

Humor's persuasive power appears in multiple places in the workplace and education. Advertisements can benefit from humor by mere association. Simply placing a picture of a product near a funny cartoon can make the product more desirable. Humor can create a happy mood, leading people to process messages peripherally—relying on their gut impressions rather than complicated reasoning. Funny messages also can persuade, but only in a handful of situations. A joking rendition of an important message can make people like the messenger more, but it might also make them take the message less seriously. A funny approach can help messages that folks might not want to hear, particularly threatening information about illnesses like cancer and AIDS.

Humor's impact on thought tells us a lot about comedy but even more about our own minds. Creativity and humor appear to go hand in hand. Some researchers view humor as another form of innovative, inspired flair. Creative folks are funnier, perhaps because of links among each of these, intelligence, and extraversion. A few minutes of comedy, if it leads to genuine guffaws, can make folks happy and innovative. A good mood enhances creativity anyway, at least up to a point. Telling people to think funny can also improve creative performance on many tasks, particularly unstructured, open-ended ones (but probably not changing a tire or performing a vasectomy.) Humor alters memory in a couple of ways. People remember the gist of funny material well, though they don't often recall it word for word. This may be why we can recognize a joke once someone starts telling it even if we can't tell it perfectly ourselves. Better memory for funny material can sometimes come at the expense of forgetting the unfunny stuff. This result might help explain why humorous educational material doesn't always lead to improved learning.

Humor appears to have a role in learning more generally. Funny instructors get higher teacher ratings, perhaps because of humor's effect on immediacy—the sense that an instructor is present and attentive with students. Small studies of humor's impact on learning aren't always supportive of wit in the short run, but a full semester of instruction that includes relevant jokes that illustrate key concepts leads to better scores on final exams. Hostile humor of any sort can breed fear in the classroom and undermine motivation and learning. Despite their popularity, funny exam questions don't seem to help performance much. In a subset of students, they can be distracting and infuriating. Others seem to like them, but probably only when they know the material well. Students seem to enjoy jocular textbooks more than staid ones, but these books don't seem to lead students to learn more in the short run. No studies have examined whether or not a humorous text leads to better learning over a whole semester. Obvious extensions of this work to physical health and psychological well-being seem warranted. Some of these have already been done. Take a look at these in the following chapters, and I'll throw in my pet frog.

Humor and Health

At the height of the Cold War, Norman Cousins, a famed political activist, journalist, and editor, labored tirelessly for the Committee for Sane Nuclear Policy. This committee was no joke. At the time, it seemed like an atom bomb might drop in a flash. But while others all around the world were quivering in their sneakers, Cousins helped establish the treaty between the former USSR and the US that banned nuclear arms testing, earning him commendations from President Kennedy and Pope John XXIII—splendid honors in a tense and troubled time.

After an important trip to Russia in the mid-1960s, Cousins learned that he had a rare and fatal form of arthritis. Rather than taking the diagnosis lying down, he turned to diverse and unorthodox sources as part of his treatment. His health care team included humorists—everyone from E. B. White to the Marx Brothers. At the time, biological science suggested that medical mirth was ridiculous. The idea of comedy as a cure, however, may be as old as the Bible. As stated in Proverbs 17:22, "A merry heart doeth good like a medicine...." Although I don't see God doing a ton of laughing in that text, the idea of good cheer aligning with good health seems ancient. Cousins's treatment included a lot more than Harpo's honking horn. He declined the trays of food filled with white sugar and flour that they served him at the medical center where he received treatment. He turned to wholesome eats instead of Pot Noodles. He took the health establishment to task for knee-jerk, short-sighted approaches that paid little attention to anything but prescription drugs. He felt that certain medicines were doing him more harm than good, and ended up staying away from aspirin and other over-the-counter pain relievers.

This refusal to take such medications left him few options for his debilitating pain. Indeed, he could turn to strong opiates, with their odd side effects, or simply suffer. Instead, he hoped that humor could come to his rescue. Perhaps several minutes of chuckles were a good way to keep the agony away. Well, except for the agony that his guffaws would create for other hospital patients. The hospital was depressing anyway, so he moved out of it to give himself incomprehensibly large doses of intravenous vitamin C, building up to 25 grams per day. (Do not try this at home.) He spent time admiring the zest and optimism of remarkable nonagenarians like the medical missionary Albert Schweitzer and the virtuoso cellist Pablo Casals. He emulated their devotion to music, their will to live, and their passionate sense of purpose. And of course, outside the hospital, he could watch all the funny flicks that he thought would ease his aches and agony. But would all of this work?

OH, THE PAIN!

Pain is a complicated phenomenon. It waxes or wanes with attention, mood, hunger, and fatigue—and how loudly my kids are playing. Cousins decided that laughter worked as a great way to tackle his aches. Groucho Marx helped ease his hurts.

Since then, humor's impact on pain has actually become quite well established. Laboratory experiments on the topic usually present a funny video, or one that is equally interesting but less funny, and then expose participants to a painful stimulus. The most popular of these aversive stimuli is the cold pressor test—a euphemism for having people stick their hands in freezing water until they can't stand it anymore. Although not every study supports comedy as a painkiller, the studies that didn't support humor's analgesic effects often had samples too small to detect anything. Most of the big studies support Cousins's anecdotes, with a few caveats.

Humor As An Analgesic

The comedy-and-pain research gets complicated. The studies reveal several general themes. First, humor can reduce pain, but the mechanism behind the analgesia is unclear. Second, the more enjoyable the humor, the better the pain relief. Even my grandmother could have told Norman Cousins that, but the lab results are more convincing than she would have been. Third, comedy's impact might vary with a person's sense of humor. Finally, humor helps best when people believe it will. This literature is growing, but a couple of experiments illustrate these points well.

First, mirth improves our threshold and tolerance for pain. In a classic report, folks who listened to a Lily Tomlin stand-up routine later withstood more discomfort than those who waited quietly or who listened to an ethics lecture (Cogan, Cogan, Waltz, & McCue, 1987). The ethics lecture was not supposed to be the painful stimulus. Instead, experimenters pumped up a blood pressure cuff until participants cried "Uncle!" Sure enough, folks who viewed something funny could take more pressure before they claimed to feel any agony. Chalk up one for humor helping pain.

Second, other labs have confirmed that comedy creates analgesia. They also extended the findings to reveal the import of the duration and timing of comedy. More is better when it comes to comedy helping pain. Though Cousins emphasized that 15 minutes of chuckles would often do the trick for him to fall sleep, a 45-minute film reduced pain more than shorter clips did. The timing was also critical, as is so often the case with humor. Comedy's superior effect over a neutral alligator documentary or a depressing Holocaust flick showed up only a half hour after the movies were over, not while folks watched them (Weisenberg, Raz, & Hener, 1998). Generally, humor's analgesic effects improve after the comedy is over (e.g., see Nevo, Keinana, & Teshimovsky-Arditi, 1993). Better to hear George Carlin for a while before your arm has to go in the freezing water than get the first punch line when your elbow's already an icicle. And even comic reruns beat the distracting dead bodies of *Night and Fog*. The delayed onset of analgesia seems to work for adults, but not children. One study with kids showed that they tolerated pain better during a funny video rather than after it (Stuber et al., 2009). Perhaps comedy takes longer to kick in as we age. That's certainly the case with lots of other stimulation. Cousins didn't mention this delay, but his pain was from a genuine disease rather than an irritating stimulus (or experimenter).

The laboratory work provides splendid experimental control, but few of us spend a lot of time dunking our hands in ice water or squishing our arms with a blood pressure cuff. Experiments with more natural sources of pain are not as common. One shows that patients recovering from surgery, who watched funny movies of their own choosing, used smaller amounts of minor painkillers, like aspirin, than patients who watched dramatic flicks. Unfortunately, the humor did not alter the use of major analgesics like opiate drugs (Rotton & Shats, 1996). Results like these make it hard to say if humor's impact on pain has practical implications. More work with natural sources of pain, like tooth extractions or medical procedures, could add important information to this literature. Of course, it worked for Cousins, so he didn't wait around for articles to publish.

Mechanisms of Mirth

So humor can decrease pain. The question, of course, is, How? There might be more than one mechanism here—see Figure 5.1. Cousins hypothesized about a lot of ways that humor could turn into analgesia, but he had no way to test his ideas.

Endorphins?

My reductionistic pals are quick to jump to the idea that endorphins (the body's natural source of analgesia and euphoria) squirt happily in response to every chuckle, leading to delighted numbness. The laughter movement loves this notion, too. Two studies have failed to find that comedy increases blood levels of endorphins appreciably (Berk et al., 1989; Itami, Nobori, & Teshima., 1994). Psychologists, particularly those who hate to see biology take over the field, seem to like this finding. In contrast, other simple interventions that can decrease sensitivity to pain increase blood levels of endorphins quite well. For example, a brief run on a treadmill (Oktedalen, Solberg, Haugen, &

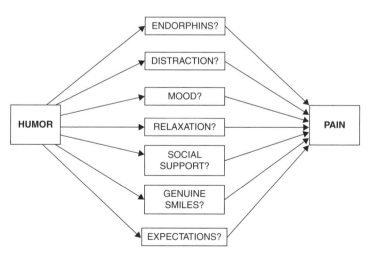

FIGURE 5.1 Ways that humor could combat pain.

Opstad, 2001), or some quick pokes from acupuncture needles (Agro, Liguori, Petti, Cataldo, & Totonelli, 2005), decrease pain and crank up endorphins.

These results make humor sound extra special, as if it can decrease pain through some mysterious mechanism that sidesteps body chemicals. I hate to miss a chance to rib reductionists or the laughter movement, but it's hard to argue that humor doesn't alter endorphins, based on these two studies. The samples are simply too small. For example, the Berk experiment cited above, which showed no impact of humor on endorphins, had five guys who watched a funny flick and five who did not. It's hard to conclude that, based on 10 people, something doesn't happen. Even if endorphin release had doubled, it might still not have been significant for a sample so small. The impact of humor on endorphins needs more work with bigger samples. Until that research is done, endorphins may have to remain in the running as one way that humor might alter pain. Nevertheless, a few mechanisms bigger than your average polypeptide are worth examining, too.

Distraction and Mood?

Although endorphins don't seem to explain humor's impact on pain, explanations related to distraction or improved mood seemed worthy of investigation. Perhaps humor takes our minds off our aches and stings. Cousins mentioned this option in his work. Distraction certainly can help pain, as several experiments emphasize. Encouraging folks to "fugget about it" can dull anything that smarts, and not just among Italians (e.g., see Wender et al., 2009). But humor may work even better than simple diversions. One experiment (Cogan et al., 1987) revealed that listening to Bill Cosby alleviated pain better than various distracting tasks did, including hearing one of Edgar Allan Poe's riveting tales. The Poe story and the Cosby monologue were comparably distracting, but comedy improved tolerance for pain better. The superiority of comedy suggests that its impact might arise from more than diversion alone. In addition, as I mentioned, subsequent work showed that humor's analgesic effect kicks in primarily *after* exposure to comedy rather than right away. The pain relief remains for at least 20 minutes after the jokes are over, too. This delayed and sustained effect is also inconsistent with the idea that distraction explains humor's impact (Zweyer et al., 2004). Cosby can't help your pain via distraction if you're not listening to him anymore. An improved mood seems like a reasonable explanation for this effect. But the pain relief remains even after changes in mood have dissipated (Weisenberg et al., 1998; Zweyer, Velker & Ruch, 2004). Folks still don't hurt even when the happiness has worn off. So at least part of humor's impact on pain must arise from something other than distraction or mood.

Relaxation?

With mood or distraction out of the running as the sole source of comedy's analgesic effect, another obvious guess concerns relaxation. The idea that the humor works via relaxation alone doesn't quite fly, either. Researchers have yet to do the definitive experiment on this idea. Laughter is actually more arousing than relaxing. That's why I can't laugh my children to sleep. Chuckles tend to increase physiological measures of arousal like heart beat or sweating, or they have little to no effect on arousal at all (Ruch, 1993; Sakuragi, Sugiyama, & Takeuchi, 2002). This result seems at odds with most recommendations involved in pain management, the techniques designed to keep agony at bay. Most treatments designed to help with pain take huge steps to reduce arousal rather than increase it, but laughter heightens arousal rather than reducing it (Weisenberg, Tepper, & Schwarzwald, 1995). Relaxation battled pain nicely in many of these same studies on humor's impact, with both strategies working equally well (Cogan et al., 1997; Dale et al., 1991). It's nice to know that mellowing out can ease pain when folks simply don't feel like joking around. In addition, there are times when relaxation techniques sound dry and dull, so comedy may be the best choice.

Social Support?

Another explanation that has always haunted me when I look at this work concerns social support. We've seen that plenty of humor involves having other people around. Social support helps combat pain in multiple studies. The mere presence of a supportive friend in the room decreases pain ratings in a couple of experiments. One of my personal favorites takes this result one step further (Master et al., 2009). Heterosexual women reported less pain in response to an aversive temperature probe if they could gaze at a photo of a boyfriend. (It was just a little piece of metal that heated up, so the ethics committee let it slide.) Gazing at a photo of some other guy or a chair didn't do the trick. A particularly crafty aspect of this experiment helped rule out distraction, too. The women had to hit a button as quickly as they could whenever they heard the computer beep—a task that measures what is called "secondary reaction time." Those who were more distracted should have taken longer to respond to the beep, but they were equally fast regardless of what photo they viewed. So the superior pain relief doesn't appear to arise from the distracting effects of a partner's beauty. Something about the social-support aspect of viewing a boyfriend's picture helped pain tolerance, and it wasn't just distraction from the pain.

Obviously, social support can help analgesia. Cousins stressed the import of good relationships between doctors and patients, leading him to better communication with his own physician. Turning relationships with health care providers into social support sounds great for all aspects of medicine. We've seen how inherently interactive and interpersonal humor is. Perhaps humor's impact on pain works via this path, too. Although watching a comedian might not seem much like gazing at a photo of a romantic partner, there's something a little more social about it than reading or listening to Poe's *The Raven*. For most stand-up performances, it feels as if the comic is talking directly to the audience. In contrast, Poe's short stories don't address the reader or listener quite as directly. He doesn't seem to be interacting with an audience in the way a good comedian can. I'd bet that hearing a best pal or a dreamy date tell some good jokes might decrease pain even more. There is no harm in using social support and humor together.

Sincere Smiles

Several experiments reveal that people can endure more discomfort after watching funny material than after watching less funny stuff, even if the material is equally engaging. Further support for the idea appears in a study that linked genuine smiles, rather than polite grins, to pain tolerance (Zweyer et al., 2004). These researchers videotaped participants while they watched *Mr. Bean at the Dentist* and recorded what are called "Duchenne smiles." Guillaume Duchenne, a French neurologist of the 1800s, distinguished between truly happy smiles and other smirks. Plenty of people can fake a smile by turning up the corners of their mouths, no matter how mortified or depressed they feel. Duchenne pointed out that truly delighted smiles also include raised cheeks and a crinkling of flesh around the eyes (crow's feet), thanks to the orbicularis muscles around the eyes.

Folks in the Zweyer study who showed more Duchenne smiles held their hands in ice water longer before they said that their hands hurt. They also kept their hands in the water longer than folks who showed fewer Duchenne smiles. The smiles data were particularly interesting because they varied with pain while subjective reports of enjoyment did not. More of the genuine smiles meant less pain, but more of the reported enjoyment did not. Saying you're happy and actually being happy might be two different things. This is a nice example of how a subtle behavioral measure of amusement can be better than subjective reports. We can fake our responses on a questionnaire, but it's hard to fake a true smile. If you do find yourself in a predicament where you have to smile and make it look genuine, try to think of something sincerely amusing. Our smiles may tell more than our words or even our laughter. Laughter, which can also be faked, didn't predict pain. A particularly ingenious aspect of this experiment required some participants to exaggerate their laughter and smiling while they watched the film. This condition parallels some of the laughter movement's practices, where people sit in a circle and laugh at nothing for minutes on end—a situation frighteningly similar to moments I've witnessed in a psychiatric ward. Those who forced their laughter in this study tolerated less pain than those who really laughed. Genuine enjoyment with sincere smiles helps ease pain, but feigned reactions don't help.

Expectancy: Does Thinking Make It So?

One last caveat about pain concerns expectations. Plenty of research in my lab and others shows that many things happen because we think that they will. For example, people who think that alcohol will make them hostile are more likely to get in fights after drinking (Smucker-Barnwell, Borders, & Earleywine, 2006). Expectations prove important for humor and pain, too. In one experiment, some participants read a paragraph that led them to believe that humor made pain worse; others read a paragraph that made them think that humor made pain less severe. They then watched the infamous "Soup Nazi" episode of *Seinfeld*, and endured the ubiquitous blood-pressure-cuff test for discomfort. Those told that humor would make pain worse found the cuff uncomfortable at much less pressure than those told that humor should make tolerance for pain better. They even did worse than participants who weren't told anything at all about pain and humor (Mahony, Burroughs, & Hieatt, 2001). Apparently, at least part of the impact of humor on pain stems from our belief that it should help. Cousins certainly bought the idea, much to his benefit.

PUTTING CARTS BEFORE HORSES

By the 1970s, Cousins's use of comedy made the headlines. It spread like a viral video of naked celebrities. The connection between humor and health started a flurry of oddball claims for the power of laughter. Some of the hysteria around Cousins and his treatment is understandable. Frustration with medicine was high at the time. Societal perceptions of physicians as cold and aloof were even worse than they are today. The idea that the medical establishment needed more levity struck a public neuron. There had to be a better way to get better. The thought of grins and giggles working better than pills and potions had an undeniable appeal.

But the culture took the idea of the healing powers of humor and went well beyond the data. Suddenly everyone from CEOs to cab drivers had clown troupes and mirth ninjas pestering them to pay for humor-enhanced programs designed to combat the dreaded sniffles. Pseudoprofessional "joyologists" started hawking newsletters, "readers' di-jests," and "funliners" that advertised their "funsulting" firms. Laughter clubs with names containing moan-worthy puns sprung up in every state. (I'll spare you.) Suddenly any fool could burn a weekend and a few hundred bucks to become a Certified Laughter Leader. I wish that I were kidding. Each organization mentioned Cousins almost invariably, citing his work as if it were definitive, divine evidence that chuckles cured cancer, even though he had in fact had arthritis. We've seen that humor can genuinely help ease pain. A close look at the research on immune function, allergies, erectile dysfunction, and longevity reveals some promise for laughter's health benefits. Nevertheless, throwing away antibiotics in favor of animation is ill advised. In addition, a blithe, nonchalant attitude about symptoms of sickness might lead people to avoid health professionals, making illness worse.

CAN LAUGHTER CURE THE COMMON COLD?

Dr. Patch Adams, the fun-loving physician with a toy duck on his head, defied stereotypes of the grumpy, overworked practitioners who rush dozens of patients a day out the door with a quick poke and a prescription. Robin Williams played the jocular doctor in the movie named after the man. He mentions that laughter is supposed to enhance biological functions galore, including those that would improve immunity. Perhaps old Dr. Adams is right. The reasoning behind this work is simple. Yucking it up might fire immune cells, protecting folks against various viruses and bugs. Two lines of research have examined this idea. Laboratory experiments show folks comedies and measure various antibodies in blood or saliva. Correlational studies ask people about their sense of humor and any physical symptoms. The results have been inconsistent, and many of the studies have had methodological quirks. Jokes aren't going to replace the flu shot anytime soon. Nevertheless, comedy has some potential for keeping immunity rolling.

The human immune system is a phenomenally intricate set of interacting biological structures. Hormones, proteins, cells, and enzymes work dynamically to protect us against toxic nastiness. This elaborate system adapts to everything from bacteria to parasites. It essentially learns to recognize these noxious agents and neutralize them quickly. The fact that our bodies can remember some previous bug and battle it efficiently is marvelous. The immune system is vital to all our vaccinations against the diseases that few ever get anymore—mumps, measles, rubella, and polio. No single aspect of this complex system is the perfect measure of immune function, but a couple of components that appear in saliva and blood are good predictors of who will and who won't get sick. That's why many undergraduates have donated bodily fluids in the name of humor science.

Secretory immunoglobulin A (S-IgA), an antibody found in saliva, is a decent measure of protection against respiratory infections. White blood cells of various types (lymphocytes like natural killer and T cells) play an integral role in the battle against illness. Most experiments on humor and health focus on these indices by sampling a test tube full of blood or spit. Studies like these are pricey. Finding out the exact number of antibodies in human fluids is not a kitchen-sink exercise. Getting grants for humor research of this type is an uphill battle, too. Nevertheless, researchers put together as much data as possible on shoestring budgets. I should emphasize that relaxation, imagery, writing poems, hypnosis, and even a stressful task can improve S-IgA measures, too (see Benham, Nash, & Baldwin, 2009). But humor may be more fun than searching for a rhyme for "tangerine."

One early study showed that a video of one of Richard Pryor's stand-up comedy routines increased S-IgA levels, but a comparably interesting, less funny film did not. Although the sample was a mere nine people, and nobody is as funny as Richard is, these data still offered hope that comedy might enhance immune function. Another set of three experiments offered further support for the idea, but again with small samples (Lefcourt, Davidson-Katz, & Kueneman, 1990). Participants exposed to comedy showed improved S-IgA, which looked quite encouraging. But a closer look at these data reveals that the baseline S-IgA measures before the humor intervention weren't always taken on the same day or in the same locale, weakening conclusions. These measures of immune function can vary dramatically across time and places. With a sample this small, a couple of odd readings that stem from a change in date or location can make the results look as if comedy is helping when really the improvement arose from something else. In subsequent experiments, humor helped increase S-IgA levels in some folks, but provided no help to others (Labott, Ahleman, Wolever, & Martin, 1990; Lambert & Lambert, 1995; Perera, Sabin, Nelson, & Lowe, 1998). Other work either failed to replicate any effects, or found that comedy actually reduced immune function. For example, an experiment with eight male medical students revealed that natural killer cell activity dropped after they watched a comedy video (Kamei, Kumano, & Masumura, 1997). It wasn't clear at the time why sometimes humor was working, while other times it wasn't.

Not Just Comedy, but Laughter

Anytime a literature is this mixed, with effects appearing in some studies but not in others, a few things could be going on. The simplest explanations involve subsets and small samples. The research on comedy and immune function is no different. Often, either humor works only for a subset of people, like those who laughed genuinely or folks with a great sense of humor, or else the samples are all too small to detect humor's impact consistently. An illustrative study looked at natural killer cells—the wonderful little corpuscles floating around our bodies, eager to assassinate any budding tumor or virus—in 33 women (Bennett, Zeller, Rosenberg, & McCann, 2003). Those in the humor group watched a stand-up routine in the company of other women in the same condition. The other group watched a distracting video, also with other women who were participating. Comparisons between those who watched the comedy routine and those who didn't revealed—drum roll, please—a big fat nothing. The comedy routine didn't alter their immune function either way.

But once the researchers looked at those who did and who didn't show mirthful laughter while watching the comedy routine, an interesting pattern of results appeared. Laughter, not just comedy, may be the key to health. Comedy enhanced immune function for those who laughed at it, but not for those who didn't. The subset of folks who laughed had comedy improve their immunity. The eight women who didn't laugh at the video (based on observer ratings of giggles) showed a significant *drop* in their natural killer cell activity. Sitting around watching something that's supposed to be funny can be a drag if you don't think it's worth a chuckle. It must be even worse when you're in a group of other folks who are laughing. These data suggest it decreased immune function. In contrast, the nine women who did laugh showed increased natural killer cell activity. Their immune function was also significantly higher than the immune function of everyone else in the study, too.

So the effect appears only for the people who laugh. Perhaps previous studies that show no impact of comedy on immunity missed humor's impact because they failed to assess laughter. Some of the participants in the comedy groups of these studies might have laughed and improved their immune function, but their improvement got washed out by the declines experienced by those who watched the comedy routine, but didn't laugh. By ignoring laughter, the studies suggest that humor has no impact when really there's an effect for a subset of folks.

The Curse of Small Samples

The small sample sizes in the humor and immune function research create another issue. In fact, the problem of small samples has been rampant in a lot of humor research. It's been an issue in all of psychology for decades. Statisticians assume that a result from a bigger group of people is more likely to generalize to everyone. Data from a thousand people are worth more than data from two. Imagine that you heard that watching "The Psychology Comedy Hour" improved immune function. Those who watched it had better immune function than those who watched an equally riveting show that wasn't funny—say, "The Psychology Drama Hour." Then you learn that the study had a million people in each group. Sounds impressive. Now imagine that you heard it worked for five people. Obviously, you'd be more skeptical. Something that worked for the million people who watched the comedy show is probably going to apply to almost everybody similar to the folks in the experiment. Something that worked for a couple of Janes or Joes might be a fluke.

For this reason, studies of huge samples can be statistically significant even if the effect is small. The huge groups who watched the comedy show need not differ a ton from those who didn't, but the effect is still considered significant because the sample is so big. Immune function might improve only by a small percentage in the study where a million people watched a funny flick. But since the result appeared in so many people, it'll count as statistically significant. In contrast, immune function could double in the study of five people and it still might not be significant. Statisticians just don't trust small samples as much because they are too likely to fail to represent everybody else who is relevant. So if the sample is small, only a huge effect counts as significant.

As I've mentioned, many of the humor and immune function studies rely on small samples. Funding is tight and these are expensive measures. Since the samples are small, some studies may fail to find any impact of humor on immune function even though it's genuine. The inconsistent findings may arise simply because each of the studies don't have very many participants. To show how a small effect can be hard to replicate, let's assume that the comparison between those who laughed and those who didn't in the Bennett study on natural killer cells was the True Effect. I mean capital T true, the size of the effect in the population. That is, if we asked some omniscient deity how big the difference was between all of those people in the world who would have laughed and who wouldn't have laughed, it would turn out to be exactly the same as the Bennett data. For atheists, assume we got everyone in the world to watch comedy. Some laughed; some didn't. Let's assume that the difference between those who laughed and those who didn't was the exact same difference as the one found in Bennett's study. (For my propeller-headed statistician friends, this was a d of .74—a large effect for the field of psychology.) Let's assume that's the true effect in the population. What would that mean for studies that are small? Some would definitely show significant effects, but many small ones would miss it. Please let me explain.

Obviously, it's too costly to get everyone in the world to watch the Marx Brothers movie *Monkey Business*, so we'll take a sample of people. It seems like this should be easy enough. We could grab the same number of people as Bennett did (33), and things ought to turn out the same for us as they did for her. But there's a chance it might not work for us even though it worked for Bennett. Even if the effect is true in the population, a sample this small might miss an effect of this size. We simply wouldn't have enough people to detect it. How come? Some of the folks who have less of a response to the comedy (good or bad) might end up in our sample, simply by accident. We might catch someone on a bad day who behaved oddly and didn't laugh when she might have under other circumstances. We might grab someone whose immune function was a little out of whack for reasons we don't know. The math is a little hairy, but it turns out that the chance of finding this effect again with the same sample sizes (9 who laughed, 24 who didn't) is a shade less than .60. That's a 60% chance of finding the effect even though it's true. Seems like a lot of work for only a 60% chance of payoff. There ought to be a way to improve our chances of finding the effect in our sample, especially if it's true in the real world.

Fortunately, there's a way. Increasing our chances of finding the significant difference would require more people. To replicate this result of improved immune function, we'd need 24 in each group (48 in total) to have a good chance (80%) of finding this effect again. Why is the bigger sample better? Now, if we happen to grab someone who's having a bad day, we've got a better chance of finding someone else who is having a good day to balance it out. We've also got more chances of finding folks who are having normal days. If we happen to grab someone whose immune function was whacky, we've got a better chance of grabbing someone else whose immune function is whacky in the opposite way. If we wanted even better odds—say, a 95% chance—we'd need 82 people (41 who laughed and 41 who didn't). In short, to replicate this effect, even if it's the Absolute Truth, we'd need to run a big experiment. In fact, it would take an experiment bigger than the combination of almost all studies on the topic so far. Humor's impact on immune function may not be much, but genuine laughter's impact might be meaningful. We won't know until someone gets fourscore and two people into the lab to give this a shot. (For my propeller-headed friends again, power of .8 and .95 with a one-tailed alpha would require the sample sizes mentioned above.)

A GOOD SENSE OF HUMOR AND IMMUNE FUNCTION

Since people who watch stand-up routines that make them laugh can improve their immune function, perhaps those with a good sense of humor have better immune function, too. Maybe those folks with a good sense of humor laugh a lot throughout the day, as if they're watching the stand-up routine of life. Research suggests that this isn't quite the case. A good sense of humor on its own failed to correlate with current cold symptoms or predict subsequent sniffles (McClelland & Cheriff, 1997). A couple of larger, more generalizable studies of a sense of humor and immune function also showed no link between the two (Labott et al., 1990; Lefcourt et al., 1990). Instead, something else seems to be going on. It's not that a sense of humor alters immune function directly; it buffers people against the immunity-zapping aspects of stress. Technically, this is a humor-moderated impact of stress on immune function. A moderator is something that alters the relationship between two other things—stress and illness in this case. Students with little sense of humor found their S-IgA levels plummet as their daily hassles increased over a 6-week period. Those with a good sense of humor maintained their immune function even as hassles mounted (Martin & Dobbin, 1988).

Humor's Impact on Folks With Allergic Reactions

As these stress, humor, and immune function results imply, comedy doesn't simply crank up antibodies directly. A series of studies performed in Japan has examined humor's impact on the lives of folks with allergic reactions. Some of these reactions arise from overactive immune function rather than from a lack of immunity. Allergies can turn one's immune function on its head. Sometimes an allergic reaction suggests that immune responses are too big rather than too small. Nevertheless, Chaplin and Mr. Bean can come to the rescue. Chaplin's *Modern Times* improved asthmatics' performance on tests of breathing (Kimata, 2004a), which requires decreasing, rather than increasing, an immune response. Comedy also altered immunoglobulin levels in the tears of folks with allergic eye reactions, so their eyes wouldn't turn red and get teary as much (Kimata, 2004b). Humor also improved sleep and altered a sleep-related hormone in kids with dermatitis (Kimata, 2007a). In addition, a comical flick increased the sleep-inducing hormone melatonin in the breast milk of moms. Their babies showed smaller allergic reactions after feeding, too (Kimata, 2007b).

Another series of studies focused on humor and dermatitis. Funny movies helped patients with skin problems, like dermatitis, keep their skin hydrated, maintain their testosterone levels (Kimata, 2007c), produce a microbe-fighting protein in their sweat (Kimata, 2007d), and even alter immunoglobulins in their sperm (Kimata, 2009). Some of these reactions required more immune cells; others required a decrease. Thus, humor doesn't simply amp up immune cells willy-nilly; it seems to alter immunity as needed. It can protect against stress, increase immune cells when they are essential, or alter other aspects of immune function, if that's what's best.

Humor's Impact on Cardiovascular Disease

As you've probably guessed by now, Cousins beat the arthritis that seemed so fatal when he first learned of it from his physician. He viewed all of his changes in diet, relationships, medications, and attitude as essential to his improvement, despite the laughter movement's focus on humor alone. Fifteen years after the diagnosis, he was living a painless, productive life, when he suddenly had a heart attack. He again took responsibility for his own care. This time humor may have had too much to battle. Systematic work on humor examining blood pressure and heart rate suggests that 6 weekly 90-minute sessions of comedy did not help as much as relaxation (White & Camarena, 1989). The investigators didn't actually code for laughter, so there may be an impact that they missed. The participants were college students, too, so their blood pressures and heart rates weren't particularly high. Humor interventions for cardiovascular problems need more work, but these data support the need for relaxation for one and all. We might soon discover that laughter helps, but we can already count on a nap.

Trait measures of a sense of humor might show a stronger link to cardiovascular functions than mere laughter does. The Situational Humor Response Questionnaire and the Coping Humor Scale showed no links to diastolic blood pressure (the lower number, which represents the pressure between heartbeats) during a cold pressor task. But for systolic blood pressure (the higher number, reflecting pressure as the heart beats), women high in humor showed lower numbers, while men high in humor showed higher numbers during the cold stressor test (Lefcourt, Davidson, Prkachin, & Mills, 1997). This gender-moderated link between humor and blood pressure reactivity may arise because men use more hostile humor. A replication using the Humor Styles Questionnaire, which assesses hostile humor more directly, would make a nice addition to this line of research.

Another study (Clark, Seidler, & Miller, 2001) found lower scores on a version of the Situational Humor Response Questionnaire in patients who had recently been diagnosed with coronary heart disease than in their healthier relatives. This result might mean that a poor sense of humor is a risk for heart disease. Nevertheless, you'll recall that this questionnaire describes oddball predicaments and asks people how funny they would find the circumstances. I doubt that even Richard Pryor and George Carlin, who both had plenty of heart attacks, would have found many situations worthy of laughter if they were filling out a questionnaire at the hospital where they learned about their coronary heart disease. A larger study, where people completed humor measures and then responded again years later about their medical condition, would offer better support for the idea that humor might be a buffer against coronary conditions. Until this kind of work is done, I'm afraid we're all stuck with eating right and exercising, rather than yucking it up to keep our hearts healthy.

Comic Viagra?

Far from immune function, allergy, heart attacks, or pain (at least for some of us) is the splendid physical function of sexual arousal. It may come as a bit of a surprise, but humor appears to improve erections. Norman Cousins never mentioned this effect, but I sure wish that I could ask him about it. I've never been a huge fan of the big emphasis on equating sexual health with erections. The rigid, fanatical focus on them seems to highlight performance over all else, potentially robbing sex of its intimacy and fun. Of course, I'm not down on erections. Erectile dysfunction is no laughing matter. George Burns described it as trying to shoot pool with a rope. Anything that can help ought to be a plus. I just hate to see closeness and joy confused with a hard penis. I'm sure that my lesbian friends agree.

An intriguing experiment related humor to erectile dysfunction. This seminal work was performed in Japan. Thirty-six guys who had dermatitis (an allergic skin reaction) and erectile dysfunction completed questionnaires and had some blood drawn to measure levels of various hormones. For the next three nights, they brought their wives to the hospital to watch films and repeat the questionnaires and blood samples. Each movie night they ran home with instructions to get it on (Kimata, 2008): "I'm not kidding, Honey. Doctor's orders." Some couples watched funny flicks first (*The Best Bits of Mr. Bean*, Charlie Chaplin's *Modern Times*, and *There's Something about Mary*) for three nights in a row. Others watched documentaries about the weather, again for three nights in a row. Two weeks later, they switched—not partners, but movies. Those who had already watched comedies now watched weather movies; those who had watched weather flicks now watched comedies.

Mr. Bean's best seemed to do the trick for naughty bits. After the first night of watching a comedy, the men showed spikes in testosterone, a hormone that can enhance erection. They also showed drops in estradiol, a hormone that can interfere with Mr. Happy's happiness. A questionnaire about erectile function revealed improvements, too. Some questions concerned how hard and penetrating their erections seemed. More importantly, additional queries emphasized how enjoyable and satisfying the sex was. Some of the effects were pretty big, with scores on satisfaction with intercourse doubling on the first night after watching a comedy. In contrast, the weather movies didn't raise a lot of interest, so to speak. A tale about tornadoes just doesn't create the same mood. The idea of comedy as foreplay has an intuitive appeal. It has a nice consistency with the evolutionary psychology material we discussed in the previous chapter, too.

The author of the study emphasized that the effects were significant only for the first day. He even began the title of the report with the words "Short-Term Improvement in Erectile Dysfunction . . . ." If the comedy works only once in a while, perhaps couples could mix it up with a steamy romance or an erotic thriller. Visual stimuli can have a dramatic impact on an erection (Janssen, Everaerd, van Lunsen, & Oerlemans, 1994). But I wouldn't get deflated about the idea that the movies worked only for one night. I think that the author is expecting too much of humor. Sure, we don't see improvements in erections on the second and the third night of comedy. But that's not Mr. Bean's fault. It certainly doesn't belittle something about Mary. The fact that watching a comedy in the hospital conference room had any impact later in the bedroom seems miraculous. The fact that another comedy, particularly one the very next night, didn't work right away again is no tragedy, for the following reasons.

Men with erectile dysfunction don't often have sex two nights in a row, never mind three nights in a row. In fact, Asian women who are the ages of the wives in this sample (32 years old on average) report having sex about only once a week. That estimate is not just from the women married to men who have dermatitis and erectile dysfunction, either. Even the women with husbands who have no skin conditions or arousal difficulties were included in the estimate of sexual frequency among Asian women (Schneidewind-Skibbe, Hayes, Koochaki, Meyer, & Dennerstein, 2008). With that fact in mind, these results linking comedy to erections seem more pronounced. Most libraries have free movie rentals, making comedies cheaper than anti-impotence drugs. And unlike Viagra, Ben Stiller never gave anyone vision problems (Pfizer, 2007). (All those concerns about masturbation creating blindness were clearly misplaced.) I think that married men the world over will emphasize that the humor has done all that anyone could expect in this study. In an informal poll, I asked over 5,000 men how frequently they had sex with their wives on three consecutive nights, excluding honeymoons. Those who had sex three nights in a row said that it happened only rarely—both of them. (Okay, I'm kidding.) Everybody loves Chaplin, but even he can't get the average, faithful, married guy laid three nights in a row.

CAN YOU LIVE LONGER WITH LAUGHTER?

Although the Bible praises laughter's curative powers, note that it does not say "Laughter will make you live forever" or even "Some laughter each day keeps the doctor away." An impressive test of comedy's impact on health would link humor and longevity. If people who appreciated, generated, or experienced a lot of humor also lived longer, the knock-knock-joke industry would undoubtedly flourish. Swapping punch lines sounds like a lot more fun than eating right, exercising, and getting plenty of rest. This type of research on jokes and longevity proves very difficult. Studies that focus on other predictors of a long life can rely on animal models, providing a lot of experimental control. For example, eating less seems to help mice and monkeys live longer (Anderson, Shanmuganayagam, & Weindruch, 2009). Researchers can randomly assign animals to receive less food, so when one group ends up living longer, we know it's from the calories consumed, and not some natural correlate of eating.

But humor research can't work this same way. Imagine randomly assigning participants to solemn or witty lives. It just can't be done. Until we get monkey troops to watch videos of another monkey slipping on a banana peel, we're stuck with correlational research. We can assess aspects of a sense of humor and wait for folks to die, but we won't know if it's comedy or one of its correlates (like extraversion or mirth) that creates the effect. Nevertheless, this correlational work makes a nice first step. If there's no correlation between humor and longevity in these kinds of studies, even with all of their problems, then there is little need to pursue more difficult work on the topic.

An intriguing, early approach to the question of humor and longevity compared comics and comedy writers to other entertainers and authors. Rotton (1992) examined encyclopedias of famous people. With a name like Rotton, he had to become a humor researcher. He compared those who were funny for a living to those who were born in the same year and who were known for something other than humorous work. Those who were funny professionally lived no longer than others did. Oddly enough, entertainers of all sorts died at a significantly younger age than other luminaries did. Entertainers lived an average of 70.5 years; other famous people (scientists, politicians, etc.) averaged about 73 years. The national average age of death at the time of the study was around 75. Perhaps an entertainer's life on the road leads to unhealthy eating, drinking, sleeping, and exercise habits. Maybe the constant pressure to be engaging and productive took its toll on them, too. Another group that seems to suffer from plenty of scrutiny and artistic demand also dies younger: poets (see Kaufman, 2001). Perhaps the life of the artist creates just too much strain.

An alternative look at humor and longevity focused on the Terman Life-Cycle Study (Friedman et al., 1993; Martin et al., 2002). In the early 1920s, Lewis Terman recruited over 1,500 high-IQ, smarty-pants kids to participate in a study on intelligence and success. These "Termites," as they were called, provided data every 5 to 10 years for over seven decades. Contrary to expectations, funny folks died sooner than their staid pals did. As many would guess, these same people were more likely to smoke cigarettes and drink alcohol, but controlling for these behaviors didn't make the effect disappear. The funny folks still died at a younger age. The humorous kids also grew up to have some riskier hobbies, like flying planes or hunting, but these didn't explain the effect, either. Something about being funny was fatal. It may be comparable to the link between extraversion and dangerous activities that I discussed previously. Or maybe funny people laugh about their illnesses and never go to the doctor.

The authors emphasized that the link between humor and longevity may not stem from one single mechanism. A lighthearted attitude about physical symptoms might lead people to minimize concerns about health. In the long run, folks who are less concerned about health might continue to overeat, drink too much, or smoke, despite negative consequences. They might drag themselves to work when they should stay in bed. They might avoid visiting the doctor when they should. All of this could add up to dying younger. Another study related to this idea (Kuiper & Nicholl, 2004) looked at humor, symptoms, and health concerns. Those with a sense of humor reported fewer physical symptoms, suggesting that comedy could improve health. Nevertheless, the humorous folks also paid less attention to bodily sensations, worried less about illness, and showed less concern about pain. It's possible that humor doesn't relate to health so much as it relates to one's perception of health. Humor might provide a false sense of security about health or a nonchalant attitude about pursuing healthy behaviors, leading funny folks to report fewer symptoms but then to wind up dying young because they didn't attend to their ills.

So humor does not provide the fountain of youth or the key to eternal life, but that's a lot to expect of any trait. One of the few personality characteristics that does predict mortality may not come as a big surprise. Conscientiousness, that devoted-to-the-details, painstaking, self-controlled approach to keeping organized and productive, appears to buy people a few more years of life (Martin, Friedman, & Schwartz, 2007). The mechanism behind this link is probably obvious. Conscientious folks are more likely to stay away from heavy drinking, tobacco, and other drugs, as well as reckless driving, risky sex, overeating, and suicidal behaviors (Bogg & Roberts, 2004). It's no wonder that they live longer. Their lives must feel particularly long. These effects of conscientiousness are more important than a love of comedy, which actually predicted earlier mortality. For what it's worth, Norman Cousins edited the *Saturday Review* for over 30 years—the type of job no one keeps without a great deal of conscientiousness. Although I'm tempted to reiterate the idea that everybody wants a great sense of humor but that it'll kill you, the real message is less pessimistic. Physical illness isn't always funny. A great sense of humor is delightful, but even the most hilarious people, those who laugh quickest and most often, still have to eat right, exercise, sleep, and go to the doctor if they want to live a long time.

HUMOR AND HEALTH IN A NUTSHELL

Humans have often assumed that humor would help health. Ever since Norman Cousins praised comedy as part of his recovery from a debilitating illness, the idea has spread like feral flames. Though good old Norman outlived the allegedly fatal form of arthritis by 16 years, and kept kicking 10 years past his first heart attack, he did not survive on chortles alone. It's a little sad to think that a guy who probably saved the world from the fiery, radioactive death of a global thermonuclear war will be remembered best for falling asleep after watching *Monkey Business.*

The humor-and-health data aren't as strong as folks might hope, but the research reveals some promise. A chuckle-worthy show can keep pain at bay in the laboratory, but we're not exactly sure why. The analgesia doesn't appear to arise solely from distraction or an improved mood. It may work best for those who believe it will, just like placebos. Comic performances can improve immune function in those who find them very funny, especially if the jokes create genuine Duchenne smiles or sincere sniggers. People with a good sense of humor seem to have a built-in buffer against stress's impact on immune function. A good comedy can decrease the overactive immune reactions that create allergies, too. So laughter may crank immune function up or down appropriately. Women with a good sense of humor might have lower blood pressure reactivity than their less humorous sisters. Men with high humor scores might show more blood pressure reactivity, perhaps because of hostile humor. A good sense of humor is not likely to lead to a longer life. In fact, those who treat the symptoms of illness as a joking matter can end up dying younger. A love of laughter and plenty of guffaws, combined with a healthy diet, regular exercise, supportive relationships, appropriate medication, and a passion for life, have the potential to keep people healthy.

A funny flick can also help in a case of erectile dysfunction, but not every night for three nights in a row. There is an obvious natural progression from erectile dysfunction in physical health to research on mental health. Sexual health invariably combines purely physiological functions with important psychological ones. Physical, biological contributors to sex rest heavily on the psychological components that make it enchanting. In many ways, the fact that humor can enhance sexual health underscores its potential contribution to psychological fitness more generally, as we'll see in the next chapter.

Humor and Psychological Well-Being

As we saw in the previous chapter, Norman Cousins's use of humor against physical disease became legendary. Although his treatment included a lot more than watching *Duck Soup*, he claimed that laughter played a key role in helping him in his arthritis. He also emphasized the interplay between his physical health and his psychological well-being. Feeling good mentally led to feeling good physically. Research offers more support for humor's impact on psychological well-being than on physical health. If Norman Cousins serves as the poster boy for humor's use against medical ills, the man who serves the same role for psychological well-being would have to be Nathan Birnbaum.

Nathan, who was much funnier than Cousins, battled other kinds of hardships and lived to be 100. He was one of 12 children and lost his father in a flu epidemic before he was

8 years old. There were no child-labor laws at the time, so little Nathan got a job making syrup at a candy store. Times were so tough that he had to steal coal from the truck on the street to keep the family's house warm. At least he had a good sense of humor about it. He shined shoes, ran errands, and sold newspapers. One of his business ideas included forming the Pee Wee Quartet. They put a hat on the sidewalk as they sang, in hopes of earning a few pennies. Unfortunately, sometimes people took coins rather than leaving them. Occasionally, they even took the hat.

The show business bug bit Nathan, even despite the stolen hats. He dropped out of school in fourth grade to attempt to make it as an entertainer. He tried trick roller skating and dancing, but eventually he settled on a vaudeville comedy act. When he was older, he and an acquaintance started a "Dumb Dora" routine at local theaters. He would ask his female colleague straightforward questions; she would answer in a scatterbrained, funny way. Audiences laughed; the new comedy team was booked time and again. Soon Nathan found himself falling in love with his "Dumb Dora," for she was actually a brilliant comedian. Alas, she was engaged to another performer. It must have hurt to write and rehearse hour after hour with an unrequited crush. Others might have lapsed into a depressive funk, but Nathan kept his sense of humor and eventually won her heart as well as her hand in marriage.

A few years later, the ups and downs of the Great Depression hit everyone hard, but Nathan stayed with it. He could have become anxious and fretful, but instead he kept working. Soon the act played radio, television, and the big screen. Nathan enlisted his brother and a couple of other writers to help craft new jokes. Some routines worked and others didn't, but Nathan and the team kept coming out on top. Many years later his beloved wife Gracie died. The death of a spouse can be one of the most devastating events in life. Nathan lost a soul mate as well as a stage partner. Again, he kept his sense of humor. He revamped the act by playing up his advancing age and incessant cigar smoking. New crowds adored his work on the stage and screen. Humor had helped him bounce back. He even got a role as the titular character, God, in the movie *Oh, God!* Of course, he used his stage name: George Burns.

A whole life spent devoted to humor this way is rare, but many people use comedy to keep stressors from spoiling their well-being. We've seen the mixed impact that humor can have on physical symptoms and have noted the problems in the published research. But the work on humor and mental health is actually more compelling. Not that you'd know it from the lives of many famous comedians. It can seem hard to argue that humor is the key to psychological well-being, particularly in light of the notorious troubles of a long list of comedians. Patton Oswalt's riffs about his clinical depression can bring anyone to tears. The legendary drug problems of Lenny Bruce, Chris Farley, John Belushi, George Carlin, Richard Pryor, Robin Williams, Sam Kinison, and Mitch Hedberg come to mind. The odd relationships with food for Louie Anderson, John Pinette, Ralphie May, John Candy, Will Sasso, and Fatty Arbuckle don't help. High-profile suicides among comic performers make the argument for humor as an aid to well-being difficult. Stand-up comedian Richard Jeni's self-inflicted death hit me particularly hard. I had seen him in a small venue long before he had HBO specials, and I had always admired his work. His death put one of his classic bits about suicide-inducing love songs into a less funny light. But these outstanding comics are the exceptions rather than the rule. It's easy to forget that plenty of humorless folks use drugs, gain weight, and kill themselves. There are also thousands of comics who don't abuse substances, struggle with their girth, or take their own lives, too.

Despite the salient exceptions in the world of stand-up, most people think that humor helps mental health. And the more humor, the better. Much of the research on this topic focuses on variations in mood. We'll get into experiments and studies that examine comedy's impact on sadness, angst, or well-being. Other projects look at people with diagnosed disorders—conditions with multiple symptoms, like depression or schizophrenia. Plenty of armchair theorists spin yarns about humor and emotional health in various forms. Others suggest that humor should be a key in battling stress and conducting successful psychotherapy. As we'll see, it's not quite this simple. Fortunately, the data have even better tales to tell.

HUMOR AND MOOD IN THE SHORT RUN

Humor makes folks cheerful. A funny routine can decrease sad moods and enhance happy ones. In fact, a sitcom episode appears to improve mood as much as an equal amount of time on the exercise bike does (Szabo, 2007), and it's a lot easier than pumping those pedals. Nevertheless, I'm not recommending three nights a week at a comedy club as a substitute for trips to the gym. The question, of course, is how a handful of gags in a story make an audience happy. Part of understanding humor's impact on mood requires a grasp of all the things that contribute to how people feel. One key source of the doldrums can be rumination—that repeated, persistent tendency to ponder the same thought. A bad mood stays bad because we keep thinking bad thoughts. This sort of chewing over the same negative thought over and over and over again definitely keeps folks bummed out, angry, nervous, or irritated. Many studies reveal that ruminating like this increases drug problems, troubles with food, anxiety, and depression (Aldao, Nolen-Hoeksema, & Schweizer, 2010). My own students have shown rumination's link to aggression, too (Borders, Smucker-Barnwell, & Earleywine, 2007). Nothing can make people want to smack their own neighbors like thinking the same thought again and again.

One study confirmed that rumination correlates with depression, especially for the humorless. Rumination was a particularly strong predictor of depressive symptoms for folks who were low on self-enhancing humor (the kind that folks use to keep their spirits high) or affiliative humor (the kind that people use to bond with buddies). In contrast, those who used jokes to remind themselves of the good things in life, or to connect with their friends, didn't let rumination turn into depression (Olson, Hugelshofer, Kwon, & Reff, 2005). In short, a good sense of humor kept repeated thoughts from transforming into gloom. This interaction between rumination and humor may arise in part from distraction—any amusing diversion that might undo those persistent thoughts. Despite our strong desires to sort through every issue in the hope of solving all our problems, once and for all (as if that could happen!), time away from the seriousness of our own thoughts can actually help a lot more. Distracting folks so that they can put an end to aversive rumination can help bad moods dissipate. This is a tough idea for some of my intellectual pals who think that the solution to every problem is more thinking.

Not all distractions work this way to help mood, of course. When I'm trying to write, my youngest daughter is sometimes banging on the piano—a distraction that does not help my cognitions. But a distraction that keeps negative thoughts out of your mind has a lot of potential. Even doing math problems can keep a bad mood from lasting long (Van Dillen & Koole, 2007), although I can never seem to convey this fact to my research-methods class. Fortunately, math is not the only way to keep away from troublesome thoughts. Humor may help mood via distraction, too, and it's a lot more fun than computing statistics (Strick, Holland, van Baaren, & van Knippenberg, 2009). An intriguing experiment reveals that part of humor's improvement of a negative mood stems from distraction. Participants who viewed nasty slides of gruesome car wrecks and hostile beatings had their moods plummet. Some of these slides were quite upsetting. But if participants saw a humorous picture right after a nasty one, their moods didn't get as bad. Chalk up one for the cartoons. But how do we know that it's humor and its distracting components that are at work here?

Humorous pictures helped mood more than equally posi-tive pictures that weren't as funny. So a nice picture of a meadow can keep mood from getting horribly bad, but it just didn't help as much as a funny photo of juggling ducks. Tests showed that these positive but unfunny photos were also less distracting. How do we know that they were less distracting? People didn't need to look at them for very long before claiming that they understood them. The positive pictures were also less likely to interfere with a memory task. The humorous ones took longer to understand; they also were more likely to make people forget an eight-digit number they'd seen right beforehand. These dif-ferences led the researchers to conclude that distraction may be part of how humor helps mood. The finding that funny, more distracting pictures alleviated a sad mood better than positive but less distracting ones seems consistent with the work on math problems and mood. These results also say a bit about how humor might function better than simpler distractions like rearranging your sock drawer with a protractor.

Even a minute of obligatory guffaws can improve mood (Foley, Matheis, & Schaefer, 2002), which I hate to admit, given my criticism of the laughter movement. These forced chuckles likely work—at least, in part, because of distraction, too. But these moments of mirth aren't what most people mean by men-tal health or well-being. The craziest among us can still laugh and joke. Even the suicidal have joyful times. Nevertheless, if a little humor helps your mood a little, perhaps a lot of comedy could improve your mental health or emotional distress a lot.

HUMOR AND MOOD IN THE LONG RUN

Unfortunately, the data offer only a little encouragement for humor's improvement of mood in the long term. For example, a sitcom episode helped improve people's mood as much as exercise did, but only for a while. After a half hour, the effect of exercise was a bit better. An hour and a half later, exercise had an obviously superior effect on mood than humor did (Szabo, 2007). Alas, sitcoms can't replace a healthy workout. In addition, adding funny flicks to daily life doesn't have as much of a positive impact on emotional well-being as one might hope. When surgery patients watched movies for a couple of days, the comedies did no better than dramas for decreasing their distress (Rotton & Shats, 1996).

Folks in an eldercare facility showed an improved mood after 6 weeks of watching comedies 3 days per week, but so did their pals who watched dramas (Adams & McGuire, 1986). Perhaps people in eldercare simply need something more to do. The idea fits some of the distraction data mentioned above. The key to a better mood might be doing more stuff that is fun or engaging. Something comparable about activity and mood seems to be going on with younger folks as well. College students who did laughter exercises for 90 minutes a week, for 6 weeks, showed an improved mood and decreased anxiety, but a similar group who went to unfunny health lectures improved, too. A third group that learned relaxation did better than those who did laughter exercises or those who went to health lectures, even though relaxation is rarely comical (White & Camarena, 1989). So much for the laughter movement. In short, comedy may help improve mood, but so do plenty of other activities.

WELL-BEING AND SENSE OF HUMOR

Although the experiments on humor and mental illness are few, the correlational studies of a sense of humor and emotional well-being are numerous. Participants usually complete measures of a sense of humor and psychological symptoms of various sorts. Some results make perfect sense. Humor increased with self-esteem and decreased with depression (Kuipers & Borowicz-Sibenik, 2005). Other results were astoundingly inconsistent at first. Humor would relate to fretting and sadness in one study but not in the next. But once researchers showed a better appreciation for humor's different facets, the results made more sense. As I noted before, some aspects of humor are healthier than other types. The development of the Humor Styles Questionnaire (Martin, Puhlik-Doris, Larsen, Gray, & Weir, 2003) helped separate the adaptive from the maladaptive aspects of humor. Separating humor styles via the questionnaire's four subscales (self-defeating, aggressive, self-enhancing, and affiliative items) helped establish consistent links with psychological distress.

For example, it's no surprise that people with high scores on the self-defeating subscale of the Humor Styles Questionnaire are depressed. Look at the questions. One self-defeating item reads, "When I am with friends or family, I often seem to be the one that other people make fun of or joke about." An item from the Center for Epidemiological Studies Depression Scale reads, "I felt that people disliked me" (Radloff, 1977). It's almost as if these two scales were measuring the same thing. But a close inspection of the research reveals that the humor and depression scales don't correlate perfectly. Other aspects of humor have a different relationship with depression. The self-enhancing subscale, which measures how folks use humor to keep from taking things too seriously, tends to go up as depression goes down, even when the self-defeating aspects of humor are taken into account (Martin et al., 2003). Other work confirms that self-enhancing humor increases with emotional well-being (like self-esteem and positive mood) and decreases with anxiety and depression. Affiliative humor, the kind of joking that helps people connect to their pals, shows comparable but smaller links. Its correlations with well-being or symptoms are a bit weaker than the ones we find with self-enhancing humor. In contrast, self-defeating humor works the opposite way. More self-deprecating jokes that attack one's own skills and abilities lead to lower emotional well-being and more symptoms of anxiety, depression, and a bad mood (Frewen, Brinker, Martin, & Dozois, 2008; Kuiper, Grimshaw, Leite, & Kirsh, 2004).

The aggressive aspects of humor seem to create the most surprises as far as well-being is concerned. Plenty of theorists think that aggressive humor should show a link to low self-esteem, depression, or anxiety. There are all kinds of conjectures that antagonistic humor stems from a poor self-image or self-loathing. In fact, aggressive humor correlated with hostility when the scale was first developed, but showed no link with self-esteem or depression (Martin et al., 2003). It did increase argumentative, critical, unempathic interactions with others (Martin & Dutrizac, 2004). Given these findings about relationships, it would make sense that aggressive humor would decrease social support and intimacy. Who wants to hang around with, let alone get close with, some biting cynic? (Okay, don't ask my wife.) But again, the data show no links among a person's reports of using aggressive humor, receiving social support, and having intimate friends and partners (Martin et al., 2003). I think that part of this lack of a relation between aggressive humor and social support or intimacy appears because the same people who report their aggressive humor also report their social support and intimacy. Folks who make hostile jokes might think that they have friends who are close, but I'd sure like to ask their friends (and spouses) about it.

Another interesting finding from the original study that developed the humor styles questionnaire concerned aggressive humor's significant link to self-defeating humor. Those who disparaged others with their jokes did the same to themselves. I can't help wondering if they simply hate the whole world, themselves and others included. Aggressive humor correlates significantly with other negative phenomena, like burnout in university lecturers (Talbot & Lumden, 2000; Tumkaya, 2007). Perhaps those with a hostile wit just disparage everything right and left, regardless if it's the people around them, themselves or their jobs. (If you thought that burnout in university lecturers is really just a stone's throw from low self-esteem, depression, and anxiety, go to the head of the class.) Perhaps aggressive humor turns into depression and low self-esteem eventually. Maybe the college students in the original study of the scale didn't show correlations between aggressive humor, depression, and low self-esteem because they hadn't had enough time to mature to their full bitterness, like older university professors might. Obviously, there is more going on here than the lay notion that more humor is better. Some aspects of humor enhance psychological well-being; others clearly detract from it.

HUMORING STRESS

The other intriguing aspect of humor and well-being involves buffering people against the impact of difficult events. The big idea at first was that a good sense of humor would make life less stressful. A few studies do reveal that as humor goes up, stress goes down. For example, health care workers who use humor to cope also report less burnout (Dorz, Novara, Sica, & Sanavio, 2003). But many other findings are more complex than simple one-to-one links where stress decreases as humor increases. Instead, humor seems to help people keep the broken shoestrings of life from sending them into fits. Generally, stressful events increase symptoms of angst and sadness for those with not much of a sense of humor, but they have less impact on those with a good sense of humor. Most of this work looks at people's tendencies to use humor to cope—the propensity to see taxing situations as potentially amusing. If the giant pile of ungraded tests on my desk can suddenly strike me as funny, they won't bother me as much. It's not that my sense of humor gets the papers graded; it just keeps them from putting me in the inpatient ward.

Researchers interested in this topic get folks to fill out a questionnaire that measures life events or daily hassles—a list of everything from traffic tickets to losing a job. They also look at a measure of disturbed mood, anxiety, or depression. One nifty study showed that women executives with a good sense

of humor reported less job burnout in a straightforward correlation, like the one with health care workers (Fry, 1995). In
addition, the effect was particularly strong when the intensity
of daily hassles was high. As hassles increased, those with a
poor sense of humor showed steep increases in burnout. Those
with a good sense of humor showed less burnout even if hassles
were dramatic. This humor-moderated link between hassles and
burnout is comparable to other evidence we've seen for humor
as a buffer. So a good sense of humor decreased burnout and
minimized the impact of stress on burnout, too.

It's great that people report that humor buffers the impact
of stress on burnout, but this study had people fill out all of
the questionnaires at the same time. It could be that folks in a
good mood, with a good sense of humor, filling out a bunch
of questionnaires once, simply said that all was well. An even
more impressive result came from longitudinal work—a study
that showed that humor could help predict the impact of stress
on well-being in the future (Nezu, Nezu, & Blissett, 1998).
Participants completed questionnaires once and repeated them
again two months later. Stressors generally made folks more
depressed overall, no matter what, but their impact was less
dramatic for people with a good sense of humor. Those who
had a good sense of humor showed only small links between
stress and depression, but their humorless pals let stress
depress them more. Oddly enough, humor didn't decrease the
link between stress and anxiety (Nezu et al., 1998). Perhaps a
good sense of humor can't keep angst and worry away even if
it does limit sadness and despair. (Poor Woody Allen.) On the
one hand, it's great that humor can keep stress from becoming
depression. On the other hand, at least for some of my colleagues, joking seems to go hand in hand with fretting and
hand wringing. It's unclear why humor would help depression
but not anxiety, and we won't know for sure without further
work. Nevertheless, it looks like a good sense of humor has
the potential to keep the impact of stress on mental health to
a minimum.

HUMOR IN THE MENTALLY ILL

Perhaps the mental health of executives and college students is strong enough to make the potential impact of humor a minor one. People who are already generally happy and functional might have less to gain by adding extra chortles to their lives. Those with disturbances that are more serious might have more at stake. Experiments related to humor with people suffering from diagnosed mental illnesses, like schizophrenia, anxiety, or mood disorders, are very rare. At first this research offered only limited support for humor as an intervention. Well, the glass may be half full.

Chronic, hospitalized schizophrenics who watched 70 comedies over three months did better than those who watched 70 dramas in the same period, but only on 6 of 21 outcomes (Gelkopf, Kreitler, & Sigal, 1993). This result seems a bit discouraging at first, as we'd expect 1 measure out of 21 to be significant only by chance. But this was the first study of its kind; it explored a lot of different measures to see what was going on. Nobody knew where humor might have its effect. A subsequent experiment using the same techniques found that comedies were superior to dramas for helping anxiety and depression in the schizophrenics. The schizophrenics in this second experiment also showed less anger after watching comedies regularly for 3 months, but those who watched dramas had a slight increase in anger (Gelkopf, Gonen, Kurs, Melamed, & Bleich, 2006). That's drama for you.

This replication—the repetition of an experiment that creates the same result—provides better support for humor's impact. These effects weren't huge, but the intervention was easy and inexpensive. It's not too hard to schedule movies every night in a hospital ward, or choose *Blazing Saddles* over *Psycho*. These results are impressive in the light of evidence that schizophrenics can have particularly odd senses of humor, too (Bozikas et al., 2007; Rosin & Cerbus, 1984). Mainstream

Hollywood comedies might not be particularly funny to the delusional (or to academics). The 10 psychotics I lived with in a halfway house while I was in graduate school seemed to find each other very funny, but they rarely laughed at movies or at me—at least not to my face. Given the impact of these comedies, a comparable study with clinically depressed or anxious people has the potential to show nice effects, when someone gets around to it.

Other forms of humor, besides movies, can help inpatients, too. Potentially funny activities decreased disruption on a psychiatric ward (Higueras et al., 2006). This experiment used highly trained clowns—which is not an oxymoron. They worked with the patients for 90 minutes a day, twice a week, for about three months. The clowns played a game of charades and imagination games, marched in funny rhythms, stretched, and danced. The patients were less likely to misbehave during those three months than they were in the previous months, when there were no clowns. They were significantly less likely to fight, try to escape, or punch the staff. Some of these effects might have stemmed simply from having more to do. Inpatient wards are notoriously dull. A lot of them offer little more than a television and some old dominoes. The funny activities might have provided more physical exercise than these patients had experienced in quite some time, too. Humor might have been part of the effect, but activity itself likely contributed a lot as well. The area of humor and its effect on serious mental illness deserves further work. A chortle or two and a good sense of humor also seem to help emotional well-being in folks involved in psychotherapy, whether or not they might qualify for a diagnosis.

HUMOR IN PSYCHOTHERAPY

Based on the assumption that humor can improve mental health, psychotherapists of nearly every ilk have recommended comedy. Some see it as a skill that therapists should develop or as a technique to use in therapy at certain times. A handful of therapists think of humor as a treatment itself. All agree that it's a double-edged sword, warning that caustic humor has no place in the process of therapy. My grandma could've given you this incredible insight, if she weren't busy being dead. The hype far exceeds the research on most of these ideas, despite their intuitive appeal. There may be more handbooks about bringing humor into therapy than there are experiments to show that it has any value.

The idea of humor as a general skill fits with what we know about psychotherapy more generally. Psychological treatments work well for many problems, but we're not exactly sure why. Extremely different therapies often work equally well. This fact led some researchers to posit that common aspects of all the therapies might be the most important. The best treatments from the best therapists usually include having the undivided attention of another human being—preferably one who is empathic, warm, and genuine. These qualities, which are not specific to any particular treatment, might be more important than any individual therapy technique—be it recording thoughts, forcing chuckles, or making people move their eyes back and forth in their heads. (Yes, that's part of a therapy called "Eye Movement Desensitization and Reprocessing," and it actually helps post-traumatic stress disorder [Ponniag & Hollon, 2009]).

The Nonspecific Factors of Therapy

The general behaviors most likely to induce change in a social interaction involve empathy, nonpossessive warmth, and genuineness. Carl Rogers emphasized these attributes in the treatment that he invented: client-centered therapy (Rogers, 1952). Despite his humility, the treatment is often called "Rogerian." The presence of these behaviors in many treatments may serve as a good explanation for why different therapies produce comparable results (Wampold et al., 1997). A healing relationship with a nonjudgmental, attentive person can facilitate change independently from a therapist's claimed theoretical orientation. Whether your therapist is monitoring your moods, interpreting your dreams, or asking you to tap yourself on the face (Don't ask!), the success of the treatment might depend upon these nonspecific factors. Empathy, warmth, and genuineness lay the foundation for any productive, therapeutic interaction. It's easy to see how the right kind of humor might facilitate all three of these.

We all know empathy, nonpossessive warmth, and genuineness when we see them, but these qualities, much like humor, prove difficult to define in the abstract. Having "empathy" means identifying with someone else's feelings. It is distinct from sympathy—feeling sorry for someone. A therapist's empathy shows that he or she understands the client's view of situations, without implying that the therapist knows what it's like to be that person. I'll never know exactly what it's like to be a 55-year-old, crack-addicted, single mom. I do, however, know what it's like to feel frustration, confusion, and disappointment. I know that it can be especially bad in the never-ending quest to be the perfect parent, while, at the same time, maintaining your own identity, trying to have fun, hoping that you'll have enough money for everything, wishing you had more time for yourself, dreaming of a better future, and realizing you should also exercise, eat right, and get plenty of rest but first you have to find your clean underwear.

I know what it's like to feel frightened, mad, and afraid in the ways that an older mom with drug problems might. Sharing this fact with her might help her feel less like the oddball or the evil one. Expressions of empathy enhance the relationship between client and therapist. In fact, they can enhance any relationship. (People who are looking for dates that actually lead somewhere, take note!) This sharing of feelings might increase the client's trust, encouraging candid disclosures. It may even inspire people to solve their own problems. Empathic therapists have clients who do better in the long run. They even do better than clients in the same kind of treatment who have less empathic therapists (Miller, 2000). More empathy equals a better outcome.

"Nonpossessive warmth" refers to a therapist's interactive style. Warmth suggests a generally good-natured approach to treatment. The nonpossessive aspect implies that the therapist does not withdraw her or his warmth if clients screw up. I'm a better therapist if I'm just as warm when clients are down as I am when they're up. My warmth does not disappear and reappear with changes in behavior. This way, my clients need not fear a bad reaction from me if they report emotions or behaviors that they consider negative. And they'll be more likely to tell the truth, the whole truth, under these circumstances. Few of us have experienced a lot of relationships that include nonpossessive warmth. Ways of demonstrating this warmth will vary with each therapist, but a sincere smile, an attentive nod, and considerate listening can't hurt.

Genuineness arises from authentic, trustworthy, realistic behaviors that are consistent with the therapist's attitudes, values, and goals. Clients rely on sincere reactions that are free of affectation or pretense. A therapist who seems natural creates a more comfortable atmosphere than one who appears scripted, stilted, or phony. Therapists who show genuineness have body language, eye contact, and facial expressions that correspond to their words. They don't claim to be interested while stifling a yawn. Essentially, the human interaction should feel more important than taking notes or following a treatment manual. I develop a lot more rapport with clients if I am myself than if I put on some kind of therapist's act. Then clients report that they're getting to know me, and that our interactions are more than a simple exchange of information. People easily recognize therapists who seem consistent, true to themselves, and real (Miller & Rollnick, 2002). Research suggests that these therapists can produce better outcomes than other therapists who are performing the same type of treatment.

Appropriate humor seems as if it could enhance empathy, warmth, and genuineness. Affiliative humor, the kind that brings people together, certainly sounds apt. A simple joke that joins therapist and client has the potential to enhance their relationship. For example, jocular comments that remind both the client and the therapist that they are part of the human condition work well. We all have many of the same struggles. I have joined with clients over the years about a love of caffeine, a disdain for awakening early, a mistrust of bureaucracy, a suspicion that those who talk too much have little to say, and a longing for just a little more cash. Almost all of us would love a bit more vacation time, sleep, or chocolate. Connecting on these similarities can keep both the client and the therapist from burning out. It can help them focus on what they have in common. It can remind them both that life is difficult but that it certainly has its moments.

Self-enhancing humor on the therapist's part also seems to have potential. This kind of humor can model ways for clients to value themselves and emphasize their strengths. Examples that are funny in the moment often fall flat on paper, but the best ones teach clients how to use self-enhancing humor of their own. For example, a socially anxious client of mine who needed to reschedule an appointment that he would have to miss in a week learned that I had no other openings to offer. "I'm popular, you know!" I added with a smile. I felt as if the news of my full schedule might suggest that many people viewed me as competent. I had hoped it might reassure him that our time together was well spent. Later in the session he listed a few people he had planned to see socially, which was a big step for him, and he added, "I'm popular, you know!" We both smiled and I was pleased to see him say something so positive about himself. If I'd been seeing a client who had no friends and nothing to do, however, I would have never joked about my own full schedule. The therapist's self-enhancing humor cannot imply something bad about the client in contrast, even if only indirectly.

Although self-enhancing humor has potential, any kind of aggressive humor would undermine the therapeutic relationship. An intriguing study examined tape recordings of therapy sessions conducted at university counseling centers (Killinger, 1987). Almost 20% of therapists' jokes seemed like ridicule or teasing. Understandably, clients did not react particularly well to these. Therapists could usually recover in the subsequent conversation, but these wisecracks tended to interrupt the discussion or turn the topic away from effective self-exploration on the client's part. A comparable study of five sessions of group therapy revealed that over half of the jokes made by the clients ribbed someone within the group, leading to less effective, less therapeutic discussion (Peterson & Pollio, 1982). Obviously, jibes like these may do little to convey empathy, genuineness, and warmth. For this reason, some clinicians have gone so far as to imply that humor has no place in psychotherapy at all (Kubie, 1994).

HOW COULD HUMOR HELP WELL-BEING?

Humor may help psychotherapy by enhancing aspects of the therapeutic relationship. The mechanism behind humor's other impacts on well-being remains a mystery. The distraction data are compelling for explaining brief, humor-induced improvements in mood, but that's about all. There has to be more here than what you could get from doing long division or balancing ionic equations. I think that there is. It's nice that comedies can keep mental patients from getting too hostile. I'm delighted that a good sense of humor can keep health care workers from burning out. And it's my sincere hope that a little levity in therapy could improve the treatment. But I've got this nagging sense that something is missing. There's a mysterious bit about humor and well-being that the research hasn't quite addressed. Appreciating humor, like appreciating any art form, is a joy unto itself (Earleywine, 2011). But I think that qualities specific to jokes and jesting have unique life lessons. Please humor me a moment while I explain.

Any fan of comedy can detail extensive, delighted hours spent chuckling at the many forms of the art. Why all the joy? Queries reveal the usual responses: the self-evident—"Because it's funny!"; the naïve—"Because it's true!"; and, best of all, the budding researcher's recommendation—"Check it out yourself!" My academic friends can pontificate about various brain structures squirting happy chemicals to explain these comedy-induced thrills. I'd like to assert that jokes in general, and some stand-up performers in particular, train listeners in the central ideas in modern psychology, the very ones that lead us to think clearly, responsibly, and happily. In a sense, current cognitive behavioral therapies teach some of the same lessons we find in comedy. The flip side may also be true: Understanding cognitive behavioral therapies may illuminate comedy a bit. It will take me a few steps to explain this. First, I'll take a look at how humor might have an impact on psychological well-being by understanding how our thoughts and actions contribute to our moods.

Thought, Action, and Mood

Though I love humor for its own sake, the best gags, witticisms, and funny interactions make us rethink our perceptions of the world. A mountain of research now supports the idea that the way we think and behave has a tremendous impact on how we feel, and vice versa. The idea probably goes back to the ancient Greek philosopher Epictetus, but we lose it and find it again across generations. We've been immersed in the idea enough lately so that it no longer sounds like abstruse aerodynamics, let alone rocket science. But for many years the field of psychology had lost touch with simple links among thought, action, and mood. These ideas got masked in the manufactured mystery of Freudian notions. Freud was a superb writer and storyteller. He was not, however, much of a scientist. His theories caught on for reasons that are hard to explain. Many therapists throughout the 1940s floated in a sea of weird, impractical, psychodynamic sewage—unfalsifiable concepts that were hard to pin down or predict. Though some promising modern treatments are rooted in Freud's work (Driessen et al., 2010), the way Freudian analysis was done at the time was inefficient at best and troublesome at worst. Freud's ideas could explain anything after the fact, but they could never explain how someone might feel in the future.

By the middle of the 1950s, a few giants (like Aaron Beck and Albert Ellis) climbed out of this sludge with clearer, more sensible, more realistic models of human functioning. Their message was simple and echoed Epictetus's words: It's not what happens to us, but what we think and do in response, that makes us genuinely miserable. This new view created the opportunity for rational, adaptive, responsible approaches to life. It relied on examining thoughts and actions, rather than interpreting dreams or slips of the tongue. This was the cognitive behavioral revolution in therapy. The approach helped minimize misery left and right. Suddenly the anxious, depressed, and traumatized had new ways to see the world and think about it, inspiring them to take contented action. But the old Freudian ideas were deeply rooted in the field, preventing the revolution from catching on more quickly.

A lot of this work in psychology began with studies of depression. Depressed people thought that their endless bouts of horrid moods and paralysis simply happened upon them. That's how depression feels, anyway. These thoughts left them essentially powerless to intervene. If a giant raincloud of despair can descend at any time, what could any mortal possibly do about it? Reductionistic notions of deviant neurotransmitters and wounded brains were popular at the time. We had some chemical mood elevators that seemed to help briefly, but many of these drugs had negative side effects or didn't work after a while. For example, physicians prescribed amphetamine for depression at the time. As you can imagine, this drug amped people up but didn't teach them how to solve problems or create a happy life (Rasmussen, 2008). Even our current antidepressants are only a shade better than placebos (Kirsch, 2005).

There was also one long, arduous, strange psychological treatment: psychoanalysis. I'm parodying a bit, but psychoanalysis essentially involved lying on a couch and free-associating. Ideally, whatever came into your head popped out of your mouth for fifty consecutive minutes. Any accidental misstatement or slip of the tongue was supposed to reveal thoughts and feelings outside your awareness. Examples of these Freudian slips abound, but the ones that make news almost invariably reveal sexual attraction. If you happened to construct a narrative about one of your dreams, that was supposed to be prime material, too. An analyst, an authority so powerful that he (and it was usually a "he" at the time) took your money hand over fist, and provided interpretations that were supposed to lead to insights. These insights purportedly uncovered unconscious material, resolved repressed conflicts, and ended guilt-ridden punishments of the self.

If you're scratching your head about how this passed for therapy, join the club. I'm not sure what all that means or how it was supposed to help. The treatment burned tons of time and cash. The successful clients spent years and thousands, and then left the ranks of the depressed to the glories of everyday unhappiness. Even Freud (1905) said that this was the goal. Other clients just spent years and thousands but probably didn't get better. But we learned one thing: Insight alone is not enough. We can make up stories about what happened to us and why, but we rarely feel better without thinking and acting differently. Insight alone doesn't bring long-lasting changes in emotion or behavior. Dwelling on ancient slights or recent mistakes tends to increase rumination and bad moods. Humor likely helps bad moods by interfering with this process, as I mentioned previously. A distracting chuckle can keep us from repeatedly mulling over depressing problems. We can't deny our own errors. It doesn't help to minimize the bad things that happened to us, no matter how nasty they were. And, of course we take our past with us everywhere we go, even if it's only in our memories. The problem with insights into the past, though, is that the past does not lend itself to change. Unless there's a time machine handy, what's done is done. Learning from the past is only good if we can apply it to the present and the future.

In a sense, what we tell ourselves about the past may be more a case of fiction than fact. Our memories are filled with vagaries, tainted by our mood at the time events happened and at the time when we recall them. Research on this selective memory usually requires getting folks into a mood, having them read a story that has an equal number of happy, sad, and neutral events, and then asking them to recall the tale (Forgas, 2008). Almost invariably, the recalled events match the mood. Folks in sad moods remember the sad stuff; those in happy moods remember the happy stuff. How we feel not only contributes to what we think, it even alters what we remember. But when someone else provides the interpretations (psychoanalysts, in this case), no matter how well trained or well paid the alleged experts might be, we should check our own experiences ourselves. No one is a better authority about our own lives than we are, as many a comedian has emphasized.

Cognitive Distortions

Other theorists who escaped the psychoanalytic bent noticed some key thoughts common to all of their clients. The distressed tended to have a tremendously negative view of themselves, the world, and the future. (See Clark & Beck [2010] for a helpful review.) Distressed folks thought that they were terrible people, that the world was a terrible place, and that it would always be this way. They felt so rotten that they perceived things as rotten, which made them feel rotten some more (Ellis, 1997). The distressed even interpret potentially positive things in a negative light. Research on the fact is crafty and intriguing. One study asked anxious folks and their happier peers to explain ambiguous sentences. They read the words "The doctor was impressed by Mary's growth." Happy campers said, "Sounds like a little girl used to be short but now she's taller." The anxious said, "Oh, no! She's got a tumor!" (Eysenck, Mogg, May, Richards, & Mathews, 1991). The ambiguity of the sentence is the beginning of the structure of humor because it's got the potential to be seen two different ways. But to the anxious, it's no joking matter.

Some folks see only the worst, no matter what the circumstances may be. The glass is not only half empty, it's poisonous. In fact, they see only the worst so badly, and it frightens them so much, that they can hardly think. In another set of studies, when asked, "What color ink is this word written in?," distressed folks took longer to name the color if the word was negative (e.g., "agony"). Clearly, they were battling their own minds, as if difficult feelings slowed their reactions in even a simple task like naming a color (Richards, French, Johnson, Naparstek, & Williams, 1992). As you can imagine, this can make for a rough day. Research also revealed that these distressed people believed tons of completely irrational, subjective, maladaptive thoughts—the kinds of things that would bum out Mother Teresa. These thoughts appeared to precede their rampant bad mood, insomnia, inactivity, and irritability. The thoughts also led people to interpret the whole world as threatening, when only parts of it are, creating overreactions and wasted efforts that perpetuated fear or hatred. I've struggled with distorted cognitions so much myself, and had clients, students, and friends resist this idea with such enthusiastic fervor, that I feel a need to elaborate on a couple of ways that thoughts can go awry.

Part of examining thoughts requires a taxonomy of the maladaptive ones, a list of telltale signs that whatever is buzzing in our heads is probably a far cry from anything that might be fun, let alone a reflection of reality. Once we know the types of thoughts that drive us crazy, we can catch them better. Note that we'll still have nutty thoughts; we'll just take them less seriously. If humor teaches us anything, that would be the lesson. None of these ideas about the detrimental impact of thoughts means that thinking is itself bad. A clear head is a key to happiness. Rational, realistic thoughts can be a huge help. If we knew the categories of maladaptive or distress-inducing thoughts, we could probably recognize them better when we thought them. It's sort of like that business with Eskimos having fine distinctions about types of snow (Widlok, 2008). I don't know many Eskimos, but devoted skiers seem to have plenty of terms for snow ("powder," "mashed potatoes," "Sierra cement," and "granular"). The words make it easy for them to recognize and discuss different types. We could do the same with types of maladaptive thoughts and keep them from wiping us out.

Dichotomous Thinking

One of the most common of these types of maladaptive thoughts involves dichotomous thinking, a ubiquitous invitation to misery (Clark & Beck, 2010). That all-or-nothing, black-or-white misperception of a planet that appears, in truth, in glorious (but messy) color, can stymie anyone. Rarely is the world completely one thing or its opposite. Dichotomous thoughts usually include words like "always," "never," "every," and "none." Thoughts with words like "best" and "worst" can lean this way, too. Lots of bad moods and troublesome acts rest on dichotomous thinking. My favorite dichotomous thought came from one of my clients at the VA Hospital, who said, "Second best is the same as last." You can imagine how a thought like that could turn anything dour. I'm not sure where to point fingers first, but institutions that seek to control others often rest on manufactured dichotomous distinctions like black/white, evil/good, and right/wrong. I have to be careful with distinctions like healthy/unhealthy, adaptive/maladaptive, and even correct/incorrect, as these distinctions may be more manufactured than real, too. Artificial dichotomies like these distort our minds to the point where personal preferences get confused with demanded duty. These thoughts create distress by leading us to think in terms of "musts" instead of "coulds"—a process Ellis dubbed *musterbation* (Ellis, 1997). Suddenly actions we *could* take become actions we *must* take, because of some manufactured *always* or *never* thought. Even the attempt to challenge them can get sucked into the same distortion (e.g., "I must never have dichotomous thoughts").

Perhaps these ideas seem minor at first, or deceptively self-evident. But they inspire acts as dramatic as a suicide bombing or as disheartening as a life spent in thoughtless toil. Throw a rock in the fields of government, religion, or academia and you're bound to hit the result of a *must*, a *should*, or an *ought* that arose from some dichotomous thought. And do me a favor—throw it hard. Most comedians poke fun at these institutions in ways that show how rigidly they can demand obedience. I think George Orwell (1946) said it best: "Every joke is a tiny act of rebellion." Rebelling against these institutions is often a rebellion against dichotomous thoughts. Note that even the idea of dichotomous thinking can't be thought about dichotomously without paying a price. Some *always* and *never* thoughts are true. We can't uniformly dismiss every single one. We must examine the evidence before we decide. But odds are high that there's some gray area in between the black and white, some silver lining, some nuanced way to see each event that will make it less debilitating. There are plenty of other cognitive distortions, but dichotomous thinking is a typical one.

Alternatives to Angst

So what did this new breed of cognitive behavioral psychologists recommend, instead of spending hours on the couch every week for years and years? All these data on thoughts and actions and their impact on mood suggested that they were the way to go. The new psychologists thought it would be better to take a look at our own thoughts for ourselves. We could emphasize that they're thoughts but often little more than that. This way, we could see which thoughts were helpful or not. We could move from there to doing the things that we love, while trying to enjoy each moment. Part of examining thoughts requires recognizing that they are thoughts and not necessarily reality. Many of our miseries arise because of key assumptions. Tons of comics make this same point in their own ways. Mitch Hedberg said, "The depressing thing about tennis is that no matter how good I get, I'll never be as good as a wall." The joke lets us know that the thrill of victory and the agony of defeat are much less dramatic once you question the assumption of a game. Humor reframes situations by getting us to question the assumptions we make.

If we can get above the battlefield in our own heads and witness our own minds, we can see these beliefs, opinions, and attitudes for what they sometimes are—interpretations of facts rather than facts themselves. Catching these thoughts as we witness them is the key. That moment when a punch line pulls the rug out from an assumption is often a great start. Thoughts will come and go. It's just part of being human. Recognizing them for what they are, before they lead us to behave in ways counter to our real values, can make the difference between delight and despair. Confusing what we think or how we feel for "the truth," with two capital "T"s, particularly in environments where our beliefs or moods are manipulated, can create genuine disadvantages. Mistaking our thoughts for truth can be downright dangerous.

Releasing the Maladaptive Thoughts

With this kind of approach to identifying and examining our own cognitions, the next step may be easier to say than do-letting the maladaptive thoughts fall away. Sometimes it seems that we can't help believing what we believe, even as evidence to the contrary mounts. These changes in beliefs, moving from maladaptive to adaptive thoughts, may not be a dichotomous, categorical enlightenment. (That would be a form of dichotomous thinking of its own.) I'd love it if every time I triumphed over an irrational thought, something dramatic would happen.

It would be great to have the rainclouds part with a crash while a giant ray of rational sunlight came shining down on my head, but it's rarely that spectacular. The gradual transition, a sort of splintering off of irrational aspects of the depressing thoughts to leave the realistic, rational ones, may be more common. We can make the sum of small movements turn into big ones over time. The vigilance required can be daunting. A lot of this process is more about losing illusions than about finding new truths. It's not that we need to learn some new thoughts as much as it is about letting go of some old, maladaptive ones.

The message in comedy is often to challenge false beliefs. There's a genuine pleasure inherent in defying rules that go unexamined. Watch Chris Rock challenge the idea that ethnicity or money or popularity or parenthood is supposed to guarantee happiness. Once he questions some of these ideas, it's hard not to feel relief as well as mirth when you realize that none of these notions are important enough to wreck your mood. Chipping away at archaic, maladaptive beliefs, or even good ideas that have gone too far, can be its own source of glee. The fact that these beliefs may arise from the government, the family, education, or religion should not make them too sacred to challenge. Comedy encourages an independence of mind. Of course, this approach also emphasizes the import of action—any action, no matter how small.

Do What You Love

The next step in the process concerns translating thoughts into deeds. What you do with your time is your own glory. Rather than leaving us all spinning in thought, cognitive behavioral therapists recommend concerted action. A whole philosophy and treatment program has developed around the intuitive idea that the key to improved moods is a dynamic life filled with behaviors consistent with your values—Behavioral Activation Therapy. It works as well or better than Big Pharma's favorite antidepressants, too. Speaking of doing what you love, behavioral activation therapy is unlikely to interfere with your orgasms. It might even enhance them. I can't say the same for antidepressants, which can be hard on erectile function and on the "big O" of orgasm (Williams, Edin, Hogue, Fehnel, & Baldwin, 2010).

See Kantor, Busch, and Rusch's (2009) book for an accessible review of behavioral activation theory. The treatment involves more than doing fun stuff, though there's plenty of that. There are few better ways to lift your mood. The therapy is all about choosing the acts that are consistent with what we think is most important, and, most importantly, doing them. The treatment encourages people to increase fun activities that are consistent with their goals so that they stop avoiding the aversive tasks in their lives. Clients get good things done each day—tasks that are consistent with their values. They also tackle projects they've shunned, often discovering that these weren't as awful as they'd feared. (That stack of reading and writing projects might not be as terrible in reality as it is in my head.) The bottom line is that sometimes humor helps well-being simply because it involves something fun to do and pokes fun at those who do things that are a drag. If we find ourselves doing things we hate over and over, it becomes obvious that it's time to stop. Comics are great at making this point in meaningful ways. Check out Lewis Black's rant about golfers on his album "Anticipation," for a good example. Black's description of lugging clubs while wearing lime green pants, and investing untold dollars to get a ball into a hole, certainly makes listeners wonder if some behaviors are not worth repeating. Even the most devoted golfer would take the activity less seriously afterward.

Increasing positive activities increases a positive mood. Sometimes this means meaningful work; sometimes it means taking a meaningful break. Few things are more important than thoughtful leisure, especially in a world filled with mundane or distracting events. Comedy sends this message often. (See Bill Hicks's [2008] proleisure discussion of cannabis and amotivation for a great example.) Of course, watching comedy is fun on its own, too. But more than simply having fun, the transition to longer bouts of pleasant emotion requires work that we value. Good work is the key to good fortune, which may include good feelings, too. Even the most irate rants of stand-up comics often end with a statement that we're the ones who need to take action to make things better. Sometimes the list of actions we need to take can seem long or overwhelming, but there's a key for making them tolerable, if not joyous: remaining mindful of our actions as we do them.

ENJOY MOMENTS MINDFULLY

A superb series of new studies in psychology confirms what every Zen meditator has said for centuries: Pay attention to the present, and delight will follow. This is what mindfulness—focusing awareness on the current moment—is all about. Mindfulness can prevent depression in intriguing ways (Williams, Teasdale, Segal, & Kabat-Zinn, 2007); it certainly helps us recognize our own thoughts, moods, and experiences. I think that comedy can do the same. These moments of mindfulness can start right now. They usually click in the millisecond when we resolve a punch line's incongruity and fix our previous, incorrect assumption. The chuckle that accompanies this shift is often the realization that we've made a mistake but, at least in the current moment, all is well.

A whole school of Zen rests on using these sorts of cognitive shifts to reach a mindful, aware, compassionate understanding of life. Practitioners contemplate perplexing stories or questions called "koans." These koans invariably make little sense at first but somehow resolve themselves with extra thought and a touch of intuition. Attempting to understand them can send the mind reeling. This reeling makes the mind itself more evident, helping people recognize their thoughts as separate from who they are. Suddenly the separation between the thought and the thinker is clearer, so the thoughts themselves seem less important. As one of my favorite bumper stickers reads: Don't believe everything you think. It's easier to question one's own thoughts when it becomes obvious that they are only thoughts.

Getting a joke is very much the same process. In fact, some koans sound remarkably like setups. What is the sound of one hand clapping? What did your face look like before your parents were born? How many psychologists does it take to change a lightbulb? Answering these questions can inspire a lot of laughter, and they just might create enlightenment (Kapleau, 1989). We don't have a ton of time on earth. Few of us know exactly when we'll die or how many days we have. The whole of mirthful laughter certainly stresses a joy in the moment, a calm, at the center of things, that is available if we only attend to it. The beauty of many jokes comes in the way that they are the incarnation of their own recommendations. Recognizing that a joke is a joke sends us a message to take all our assumptions less seriously and to hold our thoughts a little more lightly. But explaining this phenomenon is very different from experiencing it, much like explaining a joke is not the same as getting it. And so the best approach to humor or cognitive therapy may be one of the answers mentioned above in response to the question of why comedy is fun: Check it out yourself!

HOW CAN HUMOR IMPROVE THINKING?

Comedy can improve well-being. Despite the comics who seem to be living lives as a counterexample, humor makes people happy. Funny folks who aren't being humorous for a living seem to enjoy it and benefit. (The pressure to create humor nonstop might not create the same happiness.) Jokes, cartoons, routines, and movies can improve mood, probably by preventing folks from ruminating about irritation or angst. They might also encourage mindful moments and the recognition of errors in thinking. Experiments show that a little comedy lifts moods a bit. Regular use of clown troupes and funny flicks can improve behaviors on the inpatient psychiatry ward and help the worried well stay happy. A dash of humor can improve the relationship between therapists and clients, so long as there's no teasing or ridicule involved. People with a good sense of humor seem less depressed and anxious. Those who use laughter to join with others and highlight their strengths tend to flourish. A good sense of humor buffers people against the slings and arrows of stress, keeping them from bumming out or burning out. Humor may create these improvements by revealing errors in our own assumptions, encouraging us to question our own thoughts, rallying us to actions consistent with our values, and reminding us to enjoy each moment.

The experience of a joke can parallel the sort of thinking that a therapist might want to teach to a client. Comedy also frequently questions the tacit assumptions underlying the silly things that we all do. Most jokes serve as examples of seeing a topic in two different ways (Attardo, 2008). The funniest ones invariably lead us to question assumptions. A punch line often surprises us with the news that we have assumed something about the setup that wasn't correct. When we realize the mistake, we laugh, perhaps because we've questioned the original assumption.

In incongruity-resolution humor, we note that an alternative interpretation makes sense with the punch line. And that strikes us as funny. This questioning of assumptions is often the key behind modern cognitive therapies, too. These are often the assumptions that we might have failed to recognize—the very ones that might make us miserable. One humor-based therapy builds on this idea of questioning assumptions. It pushes a client's concerns to the extreme until their absurdity becomes obvious. For example, a schizophrenic inpatient went into frequent rages because she thought other patients were stealing her things. She resented any assertion that her concerns were unjustified. Instead of dismissing her worries, staff members took her very seriously. They made elaborate lists of missing items, detailing their condition and price. The list turned out to include only useless articles with a total worth of about four bucks. When the silliness inherent in flying into a rage over these items became obvious to the patient, she was eventually able to laugh each time she mentioned another missing toothbrush or sweater (Witztum, Briskin, & Lerner, 1999).

Cognitive therapy asks us to check out how our own thoughts can make us more depressed than anything that might happen to us. A handful of the best comedians also offer ideal examples of adaptive ways to view the world. They can communicate difficult emotions thinly veiled with humor. (See Richard Pryor's uncompromising criticism of racism in "Live on the Sunset Strip.") They even rally resources to motivate action. (Check out Sam Kinison's recommendations for keeping relationships together, in "Breaking the Rules.") Comics often point out the forbidden, and there's nothing like tackling taboo topics as a first step toward making things better, too (Zerubavel, 2007). In fact, this might be comedy's future—improving the world by stating the truths that no one else is willing to speak.

Bringing Humor to Everyday Life

n the study of humor, there are a few recurring themes. As I mentioned previously, people tend to laugh more together than alone. When others are around, they often giggle after mundane comments as well as after crafty turns of phrase or witty jokes. Chuckles can communicate everything from sexual interest to social dominance. We each really do have a sense of humor; it has many facets that relate to intelligence and personality in complex ways. Extraversion, openness to experience, agreeableness, authoritarianism, and religious fundamentalism can help predict who's funny and who will appreciate different kinds of gags. Humor can have direct effects on physical health and psychological well-being; it can buffer folks against the slings and arrows of daily hassles. When applied with appropriate finesse, it can help in bargaining and business and marriage and friendship and dating—too bad it doesn't help long sentences. All of these results suggest that humor is worth cultivating. Many theories try to explain everything that's funny; all fall short in one way or another. But after considering all these issues in previous chapters, we're still left with the big question of how people become funny. A keen understanding of ways that people develop jokes can help us generate and appreciate them, which might make our social interactions more fun or help the occasional speech, toast, or presentation.

THE EFFORT TO GET FUNNIER

First off, I need to dispute a couple of key ideas before we go any further on the topic of becoming funny. The first idea is that funny people are born and not made. No one is born a riveting prankster—no one. I'm sure that your parents thought that you were cute (probably), but no one is consistently funny in front of mass audiences without work. Not Chris Rock or Rita Rudner or Robin Williams or Rabelais or your baby sister. An important quote on the topic, frequently attributed to everyone from Irish dramatist George Bernard Shaw to English actor Edmund Gwenn, says, "Dying is easy; comedy is hard." People love to present themselves as naturally, effortlessly funny. The wittiest comics and all the others who think that they're hilarious pretend that humor just slips from their tongues. Plenty of folks are good at maintaining the illusion that their jokes simply write themselves. It keeps the competition away. If other people believe that humorists are born and not made, they'll also think that they can never learn to be funny. Then they won't even try, leaving room for those who know it's work. The big quip among stand-ups when I was playing the circuit was, "It took me seven hours to write that ad lib." It takes effort to become humorous. Ironically, it's not the effort usually associated with trying to be funny. People who are constantly trying to be funny are often incredibly irritating. The effort has to come from thought and preparation, not a constant barrage of fart jokes.

The second idea worthy of examination is that being funny cannot be taught. Like the first idea, this one is also false. Being funny can clearly be learned. Part of the way that it is taught is through experience, the school of laughless hard knocks. Many a comedy coach can explain the craft, and I'll get into the structure of jokes here. But the social universe is the best teacher of how to be funny. The way to be funny is to go out and make mistakes. Tell some groaners. Make flip remarks and accidentally insult people. Screw up. I try to make at least one big mistake a day. Push the envelope a little. Only those who go too far know how far they can go and all that. I think a lot more people would be a lot funnier if they weren't quaking in fear of mistakes. So you tell a bad joke. So what?

One of the greatest studies on the topic of telling bad jokes, aptly named "Responses to failed humor" (Bell, 2009), shows that a bad joke never leads to death. It rarely causes physical injury. Dr. Bell and her research team of over 30 assistants all went out and told a terrible joke in a social setting: "What did the big chimney say to the little chimney? Nothing. Chimneys can't talk." Over 180 unlucky fools had to hear this horrendous excuse for a joke. No one murdered the jokester. Fourteen percent of the time, there was no response. Crickets chirped in the silence. Over a third of the people (37.1%) laughed at this lame gag. It probably wasn't more than polite laughter, but it was laughter nonetheless. People seemed to giggle more at the person's attempt than at the content of the joke itself. Almost another third (32.3%) responded with a question or a comment about the joke. These ranged from the minor ("That's not very funny") to the harsh ("What the hell kind of joke is that?"). The terms *nerd, dork,* and *douche bag* were used only once each—I'm not kidding. But here's the clincher: The negative feedback came from listeners with a closer relationship to the teller. Strangers, those poor store clerks and bellhops who had to hear this tripe, were more likely to give a neutral reaction. But intimates, the aunts and uncles and boyfriends, were more likely to let the tellers know that this joke was a bomb. So tell a bad joke. You'll find out who your friends are.

Understanding how pranksters construct a good joke can increase appreciation for humor. Becoming funny is work, but it's worth it. Why? We've noted that people think funny folks are also smart, happy, easygoing, and likable. But social skills training would probably do much of that, too. We caught the data on laughter helping pain, allergies, and cases of erectile dysfunction. But none of these is really a great justification, either. We've got a world filled with aspirin and allergy medications and Viagra. There are probably better ways to improve your physical health—dull ways like exercising, eating right, and getting plenty of rest. Relaxation and meditation probably have a better impact on psychological well-being than humor does. Developing optimism would probably have a more direct effect on handling stress than becoming a comedian would (Cann & Etzel, 2008). So why be funny? Because it's fun. It's not the most efficient path to anything else. It's just pure delight on its own. If the thought of being funny for its own sake makes sense, or at least means appreciating wit when it's around, that's the best justification for developing a good sense of humor.

Humor Means Thinking Funny

To be funny, you have to think funny. My emphasis is on the thinking part. Many folks would like to watch a hundred sitcoms and a thousand comedians and wait for opportunities to use stolen jokes. These opportunities rarely arrive, and only if you can remember the material. Trust me, that's not always easy. And remembering new material and whether or not you've already said it gets tougher as you age (Wang, Li, Metzak, He, & Woodward, 2010). And remembering new material and whether or not you've already said it gets tougher as you age, too. Reading funny material, or watching comics perform, or catching the latest comedy is certainly an enjoyable use of time. But it won't make you funny. Think of all the people you know who've seen every hilarious flick ever produced. How many of them are actually wits? Exposure alone is not enough. But once you actually understand how humor works, suddenly the opportunities are everywhere. You don't have to wait around for something to happen that reminds you of a joke that you already know. You see the potential for something funny in the usual day that is filled with straight lines, and you can come up with a joke yourself.

The indigenous people of southern Africa use a species of beetles to make the poison in their arrows. They have to learn how to find beetle tracks to gather up these little insects. Before you know what beetle tracks look like, it's hard to imagine how anyone could complete this outrageous task. Once you've learned to recognize beetle tracks, though, they're everywhere (at least in southern Africa). Every inch of bare dirt seems to have the little creepy-crawly footprints. Opportunities for humor occur the same way. Once you understand the different types of humor and the structure of a joke, the whole world is filled with beetle tracks. You'll see straight lines and setups everywhere you turn. To see more opportunities, though, first we have to have a bigger taxonomy of humor. We went into Ruch's (1992) factors in chapter 1: Incongruity, nonsense, and sexual components can account for a lot of people's reactions. Some fine distinctions can help us see humor in more spots, laying the foundation for cracking our own jokes more often.

AN ALTERNATIVE APPROACH TO RUCH'S CATEGORIES OF HUMOR: SON OF SORTS OF SILLINESS

Ruch's categories of humor based on jokes reveal a great deal about their content and their structure. The sex, incongruity-resolution, and nonsense factors dovetail nicely with theories of humor. But they seem to leave out too much. An alternative approach, based on researcher's intuitions, appeared in the Antioch Humor Test. The Antioch team sorted jokes into ten categories (Mindness, Miller, Turek, Bender, & Corbin, 1985). They have nonsense and sexual categories of jokes that overlap with Ruch's. The remaining eight types include jokes that are hostile, demeaning to men, demeaning to women, ethnic, social satire, philosophical, sick, and scatological. The first five categories all look at aggressive humor with varying targets. Hostile jokes attack an individual. The next categories disparage men, women, or members of a specific ethnic group—these seem like subsets of hostile jokes. Examples from these categories are ubiquitous. The failure to provide a category for jokes hostile to animals reflects the anthropomorphism of the time. The absence of homophobic jokes may also say something about the era when these categories appeared. As we saw in previous chapters, hostile humor is just a drag. It tends to covary with nasty things like poor relationships and burnout at work. It offers little help in getting good stuff like close friends or happy bargaining. If it's fun for you, it's probably best to keep it to yourself. It can undermine relationships in ways that hostile jesters might not realize.

Social satire ribs an institution or a policy. A quotation attributed to Will Rogers makes a good example: "There's no trick to being a humorist when you have the whole government working for you." Philosophical jokes, at least in this taxonomy, focus on the human condition. Oscar Wilde's remark, "Seriousness is the only refuge of the shallow," has a philosophical edge. Note that this is a little different from jokes that rely on some knowledge of philosophy. A favorite at the sarcastic, uppity, private high school that I attended with George Bush's cousin (who was known at the time as George Bush's nephew) was: A server asked René Descartes if he'd like some coffee. Descartes said, "I think not!" and promptly disappeared. Yeah. We were geeks. Such big geeks that my philosopher friend said, "But that's fallacious! It's denying the antecedent!"

Sick jokes target handicaps, death, or disease. I can't cite any without drawing accusations of political incorrectness, but the quadriplegic, dead-baby, "Mommy Mommy!" and leper genres certainly qualify. It's probably a sick joke if it involves someone in a wheelchair losing a hand while tossing a baby in a blender. You've got both sick and hostile if that someone happens to be a Jewish, Asian, trans-gendered, low IQ lesbian. Scatological jokes involve bodily functions or excrement (fart jokes—finally!). Comics call this "working blue," which seems odd because it usually involves discussions of body parts that are pink. An example of scatological humor that was well known at one time comes from France's Joseph Pujol, the "far-tiste." Pujol performed an amazing act at Paris's Moulin Rouge in the 1890s that included rectal impressions of cannons, smoking a cigarette through a tube in his anus, and using the smoke to play a couple of tunes on the song flute (Spinrad, 1999). Too bad he never learned Justin Bieber's "Baby."

This taxonomy is much more focused on content than Ruch's, provides a shorthand for discussion, but lacks some of the insights about joke structure and function. Nevertheless, these can give potential jokers a feel for more types of jokes, making the quest to fashion them a little simpler. Trying to think up a joke about anything is too broad a task. Narrowing it down to a category actually helps. I do not, however, recommend the song flute.

THE ARCHITECTURE OF JOKES

Hairsplitting academics have filled tons of journal space with discussions of other types of humor. The amount of quibbling over irony alone, with no sense of irony, is stunning. We have overstatements and understatements and puns and the like. The list goes on and on. Understanding these different categories of jokes and wit will help opportunities for humor appear in daily life. The best way to take advantage of these, oddly enough, is to stay paratelic. As we saw in Chapter 1, the paratelic state involves attending to the present to create mellow moments and a playful attitude. Straining to craft numerous wisecracks per minute creates too much pressure. Turning every conversation into a feverish hunt for setups can actually kill opportunities for fun. It's like trying to motivate people to relax by putting machine guns to their heads. But a playful attitude, free of pressures to produce, can be an ideal condition for generating humor. To take best advantage of the paratelic state and opportunities for wit, we have to go back to a model of humor. After all, there's little need to memorize every possible category of wit, jokes, or humor if there's an encompassing model or framework that can shed light on them all.

As we saw in Chapter 1, not one of the models of humor is perfect. Part of the problem in all of them seems to be that they are too imprecise. For example, none of them seem to be exact enough to translate into a computer program for writing jokes (Ritchie, 2004). Despite these limitations, most of the theories have something to offer when it comes to generating wit. If we hold their central ideas lightly, models of humor can inform us enough to have some application. Both the General Theory of Verbal Humor (Attardo, 2008) and the Incongruity-Resolution Model (Suls, 1972) account for a lot of what's funny. The approach of these models can help form a framework for generating humorous material. It's not an exact science, but it can be an enlightening art. To get a feel for this process, let's begin with an example, a favorite from my dad's years spent tending a bar.

A busy bartender looks up to find an enormous grasshopper seated on a barstool, eager to order and he asks:

"Did you know there's a drink named after you?"

The grasshopper asks, "Ernie?"

If we recall Attardo (2008) and the General Theory of Verbal Humor, we see that most jokes rely on the idea that a statement has a certain ambiguity. The jokes essentially contain two different scripts, a reflection of two different stories. Either one of the scripts could make sense, with the information provided in the setup, but the punch line reveals that they can't both be correct. A setup for a joke usually suggests one script with a series of associated assumptions. The setup creates what the comedy teacher extraordinaire Greg Dean (2000) calls the "first story"—the initial script that generates expectations about what's coming up next. Any time you begin a tale, whether or not it's a setup, your audience forms a mental picture that rests on one assumption (or more).

The punch line violates an assumption from the first story, but in a way that is consistent with a second story. The second story is the script that's incompatible with the first. As we discussed with the incongruity-resolution model (Suls, 1972), the reveal in the punch line can make your listener say, "Wait a minute! This new information doesn't fit my first story." Researchers beat each other over the heads (and not in a slapstick way) about whether or not this realization has to be surprising. But in the end, surprising or not, this realization has to happen. Perceivers of the joke have to sense the incongruity, even if they don't know what "incongruity" means. This realization usually accompanies the reveal—the part of the joke that indicates that the initial assumption is wrong. Ideally, the reveal appears in the punch line. Once there's that "Wait a minute" moment, then your listener can search for some alternative explanation for this new information. If the listener realizes that the first assumption was wrong and the second story makes sense, there is the potential for humor. This is the standard incongruity resolution. The punch line's reveal points out the incongruity, which the listener resolves with the second story. We can usually make something funny by resolving an incongruity with a punch line that reveals a second story and points out an incorrect assumption in the first story.

So how does this work with Ernie the grasshopper? The bartender asks, "Do you know there's a drink named after you?" and creates the first story. Most listeners leap to an inherent assumption that the bartender is discussing the delicious cocktail, The Grasshopper, named for its green color and famed for the luscious taste of cream, crème de menthe, and crème de cacao. This drink is called the "reference," the topic central to forming one of the two stories inherent in the joke. If you've never heard of this concoction, the joke's not going to work for you. You won't form the first story, which is essentially, "A bartender is about to tell a bug about a cocktail named after a type of bug."

The punch line, the grasshopper's question "Ernie?" reveals a second story. The creation of an initial story and of the subsequent, alternative story rests on an association between the two scripts. An ambiguity has to be present in the first story that can create an incongruity to resolve. Greg Dean (2000) calls this the "connector" and defines it as, literally, "one thing interpreted in at least two ways." Greg will be the first to admit that he's been influenced by Attardo (1994), but Attardo's not running comedy seminars in Los Angeles. He doesn't use cool words like "connector," either. The connector in Ernie's bartending tale is "a drink named after you." This is the ambiguous portion of the joke—the part that will be compatible with multiple stories. Most folks can interpret this expression in at least two ways. Anyone familiar with the quaffable cream of the crèmes is interpreting "a drink named after you" to be "grasshopper"—the drink. But the punch line shows an equally valid interpretation that actually makes more sense—what the grasshopper calls himself. This is the second story. It provides a reinterpretation of the connector. "A drink named after you" doesn't mean "grasshopper"; it means "Ernie." The punch line creates an incongruity, points out the ambiguity of the connector, and leads the audience to search for the second story, which can create the resolution. This second story seems to make a little more sense than the first. In all honesty, if my dad shouted from behind the bar that there was a drink named after you, would you ask, "A human?"

Examples that illustrate a joke's first story, revealing punch line, and resolving second story are all around. As E.B. White emphasized, dissecting them will kill them, so I apologize right now for the murders that follow. But like those poor, severed frogs in Biology 101, these jokes die for the sake of knowledge. A few more examples will help make understanding joke structure more automatic. This understanding, in turn, can help people generate funny material of their own. In addition, there are subtle components to delivery and a few general guidelines that help turn the incongruous or the weird into gags. These components and guidelines are difficult to break into parts. No single aspect alone seems particularly essential. You'll be able to think of funny events that contradict these ideas. They don't explain everything that's ever made anyone laugh. Plenty of nonsense humor strains these recommendations. Some jokes can't quite be forced into the model. But the combination of all of these components can be critical for making the difference between a belly laugh, a polite grin, and a groan.

Connecting the References

As I mentioned above, Ernie's punch line won't work if you've never heard of the beverage named for the grasshopper. (And if you've never tasted one, get to work.) The social aspect of jokes depends, in part, on common references. Much of what generates laughter in daily interactions is only funny in an informal, chatty, "How about those Bears?" kind of way (Provine, 1993). But these little quips communicate a shared knowledge or experience. They can even step toward the empathy that we saw in Chapter 6 was so essential in therapeutic relationships. Sharing a laugh can contribute to getting along. Part of getting along involves sharing references. One pleasant lunch I had one week was with a friend who can joke about a lot of shared topics. I'm not exaggerating when I say that we laughed about David Hume, Kato Kaelin, *The Green Hornet*, the Logical Positivists (not the band), organized religion, meta-logic, Pavlov, Lance Armstrong, and our wives. No one else could have gotten all the references. In fact, anyone else would have probably had us committed to an inpatient ward. This experience helps illustrate a prime rule for being funny: "Know your audience." The expression has become a bit of a cliché in comedy circles, though it was once as fresh as a daisy. Knowing your audience really means ensuring that your audience shares your references. If your listeners never read Dante's *Inferno* or never heard of Morgan Freeman, even the funniest jokes about them are going to fall flat. But the references alone aren't funny, as the list of my lunchtime joke topics reveals.

The Pauses and Phrases of Timing

A neglected aspect of joke delivery concerns the pause—the delay in a setup that allows listeners to make the most of a punch line. People frequently mention timing as a key element in generating laughs. Timing concerns the appropriate use of phrases and pauses to allow a gag to be as funny as possible. The movie *The Aristocrats*, which shows 100 comedians telling the same horrendously dirty joke in at least 100 different ways, is a wonderful study in timing and delivery. Incongruity resolution offers some insights into how timing works, and says a lot about appropriate pauses. Certain setups require a specific duration to tell. Ideally, setups are short but expressed with a lot of enthusiasm in an effort to maintain attention. Each setup is designed to generate the expectations inherent in a first story. Sometimes, this takes a while. An appropriate pause prior to the punch line, its associated reveal, and all the subsequent steps toward making it funny can mean the difference between a hit and a miss for a joke. These are hard to illustrate on paper, but a good one comes from the talented stand-up comic John Caparulo. He says:

> Everybody's such a know-it-all. I'm sick of it. You know? I'm sick of people who...read.

John's delivery is superb. He mentions know-it-alls up front, priming listeners with the idea. Then he stretches the setup a little more to give everyone the opportunity to generate all of their expectations about these pompous jerks. The sentences "I'm sick of it" and "You know?" might seem like filler, but they give the audience more time to construct a first story. (When I was a comic, I found that this setup time had to vary a lot from show to show. If it's late in the evening, or if the crowd is drunk, people need some time to get their first story straight.) Then John continues with the varied repetition of the words "I'm sick of people who..." letting everyone come up with all the irksome things that know-it-alls do. One of the most prominent of these irritants is that know-it-alls tell other people what to do.

John's a blue-collar guy who performs in jeans and a T-shirt, and a baseball cap sunk atop his head. It seems a sure bet that he's going to gripe about some boss he's had who's a know-it-all, or maybe some pretentious professor who gave him trouble. (Yes, they exist.) John's pause allows everyone to anticipate that he'll elaborate in this direction. In addition, he says several sentences in a row without a quick punch line, creating an opportunity for a surprise. Listeners know that he's not whipping out a series of one-liners, and they pay attention. The audience is unsure if the next sentence will be more of the setup or the impending punch line. The pause before the reveal lets everyone think of dozens of things—all potential connectors between what they've guessed John will say and what he'll actually deliver. Listeners, in this brief pause, could come up with quite a few of the things that know-it-alls do but the one that they're unlikely to think of is the word he uses: "read."

This single word generates an entire second story. It's along the lines of, "Wow! John's standards for what's annoying about know-it-alls are a lot lower than anyone had assumed!" The first story leads to an expectation that pompous posers are irritating for common reasons, ones that imply that John is smarter than these know-it-alls, who actually lack the insight that he has. But the reveal word "read" suggests that John's stand-up persona not only isn't that of an intellectual, but he actually thinks that the everyday activity of reading is annoying. If he thinks that reading tops the list of annoying habits in know-it-alls, well, it's unlikely that he's sharper than the jerks he's ridiculing. He's not winning any points with book authors, either. This punch line has a nice, self-deprecating edge. John winks at the audience as if to say, "You thought I was going to complain about something a lot more irritating than reading, didn't you? You thought I meant a smaller group of know-it-alls than everyone who picks up a book." The combination of the setup, pause, and punch communicates so much in such a short time. It gives the joke tremendous power.

This example helps illustrate a couple of other key points loosely related to pauses and timing. First, the wittiest of wits put the reveal at the end. There's no reason to talk past the part of the punch line that communicates the second story. People need a moment to process the incongruity and resolve it. If you're still talking past the reveal, they either won't hear you or they won't think about the joke. Either way, you lose out. If an early part of the punch line communicates the incongruity and gets the search for resolution going, subsequent parts will only confuse the process. It's subtle, and hard to illustrate on paper, but putting the reveal at the very end is important. For example, my father-in-law was ribbing me in front of my wife, asking, "Would you call what you have a marriage or more of a civil union?" (This is an absurd question, and a bit of non-sense humor, under the circumstances. He not only attended our wedding; he presided over it.) I replied, "I would not call this civil."

The potential connector from this sentence seemed obvious—the word "civil" implied tranquility as well as a type of legal relationship. My first thought was to say, "I wouldn't call this a CIVIL union," emphasizing the reveal with vocal inflection. Fortunately, I thought before I blurted that out. Ending with the reveal, by saying, "I wouldn't call this civil," made this expression funnier. Of course, it helps that my wife and I get along. This wouldn't have been funny if she'd just given me a black eye. In a sense, putting the reveal at the end is the ultimate pause. It leads to an interesting corollary: Once the joke is out, stop talking. I can't emphasize this one enough. If you're trying to be funny and people are laughing, shut up. They're doing exactly what you want them to do. A last point along these lines is true in any setting: Never make fun of someone's laugh. If you put some effort into getting someone to chuckle, don't punish them once they do it. They might not ever laugh in front of you again. So give folks time to generate a first story, put the reveal at the very end of the punch line, stop talking when people are chuckling, and never ridicule anyone's laugh.

Tags

Tags are additional punch lines that work off the same setup. The beauty of tags comes from their ability to keep laughs coming without a break. Greg Dean (2000) is the king of tags, so I'll steal one of his. "On Father's Day, I took my father out— permanently. I didn't like the way he said Mass." It's best heard with Greg's emphatic hand gestures—a gun to the head during the first reveal, "permanently," and then hands closed in prayer at the second reveal, "Mass." Note that there are really two different connectors here. The first rests on the meaning of "took out." We get an image of Greg chauffeuring his old man to a restaurant. The reveal suggests the alternative meaning of the second story. "Took out" means "murdered." The tag uses a different connector related to meanings of the word "father." It's not his dad; it's his priest. This permits a second reveal off the same setup, creating another laugh in very little time. Study the professionals and you'll get a great feel for tags. Since tags work from the same setup, there's no need for any additional chatting between punch lines, making the number of laughs per minute climb. The beloved Wendy Liebman is superb with tags. She mentions that her HMO is absurdly expensive—they even charged her for her own breast self-exam. Of course, it was a flat fee.

Callbacks

A "callback" refers to a previous topic, preferably a punch line that was genuinely funny. Callbacks are outstanding when they can employ a previous reveal to resolve a novel incongruity. When comics use a callback, it becomes a private joke between them and the audience. It communicates these words: "Hey, we've been together long enough to have a history." There's an intimacy to it, a sort of minireminiscence about a little personal nostalgia. It's like sharing a warm bowl of Pot Noodles with a childhood pal. For example, halfway through his *King Baby* show, Jim Gaffigan does a large string of jokes about bacon. (Bacon's the best. Even the frying of bacon sounds like applause.) He turns to a range of other topics for several minutes, including a rousing discussion of deodorants and their variety of scents. Then he asks, "You know what scent they should make? Bacon."

Any running gag can work this way. The *Simpsons* episode "The Bob Next Door" features the recurring character Sideshow Bob on one of his endless attempts to murder Bart Simpson. Fans of the show know that virtually every episode includes Bob stepping on a rake, slapping himself in the face with the handle. This bit of slapstick never fails to delight those who like nothing better than self-induced pain in pompous snobs like Bob. (Some dare to enjoy his agony because he's a Yalie Republican, but don't tell my Yalie wife.) The episode continues for over 17 minutes of Bob's rakish shenanigans, with no stepping on a rake. Just as viewers might suspect that the slap of the wooden handle isn't meant to be, Bob finally delivers. Ah! The beauty of timing and callbacks. In everyday life, callbacks will come to you once you think about them. Again, stay relaxed. There's no need to have a callback every 30 seconds. But once you've been chatting for a while, a topic will come up that will remind you of a previous funny discussion. You'll get the chance to mention it and it'll be funny.

Into the Nonsense

Plenty of humor is consistent with two scripts but doesn't quite have a resolved incongruity. It's not exactly the nonsense of flying musical submarine underwear; it's more the juxtaposition of the incompatible. Theorists who assert that resolution is not essential to humor can point to phenomena like these for evidence (Deckers, 1993). One example appeared when the deep-voiced Reverend Jesse Jackson read *Green Eggs and Ham* on *Saturday Night Live.* The juxtaposition of this serious civil rights activist and the rhyming rhythms of Dr. Seuss certainly seemed incongruous. But it happened right on television. How does the humor of this work? It's not crystal clear. There are certainly two opposing scripts. One potential first story has an assumption built in: Reverend Jackson would never repeat "Sam I Am" on television. The assumption gets shattered as Jackson says, "I would not eat them in a house ..." The incongruity never quite gets resolved, except as a sort of diminishment. As Apter (1982) emphasized, humor has to take a topic from the serious to the playful, diminishing its seriousness. The formal communication we expect from a public official is reduced to a well-known children's tale.

Placing incongruous ideas together is easy enough. Imagine an orchestrated version of the old song "I Like Big Butts," or Disney star Zac Efron singing the legendary rap tune "Slap My Bitch Up." These might have potential, but only the school of hard knocks seems to teach us which ones are funny. One way to experiment involves what comedy teacher Judy Carter has called the "act–out"—putting the punch line into motion (Carter, 2001). Many comics have taken to using a setup, revealing the punch, and then tagging with a physical performance of what they're discussing. Some of these are fine examples of nonsense humor. Ellen DeGeneres does multiple minutes mimicking a woman looking into the mirror while trying on clothes. There's no mirror there and she's not really changing clothes, but she makes all the same motions and the crowd goes wild.

How does this work? I'm not sure, exactly. There are opposing scripts in the sense that she's doing all the things that women do when they try on clothes, but she's not really trying on the clothes. Is "trying on clothes" the connector? Her actions seem so familiar. The crowd seems to recognize the universality of how trying on new clothes induces people to look at their butts. She's both trying on clothes and not trying them on, but the incongruous scripts never quite get resolved.

Robin Williams's renowned bit "Elmer Fudd sings Bruce Springsteen" can serve as a prime example of an act out, too. The sultry lyrics of The Boss's tune "Fire" don't fit Fudd's fumbling persona. The flagrant incongruity could be funny in the right context, and Robin Williams certainly knows how to create it. The first story might be: "I don't care how much opera Elmer Fudd ever sang; he certainly wouldn't sing a song like this." But the second story might be: "Wow! Robin Williams is acting this out, anyway. If Elmer Fudd ever did sing this song, it'd have to be a lot like this." An unlikely event seems to be happening right before our eyes. Well, it is and it isn't. Robin Williams isn't really Elmer Fudd, which adds another layer of incongruity. In a sense, Robin Williams becomes the connector. He is himself, Springsteen, and Fudd all at once. It makes him ambiguous, incongruous, unresolved, and funny.

But how can you try this at home? It's easy to ease into act-outs. Almost everyone had a friend in grade school who made sounds to punctuate speech. (Perhaps others thought that you were that friend.) You know the one I mean, the person who said things like: "We drove in the car—'vroom, vroom.' Then we got to my house and went up the stairs—'clump, clump, clump.' But my mom fell down them and went, 'Ah!'—thump, thump, splat.'" These aren't exactly in joke structure, but they can create some jokey nonsense. These mini-act-outs can elicit the occasional chuckle. If you happen to mention your puppy, boss, dean, or senator and then behave like her for a second, that's the start of a lifetime of act outs. Obviously, they're not for everyone and they're certainly not for every situation. As you discover which ones are funny to those around you, you might give in to the temptation to make them longer, louder, and more frequent. Soon it can seem that there are no rules for act-outs, just the natural reactions that you get from your environment. As your act-outs change, people's reactions will change, and soon you'll find the ones that work for those around you. This interactive process can be a lot of fun. When the models of humor don't quite tell you what to do, the feedback from those around you can be pretty clear. If something's not working, let it go and try something else. It can be a good model for a lot of things in life.

Any attempt at an act-out ends up seeming funnier if you're perceived as the kind of person who wouldn't do act-outs. I can usually get some mileage out of assumptions about professors during the first few meetings of a new class. Students rarely expect an instructor to be more entertaining than balsa wood. If I happen to mention a basketball player and feign shooting a free throw, it violates the expectancy right away. After a few incongruous moves, though, I've led students to anticipate that something odd should happen in the lecture. By the third class meeting, I invariably have to up the ante. By the end of the semester, I have to tie a tie around my head to get any response. It's amazing how quickly people create new expectations, and how it takes more to violate them.

Some who read all of this will soon find themselves performing little act-outs, paging through James Thurber, watching clips of Buster Keaton, venturing out to the comedy clubs, and crafting witticisms more often. Those who spend some time fashioning clever reveals and placing them at the ends of punch lines will learn some interesting things. Of course they discover what they find funny and what brings grins to those around them. They explore their strongest likes and dislikes, leading them to pay more attention to how they feel. Humor might not make every penis erect, cure cancer and AIDS, or create world peace overnight. But it can let you know more about what you really think and how you really feel. A lot of human distress seems to come from our unwillingness to experience our negative feelings (Hayes, Wilson, Gifford, Follette, & Strosahl, 1996). Avoiding our own emotions seems to be what ties us into knots. We all have moments where we feel sad, mad, afraid, and disgusted. It's not these feelings that seem to drive us batty, as much as it is our attempts to control emotions that can't be controlled. Humor just might let us feel the way we really feel. We might be less afraid of our own rage and sorrow and fright if we know that we can feel it without dying. We might be more likely to let ourselves feel the way we really feel if we know that these same emotions might be the seeds of a good joke. Watch the pros. The number of gags related to negative attitudes and feelings is staggering. Humor can help us give ourselves permission to feel.

HUMOR IN THE FUTURE

There's a Zen idea about mindfulness, when the mind pays attention to itself in the present. During moments of mindfulness, the mind has nothing to hold on to other than itself, and nothing to think about but its own contents—the present. So there is nothing to be done and no agent to do it, just the mind minding the mind. Having nothing to do and no one to do it can make a mindful mind joyful. There's no anticipation and no anxiety, because there is no goal and no striver. The path to humor in the future might have some of the same qualities. Each time we acknowledge that something is funny, we're getting a look inside our own minds. When we notice our minds leaning in one direction, making a specific assumption that gets violated by a punch line, we note that we were lost in our own thoughts. We can see how our own minds led us astray and took us away from our own immediate experience. We don't have to do anything special, we just see where our minds are. And when we catch our minds a little off the beam, we can remind ourselves to get back to the moment. In fact, the funny part of the joke might be what we were thinking before. Punch lines can encourage us to return to the present.

The way to get funny is to see that life is funny. Even tragedy can be comedy. And the way to see that life is funny is to be in it right now, right now, now. Then there's no joke to tell and no joke to miss. I'm not sure what comedies of the future will be like. In a few years, we might all find ourselves watching comedians juggle rocket fuel while ridiculing our newly elected World Emperor Kumquat. But I do know one thing: Humor will be in the present. There will still be that moment of attention, that tiny jocular shift just prior to the big guffaw. In a sense, there is no humor in the future. There can only be humor in the present. Something is funny in the present moment because that's the only moment that there is. And if the present moment isn't funny, the fact that it isn't funny just might be humorous on its own. Any moment spent recognizing humor—well, that's a moment well spent. And it has a great chance to be a happy one. Comedy can give us the optimism to know that there's always another laugh around the corner.

References

Abrahams, B. S., & Geschwind, D. H. (2008). Advances in autism genetics: On the threshold of a new neurobiology. *Nature Reviews Genetics, 9*, 341–355.

Adams, E. R., & McGuire, F. A. (1986). Is laughter the best medicine? A study of the effects of humor on perceived pain and affect. *Activities, Adaptation & Aging, 8*, 157–175.

Adelsward, V., & Oberg, B. M. (1998). The function of laughter and joking in negotiation activities. *Humor: International Journal of Humor Research, 11*, 411–429.

Adler, A. (1924). *The practice and theory of individual psychology.* Oxford: Harcourt, Brace.

Adorno, T. W., Frenkel-Brunswik, E., & Levinson, D. J. (1950). *The authoritarian personality.* New York: Harper & Brothers.

Agro, F., Liguori, A., Petti, F. B., Cataldo, R., & Totonelli, A. (2005). Does acupuncture analgesia have a bi-humoral mechanism? *The Pain Clinic, 17*, 243–244.

Aldao, A., Nolen-Hoeksema, S., & Schweizer, S. (2010). Emotion-regulation strategies across psychopathology: A meta-analytic review. *Clinical Psychology Review, 30*, 217–237.

Allen, M., Witt, P. L., & Wheeless, L. R. (2006). The role of teacher immediacy as a motivational factor in student learning: Using meta-analysis to test a causal model. *Communication Education, 55*, 21–31.

Allport, G. (1961). *Pattern and growth in personality.* New York: Holt, Rinehart & Winston.

Allport, G. W., & Odbert, H. S. (1936). Trait-names: A psycho-lexical study. *Psychological Monographs, 47*, 211.

Altemeyer, B., & Hunsberger, B. (2004). A revised religious fundamentalism scale: The short and sweet of it. *International Journal of the Psychology of Religion, 14*, 47–54.

Altemeyer, B. (2007). *The authoritarians*. Winnipeg, MB: University of Manitoba.

Altermeyer, B., & Adler, A. (1917). *The neurotic constitution: Outlines of a comparative individualistic psychology and psychotherapy in the authoritarians*. New York: Moffat, Yard, & Company.

Alujaa, A., Garciab, O., & Carciac, L. F. (2003). Relationships among extraversion, openness to experience, and sensation seeking. *Personality and Individual Differences, 35*, 671–680.

Ambady, N., & Rosenthal, R. (1993). Half a minute: Predicting teacher evaluations from thin slices of nonverbal behavior and physical attractiveness. *Journal of Personality and Social Psychology, 64*, 431–441.

Anderson, M., Shanmuganayagam, D., & Weindruch, R. (2009). Caloric restriction and aging: Studies in mice and monkeys. *Toxicologic Pathology, 37*, 47–51.

Apter, M. J. (1982). *The experience of motivation: The theory of psychological reversals*. San Diego, CA: Academic Press.

Arden, R., Gottfredson, L. S., Miller, G., & Pierce, A. (2009). Intelligence and semen quality are positively correlated. *Intelligence, 37*, 277–282.

Aristophanes. (1997). *Birds, Lysistrata, assembly-women, wealth*. New York: Oxford University Press.

Attardo, S. (1994). *Linguistic theories of humor*. Hawthorne, NY: Mouton de Gruyter.

Attardo, S. (2008). Semantics and pragmatics of humor. *Language and Linguistics Compass, 2*, 1203–1215.

Attardo, S., & Raskin, V. (1991). Script theory revis(it)ed: Joke similarity and joke representation model. *Humor: International Journal of Humor Research, 4*, 293–347.

Babad, E. Y. (1974). A multi-method approach to the assessment of humor: A critical look at humor tests. *Journal of Personality, 42*, 618–631.

Beard, F. K. (2007). *Humor in the advertising business: Theory, practice and wit*. Lanham, MD: Rowman & Littlefield Publishers.

Benham, G., Nash, M. R., & Baldwin, D. R. (2009). A comparison of changes in secretory immunoglobulin A following a stress-inducing and stress-reducing task. *Stress and Health: Journal of the International Society for the Investigation of Stress, 25*, 81–90.

Bennett, M. P., Zeller, J. M., Rosenberg, L., & McCann, J. (2003). The effect of mirthful laughter on stress and natural killer cell activity. *Alternative Therapies in Health and Medicine, 9*, 38–45.

Berk, L. S., Ta, S. A., Fr, W. F., Napier, B. J., Lee, J. W., Hubbard, R. W., et al. (1989). Neuroendocrine and stress hormone changes during mirthful laughter. *American Journal of the Medical Sciences, 296*, 390–396.

Berk, R. A., & Nanda, J. (2006). A randomized trial of humor effects on test anxiety and test performance. *Humor: International Journal of Humor Research, 19*, 425–454.

Bippus, A. M. (2000). Making sense of humor in young romantic relationships: Understanding partners' perceptions. *Humor: International Journal of Humor Research, 13*, 395–417.

Bogg, T., & Roberts, B. W. (2004). Conscientiousness and health-related behaviors: A meta-analysis of the leading behavioral contributors to mortality. *Psychological Bulletin, 130*, 887–919.

Boothroyd, R. A., McMorris, R. F., & Kipp, W. J. (in press). *Humor in tests related to anxiety and performance.*

Borders, A., Smucker-Barnwell, S. S., & Earleywine, M. (2007). Alcohol-aggression expectancies and dispositional rumination moderate the effect of alcohol consumption on alcohol-related aggression and hostility. *Aggressive Behavior, 33*, 327–338.

Borrow, G. H. (1893). *Lavengro: The scholar, the gypsy, the priest.* London: Ward, Lock, Bowden.

Bozikas, V. P., Kosmidis, M. H., Giannakou, M., Anezoulaki, D., Petrikis, P., Fokas, K., et al. (2007). Humor appreciation deficit in schizophrenia: The relevance of basic neurocognitive functioning. *Journal of Nervous and Mental Disease, 195*, 325–331.

Bressler, E. R., & Balshine, S. (2006). The influence of humor on desirability. *Evolution and Human Behavior, 27*, 29–39.

Brodinzky, D. M., & Rubien, J. (1976). Humor production as a function of sex of subject, creativity, and cartoon content. *Journal of Consulting and Clinical Psychology, 44*, 597–600.

Brooks, M., & Reiner, C. (1981). *The 2000 year old man.* New York: Warner Books.

Brown, A. S., & Itzig, J. M. (1976). *The interaction of humor and anxiety in academic test situations.* Dallas: Southern Methodist University.

Bryant, J. (1977). Degree of hostility in squelches affecting humor appreciation. In A. J. Chapman & H. C. Foot (Eds.), *It's a funny thing, humor* (pp. 321–327). Oxford: Pergamon Press.

Bryant, J., Brown, D., Silberg, A. R., & Elliot, S. M. (1981). Effects of humorous illustrations in college textbooks. *Human Communication Research, 8*, 43–57.

Buss, D. M. (1989). Sex differences in human mate preferences: Evolutionary hypotheses tested in 37 cultures. *Behavioral and Brain Sciences, 12*, 1–49.

Butler, A. C., & Roediger, H. L. (2007). Testing improves long-term retention in a simulated classroom setting. *European Journal of Cognitive Psychology, 19*, 514–527.

Callender, A. A., & McDaniel, M. A. (2009). The limited benefits of rereading educational texts. *Contemporary Educational Psychology, 34*, 30–41.

Campbell, L., Martin, R. A., & Ward, J. R. (2008). An observational study of humor use while resolving conflict in dating couples. *Personal Relationships, 15,* 41–55.

Cann, A., & Etzel, K. C. (2008). Remembering and anticipating stressors: Positive personality mediates the relationship with sense of humor. *Humor: International Journal of Humor Research, 21,* 157–178.

Cann, A., & Calhoun, L. G. (2001). Perceived personality associations with differences in sense of humor: Stereotypes of hypothetical others with high or low senses of humor. *Humor: International Journal of Humor, 13,* 1–14.

Canter, P. H., Wilder, B., & Ernst, E. (2007). The antioxidant vitamins A, C, E and selenium in the treatment of arthritis: A systematic review of randomized clinical trials. *Rheumatology, 46,* 1223–1233.

Cantor, J. R., Bryant, J., & Zillmann, D. (1974). Enhancement of humor appreciation by transferred excitation. *Journal of Personality and Social Psychology, 30,* 782–791.

Cantor, J. R. (1976). What is funny to whom? The role of gender. *Journal of Communication, 26,* 164–172.

Caprara, G. V., & Cervone, D. (2000). *Personality: Determinants, dynamics, and potentials.* New York: Cambridge University Press.

Carstensen, L. L., Gottman, J. M., & Levenson, R. W. (1995). Emotional behavior in long-term marriage. *Psychology and Aging, 10,* 140–149.

Carter, J. (2001). *The comedy bible: From stand-up to sitcom.* New York: Fireside.

Cattell, R. B. (1946). *The description and measurement of personality.* New York: World Books.

Chang, H. (2004). *Inventing temperature: Measurement and scientific progress.* New York: Oxford University Press.

Chaplin, C. (Director). (1917). *The immigrant* [motion picture]. United States: Lone Star Corporation.

Chen, M. J., Grube, J. W., Bersamin, M., Waiters, E., & Keefe, D. B. (2005). Alcohol advertising: What makes it attractive to youth? *Journal of Health and Communication, 10,* 553–565.

Claridge, G., Clark, K., Powney, E., & Hassan, E. (2008). Schizotypy and the Barnum effect. *Personality and Individual Differences, 44,* 436–444.

Clark, A., Seidler, A., & Miller, M. (2001). Inverse association between sense of humor and coronary heart disease. *International Journal of Cardiology, 80,* 87–88.

Clark, D. A., & Beck, A. T. (2010). *Cognitive science and anxiety disorders: Science and practice.* New York: Guilford Press.

Clarke, J. R. (2007). *Looking at laughter: Humor, power, and transgression in Roman visual culture, 100 B.C.–A.D. 250.* Berkeley, CA: University of California Press.

Cogan, R., Cogan, D., Waltz, W., & McCue, M. (1987). Effects of laughter and relaxation on discomfort thresholds. *Journal of Behavioral Medicine, 10,* 139–144.

Cohan, C. L., & Bradbury, T. N. (1997). Negative life events, marital interaction, and the longitudinal course of newlywed marriage. *Journal of Personality and Social Psychology, 73,* 114–128.

Collinson, D. L. (1988). "Engineering humour": Masculinity, joking and conflict in shop-floor relations. *Organization Studies, 9,* 181–199.

Consalvo, C. M. (1989). Humor in management: No laughing matter. *Humor: International Journal of Humor Research, 2,* 285–297.

Conway, M., & Laurette, D. (2002). Humor in persuasion on threatening topics: Effectiveness is a function of audience sex role. *Personality and Social Psychology Bulletin, 28,* 863–873.

Cousins, N. (1979). *The anatomy of an illness as perceived by the patient.* New York: Norton.

Crawford, M. (2003). Gender and humor in social context. *Journal of Pragmatics, 35,* 1413–1430.

Crawford, M., & Gressley, D. (1991). Creativity, caring, and context: Women's and men's accounts of humor preferences and practices. *Psychology of Women Quarterly, 15,* 217–231.

Dale, J., Alexander, M. A., Hudak, H. L., Klions, N., Yovetich, D. A., & Emanuele, S. (1991). Comedy in the face of stress incubation of threat, depression, tolerance of discomfort, and computer anxiety as a function of humor. *International Journal of Psychophysiology, 11,* 20.

Darwin, C. (1871). *The descent of man, and selection in relation to sex* (pp. 253–320). London, England: John Murray.

Davies, A. P., & Apter, M. J. (1980). Humour and its effect on learning in children. In E. P. McGhee & A. J. Chapman (Eds.), *Children's humour.* Chichester, England: John Wiley and Sons.

Davis, J. M., & Farina, A. (1970). Humor appreciation as social communication. *Journal of Personality and Social Psychology, 15,* 175–178.

Davis, M. A. (2009). Understanding the relationship between mood and creativity: A meta-analysis. *Organizational Behavior and Human Decision Processes, 108,* 25–38.

Day, N. (2009). Responses to failed humor. *Journal of Pragmatics, 41,* 1825–1836.

De Backer, C., Braeckman, J., & Farinpour, L. (2008). Mating intelligence in personal ads. In G. Geher & G. Miller (Eds.), *Mating intelligence: Sex, relationships, and the mind's reproductive system* (pp. 77–101). Mahwah, NJ: Lawrence Erlbaum Associates Publishers.

Dean, G. (2000). *Step by step to stand-up comedy.* Portsmouth, NH: Heineman Drama.

Decker, W. H. (1987). Managerial humor and subordinate satisfaction. *Social Behavior and Personality, 15,* 225–232.

Decker, W. H., & Rotondo, D. M. (2001). Relationships among gender, type of humor, and perceived leader effectiveness. *Journal of Managerial Issues, 13,* 450–465.

Deckers, L. (1993) On the validity of a weight-judging paradigm for the study of humor. *Humor: International Journal of Humor Research, 6,* 43–56.

Deckers, L., & Ruch, W. (1992). Sensation seeking and the situational humor response questionnaire—Its relationship in American and German samples. *Personality and Individual Differences,13,* 1051–1054.

Deffenbacher, J. L., Deitz, S. R., & Hazaleus, S. L. (1981). Effects of humor and test anxiety on performance, worry, and emotionality in naturally occurring exams. *Cogntive Therapy and Research, 5,* 225–228.

Derks, P., Gillikin, L. S., Bartolome-Rull, D. S., & Bogart, E. H. (1997). Laughter and electroencephalographic activity. *Humor: International Journal of Humor Research, 10,* 285–300.

Dickson, D. H., & Kelly, I. W. (1985). The 'Barnum effect' in personality assessment: A review of the literature. *Psychological Reports, 57,* 367–382.

Diener, E., Nickerson, C., Lucas, R. E., & Sandvik, E. (2002). Dispositional affect and job outcomes. *Social Indicators Research, 59,* 229–259.

Dobson, K. S., Hollon, S. D., Dimidjian, S., Schmaling, K. B., Kohlenberg, R. J., Gallop, R. J., et al. (2008). Randomized trial of behavioral activation, cognitive therapy, and antidepressant medication in the prevention of relapse and recurrence in major depression. *Journal of Consulting and Clinical Psychology, 76,* 468–477.

Dorz, S., Novara, C., Sica, C., & Sanavio, E. (2003). Predicting burnout among HIV/AIDS and oncology health care workers. *Psychology and Health, 18,* 677–684.

Driessen, E., Cuijpers, P., de Maat, S. C. M., Abbass, A. A., de Jonghe, F., & Dekker, J. J. M. (2010). The efficacy of short-term psychodynamic psychotherapy for depression: A meta-analysis. *Clinical Psychology Review, 30,* 25–36.

Dwyer, T. (1991). Humor, power, and change in organizations. *Human Relations, 44,* 1–19.

Earleywine, M. (2011). Training listeners to think, feel, and act. In J. Berti & D. Bowman (Eds.), *Rush and philosophy, always hopeful, but discontent.* Chicago: Open Court.

Earleywine, M., Finn, P. R., & Martin C. S. (1990). Personality risk for alcoholism and alcohol consumption: A latent variable analysis. *Addictive Behaviors, 15,* 183–187.

Ellis, A. (1997). Must musturbation and demandingness lead to emotional disorders? *Psychotherapy: Theory, research, practice, training, 34*, 95–98.

Eysenck, M., Mogg, J., May, J., Richards, A., & Mathews, A. (1991). Bias in interpretation of ambiguous sentences related to threat in anxiety. *Journal of Abnormal Psychology, 100*, 144–150.

Eysenk, H. J. (1942). The appreciation of humor: An experimental and theoretical study. *British Journal of Psychology, 23*, 295–309.

Fisher, S., & Fisher, R. L. (1981). *Pretend the world is funny and forever: A psychological analysis of comedians, clowns, and actors.* Hillsdale, NJ: Erlbaum.

Fleming, P. (2005). Workers' playtime? Boundaries and cynicism in a "Culture of Fun" program. *Journal of Applied Behavioral Science, 41*, 285–303.

Foley, E., Matheis, R., & Schaefer, C. (2002). Effect of forced laughter on mood. *Psychological Reports, 90*, 184.

Forer, B. R. (1949). The fallacy of personal validation: A classroom demonstration of gullibility. *Journal of Abnormal and Social Psychology, 44*, 118–123.

Forgas, J. (2008). Affect, cognition, and social behavior: The effects of mood on memory, social judgments, and social interaction. In M. A. Gluck., J. R. Anderson., & S. M. Kosslyn (Eds.), *Memory and mind: A festschrift for Gordon H. Bower* (pp. 261–279). Mahwah, NJ: Lawrence Erlbaum Associates Publishers.

Freud, S. (1905). *Jokes and their relation to the unconscious.* Leipzig, Germany: Deuticke.

Frewen, P. A., Brinker, J., Martin, R. A., & Dozois, D. J. A. (2008). Humor styles and personality-vulnerability to depression. *Humor: International Journal of Humor Research, 21*, 179–195.

Friedman, H. S., Tucker, J. S., Tomlinson-Keasey, C., Schwartz, J. E., Wingard, D. L., & Criqui, M. H. (1993). Does childhood personality predict longevity? *Journal of Personality and Social Psychology, 65*, 176–185.

Fry, P. S. (1995). Perfectionism, humor, and optimism as moderators of health outcomes and determinants of coping styles of women executives. *Genetic, Social, and General Psychology Monographs, 121*, 211–245.

Fuhr, M. (2001). Some aspects of form and function of humor in adolescence. *Humor: International Journal of Humor Research, 14*, 25–37.

Galloway, G., & Chirico, D. (2008). Personality and humor appreciation: Evidence of an association between trait neuroticism and preferences for structural features of humor. *Humor: International Journal of Humor Research, 21*, 129–142.

Gelkopf, M., Gonen, B., Kurs, R., Melamed, Y., & Bleich, A. (2006). The effect of humorous movies on inpatients with chronic schizophrenia. *Journal of Nervous and Mental Disease, 194,* 880–883.

Gelkopf, M., Kreitler, S., & Sigal, M. (1993). Laughter in a psychiatric ward. Somatic, emotional, social, and clinical influences on schizophrenic patients. *Journal of Nervous and Mental Disease, 181,* 283–289.

Giosan, C., & Wyka, K. (2009). Is a successful high-K fitness strategy associated with better mental health? *Evolutionary Psychology, 7,* 28–39.

Goethe, J. W. (1920/2000). *Selected works.* London: Everyman's Library.

Gorham, J., & Christophel, D. M. (1990). The relationship of teachers' use of humor in the classroom to immediacy and student learning. *Communication Education, 39,* 46–62.

Gottman, J. M., & Levenson, R. W. (1999a). How stable is marital interaction over time? *Family Process, 38,* 159–165.

Gottman, J. M., & Levenson, R. W. (1999b). What predicts change in maritable interaction over time? A study of alternative medicine. *Family Process, 38,* 143–158.

Gottman, J. M., Coan, J., Carrere, S., & Swanson, C. (1998). Predicting marital happiness and stability from newlywed interactions. *Journal of Marriage & the Family, 60,* 5–22.

Greengros, G., & Miller, G. F. (2008). Dissing oneself versus dissing rivals: Effects of status, personality, and sex on the short-term and long-term attractiveness of self-deprecating and other-deprecating humor. *Evolutionary Psychology, 6,* 393–408.

Greengross, G., & Miller, G. F. (2009). The big five personality traits of professional comedians compared to amateur comedians, comedy writers, and college students. *Personality and Individual Differences, 47,* 79–83.

Greven, C., Chamorro-Premuzic, T., Arteche, A., & Furnham, A. (2008). A hierarchical integration of dispositional determinants of general health in students: The Big Five, trait emotional intelligence and humour styles. *Personality and Individual Differences, 44,* 1562–1573.

Gruner, C. R. (1976). Wit and humor in mass communication. In A. J. Capman & H. C. Foot (Eds.), *Humor and laughter: Theory, research and applications* (pp. 287–311). London: John Wiley & Sons.

Gruner, C. R. (1967). Effect of humor on speaker ethos and audience information gain. *Journal of Communication, 17,* 228–233.

Gruner, C. R. (1997). *The game of humor: A comprehensive theory of why we laugh.* New Brunswick, NJ: Transaction Publishers.

Hay, J. (2000). Functions of humor in the conversations of men and women. *Journal of Pragmatics, 32,* 709–742.

Hayes, S. C., Wilson, K. G., Gifford, E. V., Follette, V. M., & Strosahl, K. (1996). Experiential avoidance and behavioral disorders: A functional dimensional approach to diagnosis and treatment. *Journal of Consulting and Clinical Psychology, 64,* 1152–1168.

Hedi, J. J., Jr., Held, J. L., & Weaver, D. B. (1981). *The effects of humor on anxiety and performance.* Paper presented at the meeting of the American Educational Research Assocation, Los Angeles, California.

Hemmasi, M., Graf, L. A., & Russ, G. S. (1994). Gender-related jokes in the workplace: Sexual humor or sexual harassment? *Journal of Applied Social Psychology, 24,* 1114–1128.

Hicks, W. (2008). *Love all the people.* New York: Soft Skull Press.

Higueras, A., Carretero-Dios, H., Munoz, J. P., Idini, E., Ortiz, A., Rincon, F., et al. (2006). Effects of a humor-centered activity on disruptive behavior in patients in a general hospital psychiatric ward. *International Journal of Clinical and Health Psychology, 6,* 53–64.

Holmes, J., & Marra, M. (2002a). Having a laugh at work: How humour contributes to workplace culture. *Journal of Pragmatics, 34,* 1683–1710.

Holmes, J., & Marra, M. (2002b). Over the edge? Subversive humor between colleagues and friends. *Humor: International Journal of Humor Research, 15,* 65–87.

Holmes, J., & Marra, M. (2006). Humor and leadership style. *Humor: International Journal of Humor Research, 19,* 119–138.

Hovland, C. I., & Weiss, W. (1951). The influence of source credibility on communication effectiveness. *Public Opinion Quarterly, 15,* 635–650.

Howrigan, D. P., & MacDonald, K. B. (2008). Humor as a mental fitness indicator. *Evolutionary Psychology, 6,* 625–666.

Hubert, W., Moller, M., & de Jong-Meyer, R. (1993). Film-induced amusement changes in saliva cortisol levels. *Psychoneuroendocrinology, 18,* 265–272.

Hughes, L. W., & Avey, J. B. (2009). Transforming with levity: Humor, leadership, and follower attitudes. *Leadership & Organization Development Journal, 30,* 540–562.

Hurren, B. L. (2006). The effects of principals' humor on teachers' job satisfaction. *Educational Studies, 32,* 373–385.

Isen, A. M., Daubman, K. A., & Nowicki, G. P. (1987). Positive affect facilitates creative problem solving. *Journal of Personality and Social Psychology, 52,* 1122–1131.

Itami, J., Nobori, M., & Teshima, H. (1994). Laughter and immunity. *Shinshin-Igaku, 34,* 565–571.

Janssen, E., Everaerd, W., van Lunsen, R. H. W., & Oerlemans, S. (1994). Visual stimulation facilitates penile responses to vibration in men with and without erectile disorder. *Journal of Consulting and Clinical Psychology, 62,* 1222–1228.

Janus, S. S. (1975). The great comedians. Personality and other factors. *American Journal of Psychoanalysis, 35,* 169–174.

Janus, S. S., Bess, B. E., & Janus, B. R. (1978). The great comediennes: Personality and other factors. *American Journal of Psychoanalysis, 38,* 367–372.

Kabat-Zinn, J. (2003). Mindfulness-based stress reduction (MBSR). *Constructivism in the Human Sciences, 8,* 73–107.

Kalichman, S. C., Simbayi, L., Jooste, S., Vermaak, R., & Cain, D. (2008). Sensation seeking and alcohol use predict HIV transmission risks: Prospective study of sexually transmitted infection clinic patients, Cape Town, South Africa. *Addictive Behaviors, 33,* 1630–1633.

Kamei, T., Kumano, H., & Masumura, S. (1997). Changes of immuno-regulatory cells associated with psychological stress and humor. *Perceptual and Motor Skills, 84,* 1296–1298.

Kane, T. R., Suls, J., & Tedeschi, J. T. (1977). Humor as a tool in social interaction. In A. J. Chapman & H. C. Foot (Eds.), *It's a funny thing, humour* (pp. 13–16). Oxford: Pergamon Press.

Kanner, L. (1943). Autistic disturbances of affective contact. *Nervous Child, 2,* 217–150.

Kant, I. (1790/2007). *Critique of judgment* (N. Walker, Trans.). Oxford: Oxford University Press.

Kantor, J., Busch, A., & Rusch, L. (2009). *Behavioral activation: Distinctive features.* New York: Routledge.

Kapleau, R. K. (1989). *The three pillars of Zen: Teaching, practice, and enlightenment.* New York: Anchor Books.

Karremans, J. C., Stroebe, W., & Claus, J. (2006). Beyond Vicary's fantasies: The impact of subliminal priming and brand choice. *Journal of Experimental Social Psychology, 42,* 792–798.

Kaufman, G., & Vosburg, S. K. (1997). "Paradoxical" mood effects on creative problem-solving. *Cognition and Emotion, 11,* 151–170.

Kaufman, J. C. (2001). The Sylvia Plath effect: Mental illness in eminent creative writers. *Journal of Creative Behavior, 35,* 37–50.

Kaufman, J. C. (2009). *Creativity 101.* New York: Springer.

Kaufman, J. C. (2003). The cost of the muse; poets die young. *Death Studies, 27,* 813–821.

Kaufman, S. B., Kozbelt, A., Bromley, M. L., & Miller, G. R. (2008). The role of creativity and humor in human mate selection. In G. Geher & G. Miller (Eds.), *Mating intelligence: Sex, relationships, and the mind's reproductive system* (pp. 227–262). Mahwah, NJ: Lawrence Erlbaum Associates Publishers.

Kazarian, S. S., & Martin, R. A. (2006). Humor styles, culture-related personality, well-being, and family adjustment among Armenians in Lebanon. *Humor: International Journal of Humor Research, 19,* 405–423.

Kenny, D. T. (1955). The contingency of humor appreciation on the stimulus-confirmation of joke-ending expectations. *The Journal of Abnormal and Social Psychology, 51,* 644–648.

Killinger, B. (1987). Humor in psychotherapy: A shift to a new perspective. In W. F. J. Fry & W. A. Salameh (Eds.), *Handbook of humor and psychotherapy: Advances in the clinical use of humor* (pp. 21–40). Sarasota, FL: Professional Resource Exchange.

Kimata, H. (2004a). Reduction of allergen-specific IgE production by laughter. *European Journal of Clinical Investigation, 34,* 76–77.

Kimata, H. (2004b). Differential effects of laughter on allergen-specific immunoglobulin and neurotrophin levels in tears. *Perceptual & Motor Skills, 98,* 901–908.

Kimata, H. (2007a). Elevation of salivary melatonin levels by viewing a humorous film in patients with atopic eczema. *Hormone and Metabolic Research, 39,* 310–311.

Kimata, H. (2007b). Laughter elevates the levels of breast-milk melatonin. *Journal of Psychosomatic Research, 62,* 699–702.

Kimata, H. (2007c). Elevation of testosterone and reduction of transepidermal water loss by viewing a humorous film in elderly patients with atopic dermatitis. *Acta Medica, 50,* 135.

Kimata, H. (2007d). Increase in dermcidin-derived peptides in sweat of patients with atopic eczema caused by a humorous video. *Journal of Psychosomatic Research, 62,* 57–59.

Kimata, H. (2008). Short-term improvement of erectile dysfunction by viewing humorous films in patients with atopic dermatitis. *Journal of Sexual Medicine, 5,* 2107–2110.

Kimata, H. (2009). Viewing a humorous film decreases IgE production by seminal B cells from patients with atopic eczema. *Journal of Psychosomatic Research, 66,* 173–175.

Kinison, B., Abbott, E., Petok, M. (Producers), & Miller, W. C. (Director). (1987). *Sam Kinison—Breaking the rules* [motion picture]. United States: Geneon.

Kirsch, I. (2005). Medication and suggestion in the treatment of depression. *Contemporary Hypnosis, 22,* 59–66.

Klein, D. M., Bryant, J., & Zillman, D. (1982). Relationship between humor in introductory textbooks and students' evaluations of the texts' appeal and effectiveness. *Psychological Reports, 50,* 235–241.

Kohler, G., & Ruch, W. (1996). Sources of variance in current sense of humor inventories: How much substance, how much method variance? *Humor: International Journal of Humor Research, 9,* 363–397.

Korotkov, D., & Hannah, T. E. (1994). Extraversion and emotionality as proposed superordinate stress moderators: A prospective analysis. *Personality and Individual Differences, 16,* 787–792.

Koviazina, M. S., & Kogan, M. A. (2008). Perception of humor in patients with localized brain lesions. *Voprosy Psychologii, 2,* 74–82.

Kraus, M. W., & Keltner, D. (2009). Signs of socioeconomic status: A thin-slicing approach. *Psychological Science, 20,* 99–106.

Kuiper, N. A., & Nicholl, S. (2004). Thoughts of feeling better? Sense of humor and physical health. *Humor: International Journal of Humor Research, 17,* 37–66.

Kuiper, N. A., Grimshaw, M., Leite, C., & Kirsh, G. (2004). Humor is not always the best medicine: Specific components of sense of humor and psychological well-being. *Humor: International Journal of Humor Research, 17,* 135–168.

Kuipers, N. A., & Borowicz-Sibenik, M. (2005). A good sense of humor doesn't always help: Agency and communion as moderators of psychological well-being. *Personality and Individual Differences, 38,* 365–377.

Kurtzburg, T. R., Naquin, C. E., & Belkin, L. Y. (2009). Humor as a relationship-building tool in online negotiations. *International Journal of Conflict Management, 20,* 377–397.

Labott, S. M., Ahleman, S., Wolever, M. E., & Martin, R. B. (1990). The physiological and psychological effects of the expression and inhibition of emotion. *Behavioral Medicine, 16,* 182–189.

LaBrie, J. W., & Earleywine, M. (2000). Sexual risk behaviors and alcohol: Higher base rates revealed using the unmatched-count technique. *The Journal of Sex Research, 37,* 321–326.

Lambert, R. B., & Lambert, N. K. (1995). The effects of humor on secretory immunoglobin A levels in school-aged children. *Pediatric Nursing, 21,* 16–19.

Lampert, M. D., & Ervin-Tripp, S. M. (1998). Exploring paradigms: The study of gender and sense of humor near the end of the 20th century. In R. Willibald (Ed.), *The sense of humor: Explorations of a personality characteristic* (pp. 231–270). Berlin, Germany: Walter de Gruyter & Co.

Larson, G. (1989). *The prehistory of the far side.* Kansas City, MO: Andrews and McMeel Publishing.

Latta, R. L. (1998). *The basic humor process: A cognitive-shift theory and the case against incongruity.* New York: Mouton de Gruyter.

Lauer, R. H., Lauer, J. C., & Kerr, S. T. (1990). The long-term marriage: Perceptions on stability and satisfaction. *The International Journal of Aging & Human Development, 31,* 189–195.

Lefcourt, H. M., & Martin, R. A. (1986). *Humor and life stress: Antidote to adversity.* New York: Springer.

Lefcourt, H., Davidson-Katz, K., & Kueneman, K. (1990). Humor and immune-system functioning. *Humor: International Journal of Humor Research, 3,* 305–321.

Lewis, P. (2006). *Cracking up: American humor in a time of conflict.* Chicago: University of Chicago Press.

Li, N. P., Griskevicius, V., Durante, K. M., Jonason, P. K., Pasisz, D. J., & Aumer, K. (2009). An evolutionary perspective on humor: Sexual selection or interest indication? *Personality and Social Psychology Bulletin, 35*, 923–936.

Linnaeus, C. (1751). *Philosophia botanica, in qua explicantur fundamenta botanica cum definitionibus partium, exemplis terminorum, observationibus rariorum, adjectis figuris aeneis.* Stockholm, Sweden: G. Kiesewetter.

Long, D. L., & Graesser, A. C. (1988). Wit and humor in discourse processing. *Discourse Processes, 11*, 35–60.

Losco, J., & Epstein, S. (1975). Humor preference as a subtle measure of attitudes toward the same and the opposite sex. *Journal of Personality, 43*, 321–334.

Lucas, R. E., & Dyrenforth, P. S. (2006). Does the existence of social relationships matter for subjective well-being? In K. D. Vohs & E. J. Finkel (Eds.), *Self and relationships: Connecting intrapersonal and interpersonal processes* (pp. 254–273). New York: Guilford Press.

Lundy, D. E., Tan, J., & Cunningham, M. R. (1998). Heterosexual romantic preferences: The importance of humor and physical attractiveness for different types of relationships. *Personal Relationships, 5*, 311–325.

Mackie, D. M., & Worth, L. T. (1989). Processing deficits and the mediation of positive affect in persuasion. *Journal of Personality and Social Psychology, 57*, 27–40.

Mahony, D. L., Burroughs, W. J., & Hieatt, A. C. (2001). The effects of laughter on discomfort thresholds: Does expectation become reality? *Journal of General Psychology, 128*, 217–226.

Martin, L. R., Friedman, H. S., & Schwartz, J. E. (2007). Personality and mortality risk across the life span: The importance of conscientiousness as a biopsychosocial attribute. *Health Psychology, 26*, 428–436.

Martin, L. R., Friedman, H. S., Tucker, J. S., Tomlinson-Keasey, C., Criqui, M. H., & Schwartz, J. E. (2002). A life course perspective on childhood cheerfulness and its relation to mortality risk. *Journal of Personality and Social Psychology, 28*, 1155–1165.

Martin, R. A., & Dutrizac, G. (2004). *Humor styles, social skills, and quality of interactions with close others: A prospective daily diary study.* Paper presented at the Annual Conference of the International Society for Humor Studies, Dijon, France.

Martin, R. A., & Lefcourt, H. M. (1984). Situational Humor Response Questionnaire: Quantitative measure of sense of humor. *Journal of Personality and Social Psychology, 47*, 145–155.

Martin, R. A. (1996). The Situational Humor Response Questionnaire (SHRQ) and Coping Humor Scale (CHS): A decade of research findings. *Humor: International Journal of Humor Research, 9,* 251–272.

Martin, R. A. (2007). *The psychology of humor: An integrative approach.* Boston, MA: Elsevier Academic Press.

Martin, R. A., & Dobbin, J. P. (1988). Sense of humor, hassles, and immunoglobin A: Evidence for a stress-moderating effect of humor. *International Journal of Psychiatry in Medicine, 18,* 93–105.

Martin, R. A., & Kuiper, N. A. (1999). Daily occurrence of laughter: Relationships with age, gender, and type A personality. *Humor: International Journal of Humor Research, 12,* 355–384.

Martin, R. A., & Lefcourt, H. M. (1983). Sense of humor as a moderator of the relation between stressors and moods. *Journal of Personality and Social Psychology, 45,* 1313–1324.

Martin, R. A., Puhlik-Doris, P., Larsen, G., Gray, J., & Weir, K. (2003). Individual differences in uses of humor and their relation to psychological well-being: Development of the Humor Styles Questionnaire. *Journal of Reasearch in Personality, 27,* 48–75.

Master, S. L., Eisenberger, N. I., Taylor, S. E., Naliboff, B. D., Shirinyan, D., & Lieberman, M. D. (2009). A picture's worth: Partner photographs reduce experimentally induced pain. *Psychological Science, 20,* 1316–1318.

Mayer, R. E., Bove, W., Bryman, A., Mars, R., & Tapangco, L. (1996). When less is more: Meaningful learning from visual and verbal summaries of science textbook lessons. *Journal of Educational Psychology, 88,* 64–73.

McClelland, D. C., & Cheriff, A. D. (1997). The immunoenhancing effects of humor on secretory IgA and resistance to respiratory infections. *Psychology and Health, 12,* 329–344.

McGhee, P. E. (1983). The role of arousal and hemispheric lateralization in humor. In P. E. McGhee & J. H. Goldstein (Eds.), *Handbook of humor research,* Vol. 1, *Basic issues* (pp. 13–37). New York: Springer-Verlag.

McMorris, R. F., Boothroyd, R. A., & Pietrangelo, D. J. (1997). Humor in educational testing: A review and discussion. *Applied Measurement in Education, 10,* 269–297.

McMorris, R. F., Urbach, S. L., & Connor, M. C. (1985). Effects of incorporating humor in test items. *Journal of Educational Measurement, 22,* 147–155.

Meehl, P. E. (1954). *Clinical vs. statistical prediction: A theoretical analysis and a review of the evidence.* Minneapolis, MN: University of Minnesota Press.

Meehl, P. E. (1956). Wanted—a good cook-book. *American Psychologist, 11,* 263–272.

Meighan, P. (Writer), & Colton, G. (Director). (2008). The road to Germany [Television series episode]. In G. Colton (Director), *Family Guy*. United States: 20th Century Fox.

Merz, E. L., Malcarne, V. L., Hansdottir, I., Furst, D. E., Clements, P. J., & Weisman, M. H. (2009). A longitudinal analysis of humor coping and quality of life in systemic sclerosis. *Psychology, Health, & Medicine, 14*, 553–556.

Middleton, R., & Moland, J. (1959). Humor in Negro and White subcultures: A study of jokes among university students. *American Sociological Review, 22*, 61–69.

Miller, G. (2009). *Spent: Sex, evolution and consumer behavior*. New York: Viking Adult.

Miller, G., Tybur, J. M., & Jordan, B. D. (2007). Ovulatory cycle effects on tip of earnings by lap dancers: Economic evidence of human estrus? *Evolution and Human Behavior, 28*, 375–381.

Miller, W. R., & Rollnick, S. (2002). *Motivational interviewing: Preparing people for change*. New York: Guilford Press.

Miller, W. R. (2000). Rediscovering fire: Small interventions, large effects. *Psychology of Addictive Behaviors, 14*, 6–18.

Mindness, H., Miller, C., Turek, J., Bender, A., & Corbin, S. (1985). *The antioch humor test: Making sense of humor*. New York: Avon Books.

Morgan, M. S., & De Marchi, N. (1994). *Higgling: Translators and their markets in the history of economics*. London: Duke University Press.

Morrison, J. (1940). A note concerning investigations on the constancy of audience laughter. *Sociometry, 3*, 179–185.

Mulkay, M., Clark, C., & Pinch, T. (1993). Laughter and the profit motive: The use of humor in a photographic shop. *Humor: International Journal of Humor Research, 6*, 163–193.

Mumford, M. D. (2010). *Leadership 101*. New York: Springer.

Murdock, M. C., & Ganim, R. M. (1993). Creativity and humor: Integration and incongruity. *Journal of Creative Behavior, 27*, 57–70.

Murstein, B. I., & Brust, R. G. (1985). Humor and interpersonal attraction. *Journal of Personality Assessment, 49*, 637–640.

Nabi, R. L., Moyer-Guse, E., & Byrne, S. (2007). All joking aside: A serious investigation into the persuasive effect of funny social issue messages. *Communication Monographs, 74*, 29–54.

Nerhardt, G. (1970). Humor and inclination to laugh: Emotional reactions to stimuli of different divergence from a range of expectancy. *Scandinavian Journal of Psychology, 11*, 185–195.

Nettle, D. (2006). Psychological profiles of professional actors. *Personality and Individual Differences, 40*, 375–383.

Nevo, O., Keinana, G., & Teshimovsky-Arditi, M. (1993). Humor and pain tolerance. *Humor: International Journal of Humor Research, 6*, 71–88.

Nezu, A. M., Nezu, C. M., & Blissett, S. E. (1998). Sense of humor as a moderator of the relation between stressful events and psychological distress: A prospective analysis. *Journal of Personality and Social Psychology, 54,* 520–525.

Nisbett, R. E., & Wilson, T. D. (1977). Telling more than we can know: Verbal reports on mental processes. *Psychological Review, 84,* 231–259.

Nowakowska, C., Strong, C. M., Santosa, C. M., Wang, P. W., & Ketter, T. A. (2005). Temperamental commonalities and differences in euthymic mood disorder patients, creative controls, and healthy controls. *Journal of Affective Disorders, 85,* 207–215.

O'Quin, K., & Aronoff, J. (1981). Humor as a technique of social influence. *Social Psychology Quarterly, 44,* 349–357.

O'Quin, K., & Derks, P. (1997). Humor and creativity: A review of the empirical literature. In M. Runco (Ed.), *Creativity research handbook* (Vol. 1, pp. 223–252). Cresskill, NJ: Hampton Press.

Oktedalen, O., Solberg, E. E., Haugen, A. H., & Opstad, P. K. (2001). The influence of physical and mental training on plasma beta-endorphin level and pain perception after intensive physical exercise. *Stress and Health: Journal of the International Society for the Investigation of Stress, 17,* 121–127.

Olson, M. L., Hugelshofer, D. S., Kwon, P., & Reff, R. C. (2005). Rumination and dysphoria: The buffering role of adaptive forms of humor. *Personality and Individual Differences, 39,* 1419–1428.

Omwake, L. (1939). Factors influencing the sense of humor. *Journal of Social Psychology, 10,* 95–104.

Orwell, G. (1946). *Critical essays.* London: Secker & Warburg.

Otis, L. (1984). Factors influencing the willingness to taste unusual foods. *Psychological Reports, 54,* 739–740.

Parish, J. R. (2008). *It's good to be a king: The seriously funny life of Mel Brooks.* Hobokon, NJ: John Wiley & Sons.

Perera, S., Sabin, E., Nelson, P., & Lowe, D. (1998). Increase in salivary lysozyme and IgA concentrations and secretory rates independent of salivary flow rates following viewing humorous videotapes. *International Journal of Behavioral Medicine, 5,* 118–128.

Peterson, C. (2006). *A primer in positive psychology.* New York: Oxford University Press.

Peterson, J. P., & Pollio, H. R. (1982). Therapeutic effectiveness of differentially targeted humorous remarks in group psychotherapy. *Group, 6,* 39–50.

Petty, R. E., & Cacioppo, J. T. (1986). *Communication and persuasion: Central and peripheral routes to attitude change.* New York: Springer-Verlag.

Pfizer. (2007). *VIAGRA®*. Retrieved from http://www.pfizer.com/files/products/uspi_viagr a.pdf

Pien, D., & Rothbart, M. K. (1976). Incongruity and resolution in children's humor: A reexamination. *Child Development, 47*, 966–971.

Platek, S. M., & Shackelford, T. K. (2006). *Female infidelity and paternal uncertainty: Evolutionary perspectives on male anti-cuckoldry tactics.* New York: Cambridge University Press.

Plato (2009). *Symposium* (R. Waterfield, Trans). New York: Oxford University Press (Originally published in 360 BCE).

Platow, M. J., Haslam, S. A., Both, A., Chew, I., Cuddon, M., Goharpey, N., et al. (2005). "It's not funny if they're laughing": Self-categorization, social influence, and responses to canned laughter. *Journal of Experimental Social Psychology, 41*, 542–550.

Pliner, P., & Melo, N. (1997). Food neophobia in humans: Effects of manipulated arousal and individual differences in sensation seeking. *Physiology and Behavior, 61*, 331–335.

Pollio, H. R., & Mers, R. W. (1974). Predictability and the appreciation of comedy. *Bulletin of the Psychonomic Society, 4*, 229–232.

Ponniag, K., & Hollon, S. D. (2009). Empirically supported psychological treatments for adult acute stress disorder and posttraumatic stress disorder: A review. *Depression and Anxiety, 26*, 1086–1109.

Prasinos, S., & Tittler, B. I. (1981). The family relationships of humor-oriented adolescents. *Journal of Personality, 49*, 295–305.

Prerost, F. J. (1984). Reactions to humorous sexual stimuli as a function of sexual activeness and satisfaction. *Psychology: A Journal of Human Behavior, 21*, 23–27.

Price, R. (2000). *Droodles—The classic droodles.* Beverly Hills: Tallfellow Press.

Priest, R. F., & Swain, J. E. (2002). Humor and its implications for leadership effectiveness. *Humor: International Journal of Humor Research, 15*, 169–189.

Priest, R. F., & Thein, M. T. (2003). Humor appreciation in marriage: Spousal similarity, associative mating, and disaffection. *Humor: International Journal of Humor Research, 16*, 63–78.

Prokosch, M. D., Cross, R. G., Scheib, J. E., & Blozis, S. A. (2009). Intelligence and mate choice: Intelligent men are always appealing. *Evolution and Human Behavior, 30*, 11–20.

Provine, R. R. (1992). Contagious laughter: Laughter is a sufficient stimulus for laughs and smiles. *Bulletin of the Psychonomic Society, 30*, 1–4.

Provine, R. R. (1993). Laughter punctuates speech: Linguistic, social and gender contexts of laughter. *Ethology, 95*, 291–298.

Pryor, R. (Producer), & Layton, J. (Director). (1982). *Live on the sunset strip* [motion picture]. United States: Sony Pictures.

Rabelais, R. (1973). *Gargantua in Rabelais: Oeuvres Complètes*. Paris: Seuil (Originally published in 1524).

Radloff, L. S. (1977). The CES-D scale: A self report depression scale for research in the general population. *Applied Psychological Measurement, 1*, 385–401.

Rammstedt, B., & Schupp, J. (2008). Only the congruent survive—Personality similarities in couples. *Personality and Individual Differences, 45*, 533–535.

Rasmussen, N. (2008). *On speed: The many lives of amphetamine*. New York: New York University Press.

Reiner, C., & Brooks, M. (1961). *The 2,000 year old man*. United States: Rhino Records.

Ruch, W., McGhee, P. E., & Hehl, F. J. (1990). Age differences in the enjoyment of incongruity-resolution and nonsense humor during adulthood. *Psychology and Aging, 5*, 348–355.

Richards, A., French, C., Johnson, W., Naparstek, J., & Williams J. (1992). Effects of mood manipulation and anxiety on performance of an emotional Stroop task. *British Journal of Psychology, 83*, 479–491.

Ritchie, G. (2004). *The linguistic analysis of jokes*. New York: Routledge.

Robbins, B. D., & Vandree, K. (2009). The self-regulation of humor expression: A mixed method, phenomenological investigation of suppressed laughter. *The Humanistic Psychologist, 37*, 49–78.

Robinson, D. T., & Smith-Lovin, L. (2001). Getting a laugh: Gender, status, and humor in task discussions. *Social Forces, 80*, 123–158.

Rocca, K. A. (2004). College student attendance: Impact of instructor immediacy and verbal aggression. *Communication Education, 53*, 185–195.

Rocca, K. A., & McCroskey, J. C. (1999). The interrelationship of student ratings of instructors' immediacy, verbal aggressiveness, homophily, and interpersonal attraction. *Communication Education, 48*, 308–316.

Rogers, C. R. (1952). "Client-centered" psychotherapy. *Scientific American, 187*, 66–74.

Romero, E. J., Alsua, C. J., Hinrichs, K. T., & Pearson, T. R. (2007). Regional humor differences in the United States: Implications for management. *Humor: International Journal of Humor Research, 20*, 189–201.

Rose, H., & Rose, S. (2000b). *Alas poor Darwin: Arguments against evolutionary psychology*. London: Harmony Books.

Rosenberg, J., & Tunney, R. J. (2008). Human vocabulary use as display. *Evolutionary Psychology, 6*, 538–549.

Rosin, S. A., & Cerbus, G. (1984). Schizophrenics' and college students' preference for and judgment of schizophrenic versus normal humorous captions. *Journal of Psychology: Interdisciplinary and Applied, 118,* 189–195.

Rotton, J. (1992). Trait humor and longevity: Do comics have the last laugh? *Health Psychology, 11,* 262–266.

Rotton, J., & Shats, M. (1996). Effects of state humor, expectancies, and choice postsurgical mood and self-medication: A field experiment. *Journal of Applied Social Psychology, 26,* 1775–1794.

Ruch, W., & Deckers, L. (1993). Do extraverts "like to laugh"? An analysis of the Situational Humor Response Questionnaire (SHRQ). *European Journal of Personality, 7,* 211–220.

Ruch, W., & Kohler, G. (1999). The measurement of state and trait cheerfulness. In I. Mervielde, I. J. Dreary, F. De Fruyt, & F. Ostendorf (Eds.), *Personality psychology in Europe* (pp. 67–83). Tilburg, Netherlands: Tilburg University Press.

Ruch, W. (1992). Assessment of appreciation of humor: Studies with the 3 WD humor test. In C. D. Spielberger & J. N. Butcher (Eds.), *Advances in personality assessment* (Vol. 9, pp. 27–75). Hillsdale, NJ: Lawrence Erlbaum Associates.

Ruch, W. (1993). Exhilaration and humor, chapter 42. In M. Lewis & J. M. Haviland (Eds.), *The handbook of emotions* (pp. 605–616). New York: Guilford Publications.

Ruch, W. (1995). Will the real relationship between facial expression and affective experience please stand up: The case of exhiliration. *Cognition and Emotion, 9,* 33–58.

Ruch, W., & Hehl, F. (1988). Attitudes to sex, sexual behaviour and enjoyment of humour. *Personality and Individual Differences, 9,* 983–994.

Ruch, W., & Köhler, G. (1998/2007). A temperament approach to humor. In W. Ruch (Ed.), *The sense of humor: Explorations of a personality characteristic* (pp. 203–230). Berlin, Germany: Mouton de Gruyter.

Ruch, W., Busse, P., & Hehl, F. (1996). Relationship between humor and proposed punishment for crimes: Beware of humorous people. *Personality and Individual Differences, 20,* 1–11.

Ruch, W., Mcghee, P. E., & Hehl, F. (1990). Age differences in the enjoyment of incongruity-resolution and nonsense humor during adulthood. *Psychology and Aging, 5,* 348–355.

Rust, J., & Goldstein, J. (1989). Humor in marital adjustment. *Humor: International Journal of Humor Research, 2,* 217–223.

Sakuragi, S., Sugiyama, Y., & Takeuchi, K. (2002). Effects of laughing and weeping on mood and heart rate variability. *Journal of Physiological Anthropology and Applied Human Science, 21,* 159–165.

Saroglou, V. (2003). Humor appreciation as function of religious dimensions. *Archiv fur Religionpsychologie, 24,* 144–153.

Sartre, J. P. (1944/1989). No exit. *No Exit and three other plays* (pp. 1–46). New York: Vintage International.

Schachter, S., & Wheeler, L. (1962). Epinephrine, chlorpromazine and amusement. *Journal of Abnormal and Social Psychology, 65,* 121–128.

Schmidt, S. R., & Williams, A. R. (2001). Memory for humorous cartoons. *Memory & Cognition, 29,* 305–311.

Schmidt, S. R. (1994). Effects of humor on sentence memory. *Journal of Experimental Psychology: Learning, Memory, and Cognition, 20,* 953–967.

Schmidt, S. R. (2002). The humour effect: Differential processing and privileged retrieval. *Memory, 10,* 127–138.

Schmitt, D. P. (2004). Patterns of universals of mate poaching across 53 nations: The effects of sex, culture, and personality on romantically attracting another person's partner. *Journal of Personality and Social Psychology, 86,* 560–584.

Schneidewind-Skibbe, A., Hayes, R. D., Koochaki, P. E., Meyer, J., & Dennerstein, L. (2008). The frequency of sexual intercourse reported by women: A review of community-based studies and factors limiting their conclusions. *Journal of Sexual Medicine, 5,* 301–335.

Shurcliff, A. (1968). Judged humor, arousal, and the relief theory. *Journal of Personality and Social Psychology, 8,* 360–363.

Sibley, C. G., & Duckitt, J. (2008). Personality and prejudice: A meta-analysis and theoretical review. *Personality and Social Psychology Review, 12,* 248–279.

Simpson, D. E., Biernat, K., & Marcdante, K. (2002). Taking a chance with your next teaching opportunity. *Academic Medicine, 77,* 457–458.

Smith, R. E., Ascough, J. C., Ettinger, R. F., & Nelson, D. A. (1971). Humor, anxiety, and task performance. *Journal of Personality and Social Psychology, 19,* 243–246.

Smucker-Barnwell, S., Borders, A., & Earleywine, M. (2006). Alcohol-aggression expectancies and dispositional aggression moderate the relationship between alcohol consumption and alcohol-related violence. *Aggressive Behavior, 32,* 517–525.

Spencer, H. (1860). The physiology of laughter. *Macmillan's Magazine, 1,* 395–402.

Spinrad, P. (1999). *The RE/Search guide to bodily fluids.* New York: PowerHouse Books.

Sprecher, S., & Regan, P. C. (2002). Liking some things (in some people) more than others: Partner preferences in romantic relationships and friendships. *Journal of Social and Personal Relationships, 19,* 463–481.

Steiner, S., Holley, L. C., Gerdes, K., & Campbell, H. E. (2006). Evaluating teaching: Listening to students while acknowledging bias. *Journal of Social Work Education, 42,* 355–376.

Strauss, N. (2007). *Rules of the game: The stylelife challenge and the style diaries.* Melbourne, Australia: Text Publishing.

Strick, M., Holland, R. W., Van Baaren, R. B., & Van Knippenberg, A. D. (2009). Finding comfort in a joke: Consolatory effects of humor through cognitive distraction. *Emotion, 9,* 574–578.

Strong, C. M., Nowakowska, C., Santosa, C. M., Wang, P. W., Kraemer, H. C., & Ketter, T. A. (2007). Temperament-creativity relationships in mood disorder patients, healthy controls and highly creative individuals. *Journal of Affective Disorders, 100*(1–3), 41–48.

Strother, G. B., Barnett, M. M., & Apostolakos, P. C. (1954). The use of cartoons as a projective device. *Journal of Clinical Psychology, 10,* 38–42.

Stuber, M., Hilber, S. D., Mintzer, L. L., Castaneda, M., Glover, D., & Zeltzer, L. (2009). Laughter, humor and pain perception in children: a pilot study. *Evidence-Based Complementary and Alternative Medicine: Ecam, 6,* 271–276.

Suls, J. (1983). Cognitive processes in humor appreciation. In P. E. McGhee & J. H. Goldstein (Eds.), *Handbook of humor research.* New York: Springer-Verlag.

Suls, J. M. (1972). A two-stage model for the appreciation of jokes and cartoons. In J. H. Goldstein & P. E. McGhee (Eds.), *The psychology of humor* (pp. 81–100). New York: Academic Press.

Surawski, M. K., & Ossoff, E. P. (2006). The effects of physical and vocal attractiveness on impression formation of politicians. *Current Psychology, 25,* 15–27.

Swami, V., Jones, J., Einon, D., & Furnham, A. (2009). Men's preferences for women's profile waist-to-hip ratio, breast size, and ethnic group in Britain and South Africa. *British Journal of Psychology, 100,* 313–325.

Szabo, A. (2007). Comparison of the psychological effects of exercise and humor. In A. M. Lane (Ed.), *Mood and human performance: Conceptual, measurement and applied issues* (pp. 201–216). Hauppauge, NY: Nova Science Publishers.

Takahashi, M., & Inoue, T. (2009). The effects of humor on memory for non-sensical pictures. *Acta Psychologica, 132,* 80–84.

Talbot, L. A., & Lumden, D. B. (2000). On the association between humor and burnout. *Humor: International Journal of Humor Research, 13,* 419–428.

Tannen, D. (2001). *You just don't understand: Women and men in conversation.* New York: Harper Paperbacks.

Terry, R. L., & Woods, M. E. (1975). Effects of humor on the test performance of elementary school children. *Psychology in the Schools, 12,* 182–185.

Thiel, A., Alizadeh, M., Giel, K., & Zipfel, S. (2008). Stereotyping of overweight children by their contemporaries. *Psychotherapie Psychosomatik Medizinische Psychologie, 58*(12), 16–24.

Thorson, J. A., & Powell, F. C. (1993). Sense of humor and dimensions of personality. *Journal of Clinical Psychology, 49,* 799–809.

Townsend, M. A., & Mahoney, P. (1981). Humor and anxiety: Effects on class test performance. *Psychology in the Schools, 18,* 228–234.

Treadwell, Y. (1970). Humor and creativity. *Psychological Reports, 26,* 55–58.

Tumkaya, S. (2007). Burnout and humor relationship among university lecturers. *Humor: International Journal of Humor Research, 20,* 73–92.

Tybur, J. M., Miller, G. F., & Gangestad, S. W. (2007). Testing controversy: An empirical examination of adaptationists' attitudes toward politics and science. *Human Nature, 18,* 313–328.

U. S. Census Bureau. (2005); data generated by Mitch Earleywine using American FactFinder. Retrieved May 7, 2010, from http://factfinder.census.gov

Van Dillen, L. F., & Koole, S. L. (2007). Clearing the mind: A working memory model of distraction from negative mood. *Emotion, 7,* 715–723.

Vernon, P. A., Martin, R. A., Schermer, J., Aitken, C., Lynn F., & Spector, T. D. (2008). Genetic and environmental contributions to humor styles: A replication study. *Twin Research and Human Genetics, 11,* 44–47.

Vinton, K. L. (1989). Humor in the workplace: Is it more than telling jokes? *Small Group Behavior, 20,* 151–166.

Vorhaus, J. (1994). *The comic toolbox: How to be funny even if you're not.* Los Angeles, CA: Silman-James Press.

Wakshlag, J. J., Day, K. D., & Zillmann, D. (1981). Selective exposure to educational television programs as a function of differently paced humorous inserts. *Journal of Educational Psychology, 73,* 27–32.

Walle, A. H. (1977). Getting picked up without being put down: Jokes and the bar rush. *Journal of the Folklore Institute, 13,* 201–217.

Wampold, B. E., Mondin, G. W., Moody, M., Stich, F., Benson, K., & Ahn, H. (1997). A meta-analysis of outcome studies comparing bona fide psychotherapies: Empiricially, "All must have prizes." *Psychological Bulletin, 122,* 203–215.

Wang, L., Li, Y., Metzak, P., He, Y., & Woodward, T. S. (2010). Age-related changes in topological patterns of large-scale brain functional networks during memory encoding and recognition. *NeuroImage, 50,* 862–872.

Wanzer, M. B., & Frymier, A. B. (1999). The relationship between student perceptions of instructor humor and students' reports of learning. *Communication Education, 48,* 48–62.

Weinberger, M. G., & Gulas, C. S. (1992). The impact of humor in advertising: A review. *Journal of Advertising, 21,* 35–59.

Weisenberg, M., Raz, T., & Hener, T. (1998). The influence of film-induced mood on pain perception. *Pain, 76,* 365–375.

Weisenberg, M., Tepper, I., & Schwarzwald, J. (1995). Humor as a cognitive technique for increasing pain tolerance. *Pain, 63,* 207–212.

Wender, R., Hoffman, H. G., Hunner, H. H., Seibel, E. J., Patterson, D. R., & Sharar, S. R. (2009). Interactivity influences the magnitude of virtual reality analgesia. *Journal of CyberTherapy and Rehabilitation, 2,* 27–33.

White, E. B. (1941/2000). *Essays of E.B. White.* New York: McGraw-Hill College.

White, S., & Camarena, P. (1989). Laughter as a stress reducer in small groups. *Humor: International Journal of Humor Research, 2,* 73–79.

Widlok, T. (2008). Landscape unbounded: Space, place, and orientation in not-equal-to Akhoe Hai//om and beyond. *Language Sciences, 30,* 362–380.

Williams, J. M. (1946). An experimental and theoretical study of humour in children. *British Journal of Educational Psychology, 16,* 43–44.

Williams, M., Teasdale, J., Segal, Z., & Kabat-Zinn, J. (2007). *The mindful way through depression: Freeing yourself from chronic unhappiness.* New York: Guilford Press.

Williams, V. S., Edin, H. M., Hogue, S. L., Fehnel, S. E., & Baldwin, D. S. (2010). Prevalence and impact of antidepressant-associated sexual dysfunction in three European countries: Replication in a cross-sectional patient survey. *Journal of Psychopharmacology, 24,* 489–496.

Witztum, E., Briskin, S., & Lerner, V. (1999). The use of humor with chronic schizophrenic patients. *Journal of Contemporary Psychotherapy, 29,* 223–234.

Wycoff, E. B., & Pryor, B. (2003). Cognitive processing, creativity, apprehension, and the humorous personality. *North American Journal of Psychology, 5,* 31–44.

Wyer, R. S. (2004). A personalized theory of theory construction. *Personality and Social Psychology Review, 8,* 201–209.

Wyer, R. S., & Collins, J. E. (1992). A theory of humor elicitation. *Psychological Review, 99,* 663–688.

Yip, J. A., & Martin, R. A. (2006). Sense of humor, emotional intelligence, and social competence. *Journal of Research in Personality, 40,* 1202–1208.

Young, M. S., & Pinsky, D. (2006). Narcissism and celebrity. *Journal of Research in Personality, 40,* 463–471.

Zerubavel, E. (2007). *The elephant in the room: Silence and denial in everyday life.* New York: Oxford University Press.

Zillmann, D., Bryant, J., & Cantor, J. R. (1974). Brutality of assault in political cartoons affecting humor appreciation. *Journal of Research in Personality, 7,* 334–345.

Ziv, A. (1976). Facilitating effects of humor on creativity. *Journal of Educational Psychology, 68*, 318–322.

Ziv, A. (1983). The influence of humorous atmosphere on divergent thinking. *Contemporary Educational Psychology, 8*, 68–75.

Ziv, A. (1988). Teaching and learning with humor: Experiment and replication. *Journal of Experimental Education, 57*, 5–15.

Ziv, A., & Gadish, O. (1989). Humor and marital satisfaction. *The Journal of Social Psychology, 129*, 759–768.

Zwerling, I. (1955). The favorite joke in diagnostic and therapeutic interviewing. *Psychoanalytic Quarterly, 24*, 104–114.

Zweyer, K., Velker, B., & Ruch, W. (2004). Do cheerfulness, exhilaration, and humor production moderate pain tolerance? *Humor: International Journal of Humor Research, 17*(1–2), 85–119.

Index